P9-BYA-530

ALLIED
BOMBERS
1939–45

THE ESSENTIAL
AIRCRAFT IDENTIFICATION GUIDE

ALLIED
BOMBERS
1939–45

CHRIS CHANT

amber
BOOKS

This edition published in 2008 by

Amber Books Ltd

Bradley's Close

74–77 White Lion Street

London N1 9PF

www.amberbooks.co.uk

Copyright © 2008 Amber Books Ltd

All rights reserved. No part of this publication may be reproduced, stored in a retrieval system or transmitted, in any form or by any means, electronic, mechanical, photocopying, recording or otherwise, without the prior written permission of the copyright holder.

A catalogue record for this book is available from the British Library.

ISBN 978-1-905704-70-5

Project Editor: Michael Spilling
Design: Hawes Design
Picture Research: Terry Forshaw

Printed in Dubai

PICTURE CREDITS
All photographs courtesy of Art-Tech/Aerospace except for page 10 courtesy of Cody Images.

All artworks courtesy of Art-Tech/Aerospace except for pages 12, 13(b), 16(t), 18–22(all), 27(t), 29(b), 33(all), 53(b), 59(t), 83(all), 85, 87(b), 88(b), 89, 91(t), 96(b), 106(t), 111(b), 119(b), 122(t), 125, 134, 140, 149, 151, 156(b), 166, 168, 171(b), 178(b), 179(t), 183(b) courtesy of Alcaniz Freson's S.A.

Contents

Introduction

Most bombers of 1939 were twin-engined
monoplanes with bomb loads in the order of 454 to 2040kg
(1000 to 4500lb) and a range of 4025km (2500 miles) for
the larger types. While Germany concentrated its efforts
on twin-engined aircraft intended primarily for the tactical
role over short ranges, the Allied countries had ambitions
to undertake the strategic as well as tactical roles.
This reached fruition with the development of Bomber
Command in Britain and the introduction of the United States
Eighth Air Force (the 'Mighty Eighth') into the European
theatre from 1942. Although ineffective in the early years of
the war, the combined bomber forces of the United Kingdom
and United States devastated Germany and German
industry, making an important contribution
to the final victory.

◀ **Liberator attack**
A formation of Consolidated B-24 Liberators carry out practice flights against mocked-up targets in the
Libyan desert, July 1943.

The early-war Allies were France and the United Kingdom. France had fallen behind the times in the mid-1930s, leaving it with a comparatively large fleet of obsolescent if not obsolete bombers, but was attempting without too much success and at too late a stage to re-equip with new types such as the Lioré-et-Olivier LeO 451, the fastest bomber in 1939.

The fighting in May and June 1940, which led to the defeat of France, also revealed the total inadequacy of the Royal Air Force's (RAF) Fairey Battle single-engined day bomber, which was slow, clumsy in the air, carried only a light bomb load, and was lost in appalling numbers to ground fire. The British also had three supposedly heavy twin-engined bombers: the Armstrong Whitworth Whitley, Handley Page Hampden and Vickers Wellington. Best of these by a considerable margin was the last, whose unusual geodetic structure, covered with fabric, proved to be very sturdy and able to absorb considerable battle damage. The Wellington could carry a substantial bomb load over long distances, and possessed considerable development potential.

Early in 1941 the UK introduced two four-engined heavy bombers, namely the Short Stirling and Handley Page Halifax, and then early in 1942 the Avro Lancaster, which was the best night heavy bomber of the war. Also becoming operational in 1942 was the twin-engined de Havilland Mosquito light bomber, which was of primarily wooden construction and carried no defensive armament as it possessed the speed to evade interception.

▼ **Night bomber**
The RAF crew of a Wellington Mk III heavy bomber finalize their route to the target before a raid over enemy territory.

Soviet tactical bombers
Soviet bombers, apart from the long-range Ilyushin Il-4, were used mainly for tactical bombing in support of ground forces. The twin-engined tactical bombing capability was initially centred on the obsolescent Tupolev SB-2, succeeded by the high-speed Petlyakov Pe-2 and, from 1943, by the more heavily-armed Tupolev Tu-2. A unique type, built in greater numbers than any other warplane, was the single-engined Ilyushin Il-2 *Shturmovik* attack warplane, in which an armoured 'bath' protected the engine and crew against ground fire.

The 'Flying Fortress'
During 1935 the USA produced the first truly modern all-metal monoplane bomber in the form of the four-engined Boeing B-17. Incorporating five defensive gun positions, this was nicknamed the 'Flying Fortress'. Sturdy and able to cruise at a high speed at high altitude, the B-17 was found in early operations to possess inadequate defensive armament and by mid-1942 had been developed into the far superior B-17G, with greater protection and the armament of 13 12.7mm (0.5in) machine guns, most of them in power-operated positions.

The B-17 was the backbone of the US Army Air Forces' daylight raids against point targets, in which it was supplemented by the four-engined Consolidated B-24 Liberator, but both of these types became truly viable only with the introduction of fighters possessing the range to escort them to and from their targets. First used by the French in May 1940, the Douglas DB-7, known to the British as the Boston and the USAAF as the A-20 Havoc, was a twin-engined attack bomber. The type was then supplemented and finally supplanted by larger twin-engined medium bombers such as the North American B-25 Mitchell and Martin B-26 Marauder, and also the Douglas A-26 Invader attack bomber.

Strategic bombing
Though in itself the epitomy of offensive warfare, strategic bombing demanded the creation of defensive tactics. The bombers that carried out the Allies' strategic air offensive against Germany needed a constant stream of revised tactics to counter the German air and ground defences. Because RAF Bomber Command undertook mostly unescorted area bombing night raids, the tactics were different from

those of the US Air Forces, whose bombers carried out daylight attacks for precision bombing of point targets. Initially the British bombers were widely dispersed when they flew to their targets and this enabled the German night-fighters of the Kammhuber Line to tackle each succeeding flight as they passed through the line's various radar-controlled 'boxes'. The British countered with the 'bomber stream', which was employed for the first time in the 'thousand-bomber' attack on Köln during May 1942: rather than converging on the target separately, the bombers assembled into one stream to pass through the Kammhuber Line in a column some 70 miles (112km) long and 1220m (4000ft) wide, which made it possible to saturate the defensive capability of the box through which it passed.

Throughout the war several types of electronic warfare equipment were introduced to degrade the German radar and misdirect the German night-fighters. Small spoof raids were also started to draw the night-fighters away from the main raid. The type most successful in the spoof role was the Mosquito, which was too speedy to be intercepted. When bombing real targets, a Mosquito force often attacked in two waves, one at low level co-ordinated with the other making a shallow dive, a tactic that split the defences. The Mosquito was also used for pathfinding, in which high-quality crews arrived just before the main raid to mark the target with special bombs and flares.

USAAF tactics
The USAAF had different tactical solutions to create for the protection of its aircraft. Until long-range fighters became available early in 1944 to escort them, the bombers were dependent on their own defensive armament, and therefore flew in formations designed to maximize their fields of mutual defensive firepower. Thus the numbers of any single formation and the formation's compactness increased as the war progressed. As they were both heavily-armed, the B-17 and B-24 were initially believed to be able to fight their way to and from their targets in formations of six aircraft, four such formations flying together at a distance of 6.4km (4 miles) from each other: this was adequate for bombing as it offered room to manoeuvre, but was defensively poor as German fighters could enter the gaps between the formations.

Thus in September 1942, 18-aircraft groups were introduced, bringing the aircraft closer together and

▲ **Douglas bombers**
At the Douglas plant in California, Bostons and Havocs await delivery to the USAAF early in 1942.

providing a tighter concentration of mutually supporting firepower. However, the formation was difficult to manoeuvre and easily dropped stragglers. The formation was improved in December 1942, but the German fighters were still able to cause a loss rate unsustainable over any length of time. In March 1943, therefore, the basic formation became the 54-aircraft combat wing: three 18-aircraft groups being compacted into a grouping 550m (600 yards) long, 2000m (2200 yards) wide and 810m (2650ft) deep. This aided defence but demanded bombing by formation rather than individual aircraft, and was soon further improved as the 'tucked-in' wing with the aircraft squeezed further together. This yielded a genuinely effective weight of fire and a smaller target for the head-on attacks of the German fighters.

The 'tucked-in' wing lasted to the advent of the long-range escort fighter early in 1944 and the appearance of massed Flak batteries for the defence of German cities early in 1945, each resulting in a change of formation. With fighters covering the bombers from the start to the finish of a raid, self-defence was less important than allowing the bombers to concentrate on more accurate bombing under control of the few aircraft fitted with electronic aids. One such aeroplane led a 12-bomber squadron, with three squadrons constituting an arrow-head group. The final arrangement, introduced in February 1945, comprised a group with four nine-bomber squadrons flying at different altitudes to make it more difficult for the Flak gunner to set their sights and shells.

Chapter 1

France and the Low Countries

Great things were expected of the bomber
during the 1930s, when many believed that bombing would
be the arbiter of any future war. But the bomber was
expensive to build, maintain and operate, so numbers were
comparatively few and, for the most part, the intended bomb
loads were also small. During the 1920s and 1930s, France
had produced several types of extraordinarily ugly, slab-
sided bombers, and only late in the 1930s
began to produce elegant, high-speed bombers such as
those from the Amiot and Lioré-et-Olivier companies.
Belgium and the Netherlands were concerned with defence
rather than offence, and therefore concentrated their limited
resources on light bombers for frontline service.

◀ **Bomb loading**
French ground crew load up a Martin 167 prior to a mission in June 1940. Designed as an attack bomber
in 1938, the US-made Martin XA-22 failed to win any production contracts with the USAAF. In 1939 Martin
looked for buyers overseas, and under the designation Model 167 (named the Maryland) sales were made
to Britain, France, and South Africa.

France
1939–40

The French were strong adherents of the bomber concept in World War I, and retained their faith in the 1920s and 1930s. But their aircraft became increasingly obsolete in concept, and the rearmament of the later 1930s proved too little and too late.

B Y THE MID-1930s, French national security was clearly threatened by the revival of German nationalism under Adolf Hitler, so Pierre Cot, the secretary of the air force, decided that national security was too important for the production of war planes to be left in the hands of private enterprise. In July 1936, the government began to nationalize France's aircraft manufacturing companies to create six large and, it was wrongly estimated, more effective regional groupings. The aircraft engine industry, even though it could not provide the number of powerful engines needed, was not nationalized.

ORGANIZATION	
French Air Force bomber dispositions *May 1940*	
Zone d'Operations Aeriennes Est (two groupements de bombardement)	Zone d'Operations Aeriennes Sud (none)
Zone d'Operations Aeriennes Nord (two groupements de bombardement and one groupement de Bombardement d'assaut)	Zone d'Operations Aeriennes des Alpes (five groupes de bombardement and one groupement de bombardement d'assaut)

Accelerated production

The announcement of the need to build more than 2500 modern warplanes was the direct government response to a remark by the current commander of the air force. He claimed that less than half of some 1400 frontline aircraft were ready for immediate service, and were in any event mostly obsolescent. Thus France tried to respond militarily to the threat of another European war via an intensive modernization programme in 1938–39.

▲ **Potez 540Bn.5**

l'Armée de l'Air

In civil markings and without armament owing to its use in transporting diplomats and negotiators, this was the 228th example of the Potez 540 family. The type first flew in 1933, and production reached 259 aircraft for France. About 70 were still in first-line service in September 1939, but were soon relegated to secondary tasks.

Specifications

Crew: 7	length 16.20 m (53ft 2in); height 3.88m
Powerplant: 2 x 515kW (690hp) Hispano-Suiza	(12ft 9in)
HS 12 Xirs/Xjrs V-12 liquid-cooled engines	Weight: 5950kg (13,115lb) loaded
Maximum speed: 310km/h (193mph)	Armament: 3-5 x 7.5mm (0.29in) MGs in
Range: 1250km (777 miles)	flexible nose, dorsal, and ventral positions;
Service ceiling: 10,000 m (32,810ft)	10 x 55kg (121lb) bombs in bomb bay when
Dimensions: span 22.10m (72ft 6in);	loaded for bombing

But it was 'too little, too late' as far as France was concerned. When war did break out in September 1939, the *Armée de l'Air* was still suffering the effects of the total chaos throughout the government, armed forces and industry, which meant that only 826 fighters and 250 bombers were anything like combat-ready. Moreover, many more aircraft were not ready when they ought to have been because of late deliveries and uncalibrated defensive armament and lack of effective bomb sight.

From 10 May 1940, France's lack of modern thinking, aircraft, weapons and communications

▲ Amiot 143M

3e Escadron / Groupe de Bombardement iI/35, Pontarlier, September 1939

First flown in the spring of 1935 and built to the extent of 138 aircraft, the Amiot 143 was typical of the French bombers of the mid-1930s with its high-drag lines, fixed landing gear and large ventral gondola.

Specifications

Crew: 5	height 5.68m (18ft 8in)
Powerplant: 2 x 640kW (870hp)	Weight: 9700kg (21,385lb) loaded
Maximum speed: 310km/h (193mph)	Armament: 4 x 7.5mm (0.295in) MGs in nose
Range: 746km (1200 miles)	turret, dorsal turret, forward-fuselage floor
Service ceiling: 7900m (25,920ft)	hatch and rear of ventral gondola; up to
Dimensions: span 24.53m (80ft 5in);	1600kg (3527lb) bombs
length 18.26m (59ft 11in);	

▲ Martin 167A.3

l'Armée de l'Air, 1939–40

Known to the British as the Maryland, the Model 167 was first manufactured for the French in two forms as the Model 167F reconnaissance bomber (115 ordered) and Model 167A.3 attack-bomber (100 ordered, of which 76 were delivered to the UK after the fall of France).

Specifications

Crew: 3	Weight: 5086kg (11,213lb) empty
Powerplant: 2 x 894kW (1200hp) Pratt &	Armament: 1 x 7.62mm (0.3in) Vickers 'K'
Whitney R-1830-S3C4-G Twin Wasp radial	trainable rearward-firing MG in the dorsal
Maximum speed: 447km/h (278 mph)	turretplus 1 x 7.7mm (0.303in) Vickers 'K'
Range: 1947km (1210 miles)	trainable rearward-firing MG in the ventral
Service ceiling: 7925m (26,000ft)	step position; 4 x 1100kg (500lb) bomb load
Dimensions: span 18.69m (61ft 4in); length	
14.22m (46ft 8in); height 4.57m (14ft 12in)	

BOMBER UNITS OF THE ZONE D'OPERATIONS AERIENNES NORD (ZOAN)		
Unit	Type	Base
GB I/12	LeO 451	Soissons-Saconin
GB II/12	LeO 451	Persan-Beaumont
GB I/34	Amiot 143	Montdidier
GB II/34	Amiot 143	Roye-Amy
GBA I/54	Bre.693	La Ferte-Gaucher
GBA II/54	Bre.693	Nangis

equipment, combined with an almost incredible shortage of many vital hardware elements such as propellers (the result of 'technical problems'), eased the task of the Germans as they advanced through France and destroyed all opposition: on 11 May, for example, nearly 20 French bombers and more than 30 escorting British fighters were shot down in an attempt to stop the Germans from crossing the Meuse river.

This was merely the beginning, for French fighter and bomber strengths became rapidly depleted during May as *Luftwaffe* fighters and ground-based flak units destroyed increasing numbers of the warplanes. Worse was the fact that the squadrons

were often out of contact with the army units they were to support, the result in part of the poor coordination of communication between the army and the air force, and in part of the outdated, communications equipment used by the army.

As it became clear that the battle of France was lost, the high command ordered the *Armée de l'Air's* remnants to withdraw to the French colonies in North Africa – in order, it believed, to continue the fight. In overall terms, during the battle of France, the French lost more than 750 aircraft while the Germans lost more than 850.

Even so, the Germans losses could be made good, and would not prevent the huge defeat inflicted on the French Army.

This is the emblem of Groupe de Bombardement d'Assaut I/54. The Groupe had a theoretical complement of 13 Breguet 693 aircraft.

▲ **Home of the Breguet 693**

An early model Breguet 693 sits in a field at Moteurs Gnome & Rhône, the birthplace of the type.

▲ **Breguet 693A.2**

Groupe de Bombardement d'Assaut I/54, Montdidier and La Ferte-Gaucher, France, May 1940

GBA I and II/54 were the component halves of the *Groupement de Bombardement d'Assaut 18*, which was the premier indigenous attack-bomber formation in the northern sector of the French air defence system in May 1940.

Specifications

Crew: 2

Powerplant: 2 x 522kW (700hp)

Maximum speed: 490km/h (304mph)

Range: 1350km (839 miles)

Service ceiling: 4000m (13,125ft)

Dimensions: span 15.37m (50ft 5in);

length 9.67m (31ft 9in);

height 3.19m (10ft 6in)

Weight: 4900kg (10,803lb) loaded

Armament: 1 x 20mm (0.79in) forward-firing cannon and 4 x 7.5mm (0.295in) MGs in nose (2), rear cockpit and ventral position; up to 400kg (882lb) of bombs carried internally

French campaign – first phase
May 1940

Instead of punching through northern Belgium and along the English Channel coast, as the Allies expected, the Germans drove through the Ardennes in southern Belgium to break through at Sedan before driving to the Channel coast and splitting the Allies in two parts for easy defeat.

THE GERMAN CAMPAIGN FELL into two parts: the battle of the Low Countries and the battle of France, the latter also falling into two phases. As the German forces struck on 10 May into the Low Countries, these called for French and British aid, and the Allies armies moved east, as already planned, to the 'Dyle Line' covering Brussels. Meanwhile, the Germans were driving most of their Panzer divisions

▲ **Breguet Bre.693AB.2**

4e Escadrille / Groupe de Bombardement d'Assaut II/54, Roy,
May 1940

Making its combat debut on 12 May 1940, the Bre.693 had a disastrous beginning, 10 out of the 11 aircraft being lost or damaged beyond repair.

Specifications	
Crew: 2	height 3.19m (10ft 6in)
Powerplant: 2 x 522kW (700hp)	Weight: 4900kg (10,803lb) loaded
Maximum speed: 490km/h (304mph)	Armament: 1 x 20mm (0.79in) forward-firing
Range: 1350km (839 miles)	cannon and 4 x 7.5mm (0.295in) MGs in nose
Service ceiling: 4000m (13,125ft)	(two), rear cockpit and ventral position; up to
Dimensions: span 15.37m (50ft 5in);	400kg (882lb) of bombs carried internally
length 9.67m (31ft 9in);	

Specifications	
Crew: 4	height 4.08m (13ft 5in)
Powerplant: 2 x 790kW (1060hp)	Weight: 11,300kg (24,912lb) loaded
Maximum speed: 480km/h (298mph)	Armament: 1 x 20mm (0.79in) trainable
Range: 2500km (1554 miles)	cannon in dorsal turret; 2 x 7.5mm (0.295in)
Service ceiling: 10,000m (32,810ft)	MGs in nose and ventral position; up to
Dimensions: span 22.83m (74ft 11in);	1200kg (2646lb) of bombs
length 14.5m (47ft 7in);	

▲ **Amiot 354B.4**

4e Escadrille / Groupe de Bombardement II/21, May 1940

First flown in January 1939 and potentially an excellent medium bomber, the Amiot 354 failed to make any real impact: although 900 such aircraft had been ordered, only about 45 had been delivered before the fall of France in June 1940. Several were later adapted as high-speed civil transports.

through the 'impassable' Ardennes. The Germans secured bridgeheads over the Meuse by the 14 May, and moved their armour forward on the night of 15–16 May, heading behind the British Expeditionary Force (BEF) and the French First and Ninth Armies. By 20 May, the Germans had reached the English Channel and established a corridor separating the Allied forces. The Allies fell back around Dunkirk, and after Boulogne and Calais had fallen on 25 and 27 May respectively, the Allies decided to evacuate by sea from Dunkirk.

ORGANIZATION

ZOAN bomber forces
May 1940

Groupement de Bombardement 6 (GB I & II/12)	Groupement de Bombardement 9 (GB I & II/34)	Groupement de Bombardement d'Assaut 18 (GBA I & II/54)

▲ Bloch MB.174A.3
l'Armée de l'Air, France, 1940

Entering service only in the later part of March 1940, the MB.174 was planned as a reconnaissance attack-bomber, but the 56 aircraft completed were used only in the reconnaissance role, more than half of the 49 operational aircraft being lost by the time of France's capitulation in June 1940.

Specifications

Crew: 3

Powerplant: 2 x 820kW (1100hp)

Maximum speed: 530km/h (329mph)

Range: 1650km (1025 miles)

Service ceiling: 11,000m (36,090ft)

Dimensions: span 17.9m (58ft 9in);
  length 12.25m (40ft 3in);

height 3.55m (11ft 8in)

Weight: 7160kg (15,784lb) loaded

Armament: 7 x 7.5mm (0.295in) MGs: two fixed on leading edge of wing, two trainable rearward ones in dorsal position, three trainable rearward ones on ventral wobble mounts; up to 500kg (1102lb) bombs

▲ Farman F.222.1Bn.5
l'Armée de l'Air, France, 1940

Some 35 F.222 heavy night-bombers were delivered to the French Air Force: 11 F.222.1s with a short nose and flat outer wing panels and 24 F.222.2s with a longer nose and dihedralled outer wing panels. These were the only four-engined heavy bombers in French service during 1939, equipping three *groupes*, two in France and the other in West Africa.

Specifications

Crew: 5

Powerplant: 4 x 723kW (970hp)

Maximum speed: 360km/h (224mph)

Range: 2000km (1243 miles)

Service ceiling: 8000m (26,245ft)

Dimensions: span 36m (118ft 1in); length 21.45m (70ft 5in); height 5.19m (17ft 1in)

Weight: 18700kg (41,226lb) loaded

Armament: 3 x 7.5mm (0.295in) MGs: one in nose turret, one in dorsal turret and one in ventral 'dustbin' position; up to 4000kg (8800lb) of either 20 x 200kg (440lb) or 40 x 100kg (220lb) bombs, or a mix of these with 50kg (110lb) bombs

French campaign – second phase
June 1940

With the Low Countries defeated and the northern part of the Allied armies captured or evacuated from Dunkirk, the Germans could concentrate all their efforts on the bulk of the French armies during the course of June 1940.

THE GERMAN PREOCCUPATION with the British evacuation of almost 340,000 men, 120,000 of them French, from Dunkirk in the period up to 4 June offered the French forces south of the Somme river a measure of respite. The French commander-in-chief now attempted to create a defensive system on the line of the Somme and Aisne rivers to protect

Paris and the interior of France against the inevitable renewal of the German offensive, but most of the French Army had lost all confidence in its leaders and even in itself. Nor were the remaining Allied forces in any condition to provide help: the British 51st

---

ORGANIZATION

ZOAA bomber forces
May 1940

Groupement de Bombardement 1 (GB I/62 & I/63)	Groupement de Bombardement 6 (GB I & II/31)	Groupement de Bombardement 7 (GB I & II/23)	Groupement de Bombardement 9 (I & II/21)

	Groupement de Bombardement 11 (GB I & II/11)	Groupement de Bombardement d'Assaut 19 (GBA II/35 and I & II/51)	

BOMBER UNITS OF THE ZONE D'OPÉRATIONS AÉRIENNES DES ALPES (ZOAA)

Unit	Type	Base
GB I/62 & I/63	Martin 167F	Orange
GB I & II/11	LeO 451, MB.210	Istres-Mas le Rue
GB I & II/21	Amiot 351/354 MB.210	Avignon
GB I & II/23	MB.210	Istres-Le Vallon
GB I & II/31	LeO 451	Lezignan
GBA I & II/51	Potez 633 Bre.691/693	Le Luc
GBA II/35	Potez 633, Bre.691	Briare

▲ **Bloch MB.200B.4**

Section de Remorquage d'Otange / l'Armée de l'Air, France, June 1940

Entering service late in 1934, the MB.200B.4 was a medium bomber wholly typical of French designers' angular approach to the creation of large aircraft at this time. Deliveries eventually totalled 208 aircraft, all used for training by May 1940.

Specifications

Crew: 4
Powerplant: 2 x 649kW (870hp)
Maximum speed: 285km/h (177mph)
Range: 1000km (621 miles)
Service ceiling: 8000m (26,245ft)
Dimensions: span 22.45m (73ft 8in);

length 16m (52ft 6in);
height 3.9m (12ft 10in)
Weight: 7480kg (16,490lb) loaded
Armament: single 7.5mm (0.295in) trainable
MGs in nose, dorsal and ventral positions; up
to 1200kg (2646lb) of bombs

(Highland) Division surrendered at St Valery-en-Caux on 12 June, and the British 52nd (Lowland) Division and the Canadian 1st Division had to be evacuated. The Germans moved south on 4 June, and had crossed the Seine river by 10 June.

Flight from Paris

On 12 June, the French government declared Paris an open city and removed itself to Bordeaux. Winston Churchill's offer of union between the UK and France was rejected, Prime Minister Paul Reynaud

resigned and his successor, Marshal Philippe Petain, accepted German terms on 22 June for an armistice. By this time, German forces had plunged deep into France, reaching western Brittany, the Spanish frontier on the Bay of Biscay, and a line between Limoges and the Swiss frontier near Geneva.

All France north and west of this line was occupied, and a new French government established itself at Vichy in the unoccupied zone. France had been comprehensively defeated, leaving only Charles de Gaulle's Free French to carry on the fight.

Specifications

Crew: 3
Powerplant: 2 x 850kW (1140hp)
Maximum speed: 540km/h (335mph)
Range: 1600km (994 miles)
Service ceiling: 8000m (26,245ft)
Dimensions: span 17.95m (58ft 11in);
 length 12.43m (40ft 9in);

height 3.55m (11ft 8in)
Weight: 5660kg (12,478lb) loaded
Armament: 7 x 7.5mm (0.295in) MGs: two fixed
 on leading edge of wing, two trainable
 rearward ones in dorsal position, three
 trainable rearward ones on ventral wobble
 mounts; up to 600kg (1323lb) bombs

▲ **Bloch MB.175B.3**

Vichy French Air Force, 1941–42

A development of the MB.174 for the dedicated light attack-bomber role, the MB.175 entered service just before the fall of France. Some 20 aircraft were delivered in June 1940, but none saw combat and 23 of the type saw service with the Vichy French air force. Another 56 were completed for the *Luftwaffe* as trainers.

The Netherlands and Belgium
MAY 1940

The Dutch and Belgians sought to remain neutral from 1939, relying on small forces and the nature of their countries to deter possible German aggression. It was in vain, and in May 1940 both countries were quickly overrun by larger and more effective German forces.

A S NOTED ABOVE, the German campaign in the west fell neatly into two parts, of which the first was the battle of the Low Countries designed to eliminate the Netherlands and Belgium as possible threats to the right flank of the Germans' main thrust and as potential bases for enlarged British forces. But the Netherlands had only eight divisions and some

ORGANIZATION

Belgian and Dutch bomber units
1939

Belgian (3rd Air Regiment with four reconnaissance bomber squadrons)

Dutch (1st Air Regiment with one bomber squadron)

Specifications

Crew: 2

Powerplant: 746kW (1000hp) Wright XR-1820-
32 piston engine

Maximum speed: 410km/h (255mph)

Range: 1240km (773 miles)

Service ceiling: 7780m (25,530ft)

Dimensions: span 12.65m (41ft 6in);
length 10.08m (33ft 1in); height 4.14m
(13ft 7in)

Weight: 2905kg (6404lb)

Armament: 2 x 12.7mm (0.5in) forward-firing
MGs

▲ **Douglas (Northrop) Model DB-8A-3N**

3rd Fighter Squadron / 2nd Air Regiment, Ypenburg, Netherlands, May 1940

The Dutch Air Force received 18 such aircraft between August and November 1939, and 12 of the aircraft were operational at the time of the German invasion on 10 May 1940. This one was lost on the ground, and of the 11 that took off seven were shot down and the surviving four were later destroyed on the ground.

▲ **Fokker T.V**

Bomber Squadron / 1st Air Regiment, Schiphol, Netherlands, May 1940

First flown in October 1937 and built to the extent of 16 aircraft intended for the long-range fighter as well as medium bomber roles, the T.V operated only as a bomber. The nine serviceable aircraft flown by the Bomber Squadron on 10 May 1940 were all destroyed during in the following five days.

Specifications

Crew: 5

Powerplant: 2 x 690kW (925hp) Bristol
Pegasus XXVI air-cooled radial engines

Maximum speed: 417km/h (257mph)

Range: 1550km (956 miles)

Service ceiling: 7700m (25,256ft)

Dimensions: span 21m (68ft 11in);

length 16m (60ft 10in);
height 5m (16ft 5in)

Weight: 7250kg (15,950lb) loaded

Armament: 1 x 20mm (0.79in) cannon in nose,
5 x 7.9mm (0.295in) MGs in dorsal, ventral,
both lateral positions and tail cupola; 1000kg
(2205lb) of bombs

125 warplanes, while Belgium had 18 divisions and some 180 aircraft to face altogether more powerful German ground and air forces, the former including three Panzer divisions.

The German campaign against the Low Countries began in the morning of 10 May 1940, when the Germans launched air attacks and parachute landings on Dutch airfields and bridges even as their ground forces moved moved west into the Netherlands and Belgium. This prompted both nations to ask for

British and French aid, initially in the form of the pre-planned Allied movement forward to the Dyle Line covering Brussels. Despite their standard recourse in the face of invasion, namely the flooding of key areas and the demolition of bridges over major water courses, the Dutch were soon compelled to back into 'Fortress Holland', bounded by Rotterdam and Amsterdam in the south and north, and the Zuider See and North Sea on the east and west. On 14 May, the German Air Force 'blitzed' the great port city of Rotterdam, and this persuaded the Dutch to surrender after a five-day campaign that had cost the Netherlands some 25 per cent casualties.

Meanwhile, further to the south the Germans had captured Fort Eben Emael, the cornerstone of the Belgian defence, with a gliderborne assault on 11 May, the day on which the bulk of the Belgian Army pulled back toward the Dyle Line. This was no longer of use, however, and the Allies pulled steadily back, Belgium surrendering on the night of 27–28 May.

BELGIAN AND DUTCH BOMBER UNITS			
Unit	Type	Base	Strength
Belgian 1/I/3	Fairey Fox III	Evere	9
Belgian 3/I/3	Fairey Fox III	Evere	9
Belgian 5/III/3	Fairey Battle	Evere	14
Belgian 7/III/3	Fairey Fox VIII	Evere	9
Dutch Bomber Squadron	Fokker T.V	Schiphol	9

▲ **Fairey Battle Mk I**

5/III / 3rd Air Regiment, Belgium, Evere, May 1940

All 18 Battle Mk I light bombers delivered to Belgium served with this squadron, which had 14 aircraft on strength at the time of the German invasion on 10 May 1940. Six out of nine such aircraft were lost while attacking a bridge over the Albert Canal on 11 May, and the other aircraft were also soon lost.

Specifications

Crew: 3

Powerplant: 2 x 768kW (1030hp) Rolls-Royce Merlin I Vee piston engines

Maximum speed: 414km/h (257mph)

Range: 1609km (1000 miles)

Service ceiling: 7620m (25,000ft)

Dimensions: span 16.46m (54ft); length 12.9m (42ft 4in); height 4.72m (15ft 6in)

Weight: 4895kg (10,792lb) loaded

Armament: 2 x 7.7mm (0.303in) Vickers MGs: one fixed-forward firing in the leading edge of the starboard wing, one Vickers 'K' trainable rearward-firing in the rear of the cockpit; up to 113kg (250lb) bombs carried internally, 2 x 113kg (250lb) carried externally

▲ **Fairey Battle Mk I**

5/III / 3rd Air Regiment, Evere, Belgium, May 1940

Like the British, the Belgians found that the Battle was wholly inadequate in speed, agility and armament to survive, let alone operate effectively, against an enemy possessing good fighters and powerful anti-aircraft (AA) defences.

Specifications

Crew: 3

Powerplant: 2 x 768kW (1030hp) Rolls-Royce Merlin I Vee piston engines

Maximum speed: 414km/h (257mph)

Range: 1609km (1000 miles)

Service ceiling: 7620m (25,000ft)

Dimensions: span 16.46m (54ft); length 12.9m (42ft 4in); height 4.72m (15ft 6in)

Weight: 4895kg (10,792lb) loaded

Armament: 2 x 7.7mm (0.303in) Vickers MGs: one fixed-forward firing in the leading edge of the starboard wing, one Vickers 'K' trainable rearward-firing in the rear of the cockpit; up to 113kg (250lb) bombs carried internally, 2 x 113kg (250lb) carried externally

Free French air forces
1940–45

The Free French Forces started with men unwilling to accept the defeat of France in 1940, but grew to include the formations of French colonies retaken by the Allies, and by 1943 were growing strongly in strength and overall capability. Their air force was very useful in 1944–45.

THE FORCES FRANÇAISES LIBRES (Free French Forces, or FFL) consisted of Frenchmen who had decided to continue fighting against Axis forces after the surrender of France. The FFL were led by the French government-in-exile under Général Charles de Gaulle, and their air arm was the *Forces Aériennes Françaises Libres* (Free French Air Force, or FAFL), distinguished by cross of Lorraine markings. It was on 17 June 1940, five days before the Franco-German armistice was signed, that the first exodus to the UK took place, as 10 men flew from Bordeaux-Mérignac.

Answering the call

Others rallied to de Gaulle from France and French North Africa over the next two years. From a strength of 500 on July 1940, the FAFL had grown to

ORGANIZATION

	French I Air Corps	
	October 1944	
French 1st Fighter Group (Nos 326, 327 & 328 Squadrons)	French 4th Fighter Group (GC II/5, II/3 & I/4)	French Reconnaissance Group (GR II/3)

900 by 1941, including 200 airmen. De Gaulle appointed Colonel Martin Valin as the FAFL's commander in the summer of 1940, but this officer assumed command only on 9 July 1941 from Amiral Emile Muselier.

The FAFL was formed with one mixed unit at Odiham on 29 August 1940. De Gaulle saw one of his first tasks as being the seduction of French

▲ **Consolidated PBY-5A Catalina**

Free French squadron, Morocco, 1943

The French ordered the PBY in 1939 but received no such 'boats' before the fall of France. In 1943, two squadrons (one with Free French and the other with ex-Vichy French personnel) were formed with 28 PBY-5A amphibious flying boats for service off Morocco under operational control of the US Navy.

Specifications

Crew: 7/9	height 6.15m (20ft 2in)
Powerplant: 2 x 895kW (1200hp)	Weight: 16,066kg (35,420lb) loaded
Maximum speed: 288km/h (179mph)	Armament: 3 x 7.62mm (0.3in) trainable MGs:
Range: 4096km (2545 miles)	two in the bow turret, one firing aft of the
Service ceiling: 4480m (14,700ft)	hull step; 1 x 12.7mm (0.5in) MG in each of
Dimensions: span 31.7m (104ft);	the two beam positions; up to 1814kg
length 19.47m (63ft 11in);	(4000lb) of bombs or depth charges

The badge of No. 342 Squadron 'Lorraine', RAF, sports the usual Free French cross of Lorraine. The squadron was formed after the French *escadrilles* (squadrons) 'Metz' and 'Nancy' were transferred to the UK from the Mediterranean and combined in April 1943.

Specifications

Douglas A-20G Havoc

Crew: 3

Powerplant: 2 x 1194kW (1600hp) Wright Cyclone R-2600-23 air-cooled radial piston

Maximum speed: 546km/h (339mph)

Range: 1755km (1090 miles)

Service ceiling: 7650m (25,100ft)

Dimensions: span 18.69m (61ft 4in); length 14.63m (48ft); height 5.36m (17ft 7in)

Weight: 12,338kg (27,200lb) loaded

Armament: up to 8 x 12.7mm (0.5in) MGs; 1814kg (4000lb) of bombs

▲ Douglas Boston Mk IIIA

No. 342 Squadron 'Lorraine' / RAF, Hartford Bridge, UK, 1944

No. 342 Squadron was an RAF unit manned by Free French personnel, and was allocated to No. 2 Bomber Group of the 2nd Tactical Air Force (TAF) for service in support of the Allied landings of June 1944 in Normandy, and then the subsequent land campaign.

Specifications

Crew: 5

Powerplant: 2 x 1491kW (2000hp)

Maximum speed: 518km/h (322mph)

Range: 2671km (1660 miles)

Service ceiling: 8016m (26,300ft)

Dimensions: span 19.96m (65ft 6in); length 15.77m (51ft 9in); height 11m (11ft)

Weight: 15,422kg (34,000lb) loaded

Armament: 5 x 12.7mm (0.5in) MGs: two fixed in nose, three fixed in undernose gun pack; 2 x 12.7 (0.5in) trainable in dorsal turret; 2 x 7.62mm (0.3in) trainables in rearward firing ventral position; bomb load 6 x 227kg (500lb) internally, 2 x 454kg (1000lb) externally, 1 x MK13-2 torpedo or 6 x 147kg (325lb) depth charges

▲ Lockheed PV-1 Ventura

Flottille 6F / Aeronavale, France, 1944–45

The revived French naval air arm operated a small number of PV-1 patrol bombers from 1944, and these were eventually replaced after the end of World War II by Bloch MB.175 aircraft.

colonies from adherence to Vichy France, and an operation was mounted against Dakar in French West Africa. This included the FAFL's *Groupe de Combat Mixte* 1, comprising four squadrons of Bristol Blenheim bombers and Westland Lysander army cooperation aircraft. The operation failed, and the FAFL's envoys were incarcerated at Dakar by the Vichy authorities. However, the forces in Cameroon and Chad rallied to the Gaullist cause.

There were three detachments of French Air Force units based at Fort Lamy, Douala and Pointe Noire with a miscellany of Potez and Bloch aircraft, and they thus became part of the FAFL. However, Gabon remained loyal to Vichy, so, in October 1940, FAFL squadrons set out on photo-reconnaissance and leaflet-dropping missions. The first Vichy-versus-FAFL combats occurred on 6 November 1940, when two Vichy French aircraft tackled two FAFL Lysanders near Libreville, resulting in both aircraft sustaining damage. Two days later, the first FAFL airmen were shot down and taken prisoner. Further north, a mission by the recently formed *Groupe de Bombardement* 1 'Lorraine' on 4 February 1941 ended in disaster when only one of four Blenheims sent to bomb Koufra returned.

Groupe 'Bretagne'

The Groupe 'Bretagne' was formed on 1 January for long-range reconnaissance with the Martin Maryland, army cooperation with the Lysander and

FRENCH SQUADRONS ON THE RAF ESTABLISHMENT, JUNE 1944		
Unit	Type	Base
No. 329 Sqn	Supermarine Spitfire Mk IX	Merston
No. 340 Sqn	Supermarine Spitfire Mk IX	Merston
No. 341 Sqn	Supermarine Spitfire Mk IX	Merston
No. 342 Sqn	Douglas Boston Mk III	Hartford Bridge
No. 346 Sqn	Handley Page Halifax Mk III	Elvington
No. 347 Sqn	Handley Page Halifax Mk III	Elvington

transport with Potez aircraft. It was not until 3 March, however, that the first missions were flown from Uigh-el-Kébir. For most of 1942, the Groupe 'Bretagne' concentrated on liaison and training flights, but from late in 1942 the group's 'Rennes' Squadron engaged Italian forces and operations continued to the fall of Tripoli on 23 January 1943.

November 1942 marked the start of the rebirth of the French Air Force as a result of Franklin D. Roosevelt's agreement to deliver 1000 US aircraft. On 1 July 1943 different elements of the French air forces in Africa came under the control of Général Bouscat, who reorganized his command, which included about 20 *groupes*. The new French Air Force was then active in the Italian campaign, while other elements fought with the RAF in north-west Europe, and a much enlarged and upgraded air force played a major part in the French campaign of 1944–45.

Specifications

Crew: 7

Powerplant: 4 x 1204kW (1615hp) Bristol Hercules XVI

Maximum speed: 454km/h (282mph)

Range: 1658km (1030 miles)

Service ceiling: 7315m (24,000ft)

Dimensions: span 31.75m (104ft 2in);

length 21.36m (70ft 1in);

height 6.32m (20ft 9in)

Weight: 29,484kg (65,000lb) loaded

Armament: 9 x 7.7mm (0.303in) MGs: one on flexible mount in nose; four each on dorsal and tail turrets; 5897kg (13,000lb) bomb load

▲ Handley Page Halifax Mk III

No. 346 Squadron 'Guyenne' / RAF, Elvington, UK, 1944

No. 346 Squadron was manned by Free French personnel, and in June 1944 was a heavy bomber unit of No. 4 Bomber Group within the Royal Air Force's Bomber Command.

Chapter 2

United Kingdom and Commonwealth

Great things were expected of RAF Bomber Command right from the start of the war, but expectations were initially confounded. Light bombers proved wholly inadequate, medium bombers were very vulnerable by day, bomb weights were too light, and the accuracy of bombing and night navigation was woeful. Gradually the situation improved as night area bombing became the norm, twin-engined medium bombers were replaced by altogether more capable four-engined heavy bombers, and better navigation and bombing equipment were introduced. From later in 1943, Bomber Command became a formidable strategic and, at times, tactical force.

◀ **Flight of Lancasters**
Three Lancaster bombers from No. 207 Squadron fly over British countryside, 1943. The squadron started World War II flying Avro Manchester bombers but switched to Lancasters in June 1942.

RAF Bomber Command
1936–45

The bomber forces with which the UK entered World War II were modest in size and very limited in their capabilities. The light bombers were largely obsolete, and of the medium bombers only the Vickers Wellington offered any genuine capability. There was to be a steep learning curve.

RAF BOMBER COMMAND controlled the RAF's bomber forces, and was formed on 14 July 1936 from the bomber element of the Air Defence of Great Britain. From 12 September 1937 its commander was Air Chief Marshal Sir Edgar Ludlow-Hewitt, replaced on 3 April 1940 by Air Marshal Sir Charles Portal. He, in turn, was replaced on 5 October 1940 by Air Marshal Sir Richard Peirse, and from 22 February 1942, and for the rest of the war, Air Chief Marshal Sir Arthur Harris took over. Bomber Command destroyed a major part of Germany's industries and many of her cities, and it should be noted that many of Bomber Command's personnel and squadrons during the war were not British: a significant proportion came from commonwealth countries or were exiles from occupied Europe.

'Bombers will always get through'

When Bomber Command was created, General Giulio Douhet's aphorism that 'the bomber will always get through' was believed by the public, service

ORGANIZATION

Royal Air Force Home Commands
September 1939

Bomber Command	Fighter Command	Coastal Command	Army Cooperation Command

personnel and politicians. Until the advent of radar in the late 1930s, this belief was in fact true, for attacking bombers could not be detected early enough for a fighter force to be assembled and intercept the bombers before the latter reached their targets. Some damage might be done by AA guns and by fighters as the bombers turned back after bombing, but this was not an effective defence.

Thus Bomber Command was seen as a force that could threaten an enemy with total destruction, and serve as a deterrent to war. However, even if the bomber could actually get through, its potential for inflicting decisive damage was hugely overrated. The problem was that the British government was basing

▲ Fairey Battle Mk I

No. 106 Squadron, Abingdon, Oxfordshire, August 1938

The Battle was maintained in production well after the time it was appreciated that the type was too slow, too lightly armed (both offensively and defensively) and too lacking in agility for the battlefield bombing role. Such persistence was because there was no successor, and production could not be interrupted.

Specifications

Crew: 3

Powerplant: one 768kW (1030hp) Rolls-Royce
  Merlin II liquid-cooled V-12 piston engine

Maximum speed: 388km/h (241mph)

Range: 1450km (900 miles)

Service ceiling: 7620m (25,000ft)

Dimensions: span 16.46m (54ft 0in);
  length 12.9m (42ft 4in);
  height 4.72m (15ft 6in)

Weight: 4895kg (10,792lb) loaded

Armament: 2 x 7.7mm (0.303in) MGs; 113kg
  (250lb) bomb load

its data on a casualty rate of 50 per ton of bombs dropped, and thus the government and public saw the bomber as a weapon more terrible than it was in operational reality.

At the start of World War II, Bomber Command was hampered by a lack of size for strategic capability,

The red and blue roundel was most generally associated with night bombers, in which the otherwise standard white intermediate ring was thought too obtrusive and therefore noticeable.

BOMBER COMMAND, NO. 2 GROUP (SEPTEMBER 1939)

Unit	Type	Base
No. 21 Sqn	Blenheim IV	Watton
No. 82 Sqn	Blenheim IV	Watton
No. 101 Sqn	Blenheim IV	West Raynham
No. 107 Sqn	Blenheim IV	Wattisham
No. 110 Sqn	Blenheim IV	Wattisham
No. 114 Sqn	Blenheim IV	Wyton
No. 139 Sqn	Blenheim IV	Wyton

▲ **Bristol Blenheim Mk I**

No. 57 Squadron / Air Component of the BEF, France, 1939–40

No. 57 Squadron re-equipped from the Hawker Hind single-engined biplane to the Blenheim twin-engined monoplane in 1938, and was transferred to France in September 1939. The unit suffered heavy losses in the first 10 days of the German advance into France as it attacked troop and transport columns, and was then withdrawn to England to recuperate and rebuild.

Specifications
Crew: 3
Powerplant: 627kW (840hp) Bristol Mercury VIII 9-cylinder single-row radial engines
Maximum speed: 459km/h (285mph)
Range: 1810km (1125 miles)
Service ceiling: 8315m (27,280ft)
Dimensions: span 17.17m (56ft 4in); length 12.12m (39ft 9in); height 3m (9ft 10in)
Weight: 4031kg (8839lb) loaded
Armament: 2 x 7.7mm (0.303in) MGs and 454kg (1000lb) bomb load

Specifications
Crew: 2
Powerplant: 1 x 708kW (950hp) Bristol Pegasus radial piston engine
Maximum speed: 367km/h (228mph)
Range: 1786km (1110 miles)
Service ceiling: 10,058m (33,000ft)
Dimensions: span 22.73m (74ft 7in); length 11.96m (39ft 3in); height 3.76m (12ft 4in)
Weight: 5035kg (11,100lb) loaded
Armament: 1 x 7.7mm (0.303in) MG and 1 x Vickers MG in rear cockpit; up to 907kg (2000lb) bombs

▲ **Vickers Wellesley**

No. 76 Squadron, Finningley, Yorkshire, 1939

Designed for the general-purpose role but technically and tactically obsolete by the start of World War II, the Wellesley nonetheless saw limited but useful operational service in North Africa and, more importantly, the Middle East and East Africa during the first part of the war.

the rules of engagement that limited the targets the command was permitted to attack, and a lack of adequate aircraft. The command's standard warplanes at the start of the war were the Battle, Blenheim, Hampden, Wellesley, Wellington and Whitley, and even the best of these, the Wellington, did not possess the bomb load and range for anything but a limited strategic offensive.

Bomber Command was further reduced in size after the declaration of war. No. 1 Group, with its Battle squadrons, left for France to form the Advanced Air Striking Force (AASF), providing the

Specifications

Crew: 2	Dimensions: span 16.46m (54ft 0in);
Powerplant: one 768kW (1030hp) Rolls-Royce	length 12.9m (42ft 4in);
Merlin I inline piston engine	height 4.72m (15ft 6in)
Maximum speed: 414km/h (257mph)	Weight: 4895kg (10,792lb) loaded
Range: 1609km (1000 miles)	Armament: 1 x 7.7mm (0.303in) MG; 1 x
Service ceiling: 7620m (25,000ft)	Vickers K MG; 454kg (1000lb) bomb load

▲ **Fairey Battle Mk I**

No. 12 Squadron / Advanced Air Striking Force / RAF, France, 1939–40

This aeroplane sports the standard day-bomber camouflage and markings of the 'Phoney War' period. The squadron was initially tasked with reconnaissance and leaflet dropping, but from 10 May 1940 was committed, with disastrous losses, against the advancing Germans.

Specifications

Crew: 2	Dimensions: span 16.46m (54ft 0in);
Powerplant: one 768kW (1030hp) Rolls-Royce	length 12.9m (42ft 4in);
Merlin I inline piston engine	height 4.72m (15ft 6in)
Maximum speed: 414km/h (257mph)	Weight: 4895kg (10,792lb) loaded
Range: 1609km (1000 miles)	Armament: one 7.7mm (0.303in) MG, one
Service ceiling: 7620m (25,000ft)	Vickers K MG; 454kg (1000lb) bomb load

▲ **Fairey Battle Mk I**

No. 218 Squadron / Advanced Air Striking Force / RAF, France, 1939–40

Issued to No. 218 Squadron at Boscombe Down early in 1939, this Battle Mk I went with its squadron to France in September of the same year, flew through the 'Phoney War', and was then lost on 13 May 1940, the fourth day of the German offensive into France.

British Expeditionary Force (BEF) with air striking power, and allowing the Battle to operate against German targets, since it lacked the range to do so from British airfields. The *Sitzkrieg* (lit. 'sitting down war') between September 1939 and May 1940 affected Bomber Command in France, for its squadrons flew many missions, lost men and aircraft, but did virtually no damage, as most of the missions either failed to find their intended targets, or were limited to the dropping of leaflets rather than bombs. The German attack to the west, launched on 10 May 1940, then changed all this.

▲ Short Stirling Mk I Series 1

No. 7 Squadron / No. 3 Group / RAF Bomber Command, 1940

No. 7 Squadron was the first unit to receive the Stirling, the squadron getting its first aircraft at Leeming in Yorkshire during August 1940. MG-D was the first of the aircraft to be delivered.

Specifications

Crew: 7

Powerplant: 4 x 1030kW (1375hp) Bristol Hercules radial engines

Maximum speed: 410km/h (255mph)

Range: 3750km (2330 miles)

Service ceiling: 5030m (16,500ft)

Dimensions: span 30.2m (99ft 1in)

length 26.6m (87ft 3in);

height 8.8m (28ft 10in)

Weight: 31,750kg (70,000lb) loaded

Armament: 8 x 7.7mm (0.303in) Browning MGs: two in the nose, four in the tail, two dorsal; up to 8164kg (18,000lb) of bombs

▲ Bristol Blenheim Mk I

No. 18 Squadron / Air Component of the BEF, France, 1939–40

No. 18 Squadron transitioned from the Hawker Hind to the Blenheim in the autumn of 1938, at about the time of the Munich crisis, whose solution delayed the start of World War I for a year. The squadron moved to France in 1939, but by May 1940 had re-equipped with the longer-nose Blenheim Mk IV.

Specifications

Crew: 3

Powerplant: 627kW (840hp) Bristol Mercury VIII 9-cylinder single-row radial engines

Maximum speed: 459km/h (285mph)

Range: 1810km (1125 miles)

Service ceiling: 8315m (27,280ft)

Dimensions: span 17.17m (56ft 4in);

length 12.12m (39ft 9in);

height 3m (9ft 10in)

Weight: 4031kg (8839lb) loaded

Armament: 2 x 7.7mm (0.3in) MGs; 454kg (1000lb) bomb load

'Nickel' leaflet raids
1939–40

Unwilling to attack Germany directly, which would cause the death of civilians and damage to private property, Bomber Command was initially limited to 'attacking' Germany with leaflets designed, futilely, to persuade the German people to reach a peaceful solution with the Allies.

RAF BOMBER COMMAND started with war with night leaflet flights and day reconnaissance of German naval bases. The Whitleys of No. 4 Group carried out the first operation and the other groups shared the second. An important factor of this period of the war was the neutrality of the Netherlands and and Belgium, which prevented any direct approach to Germany from British bases, and thus demanded long approach flights in across the German coast over the North Sea or in the south over France. Dutch and Belgian defences often fired on damaged or lost Whitleys flying over their territory.

The leaflet raids continued throughout the 'Phoney War' and were almost free from losses, except those resulting from adverse weather in the long winter nights.

One positive aspect of operations in this period was the high serviceability rate of aircraft maintained by the well-trained ground crew of the prewar era, combined with the fact that the night squadrons were never called upon to dispatch more than a proportion of their available strength. The range of the leaflet flights was increased when some of the Whitleys started to refuel at French airfields in the early

months of 1940, and leaflets were then delivered to cities as distant as Prague, Vienna and Warsaw. It is unlikely that the leaflets had any real effect on German morale, but Bomber Command gained valuable night experience at modest cost.

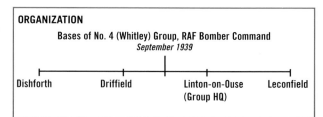

ORGANIZATION

Bases of No. 4 (Whitley) Group, RAF Bomber Command
September 1939

| Dishforth | Driffield | Linton-on-Ouse (Group HQ) | Leconfield |

BOMBER COMMAND, NO. 4 GROUP (SEPTEMBER 1939)

Unit	Type	Base
No. 10 Sqn	Whitley	Dishforth
No. 51 Sqn	Whitley	Linton-on-Ouse
No. 58 Sqn	Whitley	Linton-on-Ouse
No. 77 Sqn	Whitley	Driffield
No. 78 Sqn	Whitley	Dishforth
No. 102 Sqn	Whitley	Driffield

Specifications
Crew: 5

Powerplant: 2 x 593kW (795hp) Tiger IX

Maximum speed: 362km/h (225mph)

Range: 2414km (1315 miles)

Service ceiling: 7925m (26,001ft)

Dimensions: span 25.6m (84ft);

length 21.1m (69ft 3in); height 4.57m (15ft)

Weight: 15,196kg (33,501lb) loaded

Armament: 1 x 7.7mm (0.303in) Lewis gun

mounted in front and rear turrets; 1135kg

(2500lb) bomb load

▲ **Armstrong Whitworth Whitley Mk I**

No. 10 Squadron / RAF, Dishforth, Yorkshire, 1939–40

This aeroplane is depicted in the standard camouflage and markings of the period with yellow-ringed fuselage roundels, black under surfaces, and dark-green and dark-earth upper surfaces.

From day to night bombing
1940–41

The British bombing effort began in earnest during and after the battle of France, and at first Bomber Command hoped to strike accurately by day against point targets. The losses were so heavy, though, that the command rapidly switched to nocturnal attacks of area targets.

THE FAIREY BATTLE light bomber element of the AASF was badly damaged by German attacks on its airfields at the start of the invasion of France, but not all of this element was caught on the ground, and in the air the Battles proved to be appallingly vulnerable to ground and air fire. On many occasions Battle units were almost wholly destroyed against German chokepoints such as river-crossings.

Defeat in France

The main strength of Bomber Command was itself soon fully committed to battle. France's quick defeat seemed to presage a German invasion of the UK, and as part of its contribution to the Battle of Britain, Bomber Command was tasked with the destruction of the craft being assembled on the southern side of the English Channel for the invasion forces. This effort was unseen by the British people and never gained any coverage akin to that lavished on Fighter Command, but was nonetheless vital and very dangerous work.

ORGANIZATION

British air units in France
September 1939

| AASF (eight sqns of Battles) | AASF (two sqns of Hurricanes) | | | Air Component (four sqns of Blenheims) |

| | Air Component (two sqns of Hurricanes) | Air Component (one sqn of Lysanders) | |

▲ **Vickers Wellington Mk IC**

No. 99 Squadron / No. 3 Group / RAF Bomber Command, Newmarket, Cambridgeshire, 1940

Features of the Wellington Mk IC were two beam guns in place of one ventral gun, and larger main wheels that extended below the engine nacelle when retracted.

Specifications

Crew: 6

Powerplant: 2 x 783kW (1050hp) Bristol Pegasus XVIII 9 cylinder radial engines

Maximum speed: 378km/h (235mph)

Range: 2905km (805 miles)

Service ceiling: 5486m (18,000ft)

Dimensions: span 26.26m (86ft 2in);

length 18.54m (60ft 10in);

height 5.33m (17ft 6in)

Weight: 12,927kg (28,500lb) loaded

Armament: 2 x 7.7mm (0.303in) Browning MGs in both nose and tail; 2 x 7.7mm (0.303in) beam guns; 2041kg (4500lb) bomb load

Whitley tail gun

The Armstrong Whitley was notable as the first British bomber to carry a heavy defensive armament, specifically, the manually-operated four-gun tail turret.

From July 1940 to the end of the same year, Bomber Command lost nearly 330 aircraft and more than 1400 men killed, missing or taken prisoner. Bomber Command was also responsible, in part and somewhat indirectly, for the *Luftwaffe*'s change of focus away from Fighter Command to the bombing of civilian targets. After a German bomber had become lost and dropped its bombs on London, Prime Minister Winston Churchill ordered

retaliation in the form of a raid on Berlin, the German capital. This very minor effort enraged Hitler, who ordered the *Luftwaffe* to level British cities, so beginning the *Blitz*.

Like the Americans did later in the war, Bomber Command initially tried to fly 'precision' daylight attacks. Several raids late in 1939 were savaged by the well-organized German defences, however, and Bomber Command had perforce to switch to night attacks. This raised a fresh crop of problems, though, with those of the German defences replaced with those of finding the target and attacking it by night. Nocturnal navigation deficiencies in the early years of the war were so great that it was not uncommon for bombers flying by dead reckoning to miss whole urban areas.

Surveys of bombing photographs and other sources during August 1941 indicated that less than 10 per cent of bombs fell within 8km (5 miles) of their intended target. One of Bomber Command's most pressing needs was therefore to develop the technical aids for accurate night navigation.

Bomber Command comprised several groups, starting the war with Nos 1, 2, 3, 4 and 5 Groups. No. 1 Group was detached to France but returned to Bomber Command after the evacuation. No. 2

The yellow outer ring round the tri-colour roundel on the fuselage sides of British day-bombers was standard right into 1941.

Armstrong Whitworth Whitley Mk V

No. 77 Squadron / RAF Bomber Command, Linton-on-Ouse, Yorkshire, 1940

This aeroplane carries the standard camouflage of dark-green/dark-earth upper surfaces and black under surfaces, the latter carried unusually high onto the sides of the fuselage.

Specifications

Crew: 5	length 21.1m (69ft 3in);
Powerplant: 2 x 593kW (795hp) Tiger IX	height 4.57m (15ft)
Maximum speed: 362km/h (225mph)	Weight: 15,196kg (33,501lb) loaded
Range: 2414km (1315 miles)	Armament: 1 x 7.7mm (0.303in) Lewis gun in
Service ceiling: 7925m (26,001ft)	front and rear turrets; 1135kg (2500lb) bomb
Dimensions: span 25.6m (84ft);	load

Group consisted of light and medium bombers, and remained part of Bomber Command until 1943, when it was reallocated to the 2nd TAF. Bomber Command also gained two new groups during the war: the Royal Canadian Air Force (RCAF) contributed No. 6 Group, and No. 8 Group was established as the Pathfinder Force to lead the Main Force bombers to their targets.

▼ RAF Bomber Command light bomber squadron, early 1940

The typical British light bomber squadron of September 1939 – May 1940 comprised 12 Bristol Blenheim Mk IV aircraft divided into three flights, each of four aircraft.

1st Flight **2nd Flight** **3rd Flight**

▲ Bristol Blenheim Mk IV

RAF Bomber Command, 1939–40

This was an aeroplane of Bristol's third production batch (70 aircraft) of the improved Blenheim Mk IV.

Specifications

Crew: 3

Powerplant: 675kW (905hp) Bristol Mercury XV radial piston engines

Maximum speed: 428km/h (266mph)

Range: 2350km (1460 miles)

Service ceiling: 8310m (27,260ft)

Dimensions: span 17.17m (56ft 4in);

length 12.98m (42ft 7in);

height 3m (9ft 10in)

Weight: 65.32kg (14,400lb) loaded

Armament: 5 x 7.7mm (0.303in) MGs; up to 434kg (1000lb) bombs internally and 145kg (320lb) externally

▲ **Bristol Blenheim Mk IV**

No. 139 Squadron / RAF Bomber Command, Horsham St Faith, Norfolk, 1940
The nose of the Blenheim Mk IV was longer than that of the Mk I to improve the
navigator's accommodation, and its upper portion was downward-scalloped on the
port side so that the pilot's field of vision would not be degraded. This aeroplane
remained in first-line service to 1944, when it was relegated to the training role.

Specifications

Crew: 3

Powerplant: 675kW (905hp) Bristol Mercury XV
  radial piston engines

Maximum speed: 428km/h (266mph)

Range: 2350km (1460 miles)

Service ceiling: 8310m (27,260ft)

Dimensions: span 17.17m (56ft 4in);
  length 12.98m (42ft 7in); height 3m (9ft 10in)

Weight: 65.32kg (14,400lb) loaded

Armament: 5 x 7.7mm (0.303in) MGs; up to
  454kg (1000lb) of bombs internally and
  145kg (320lb) externally

Day bombing of German naval bases
1939–40

**The British entered the war with the concept that bomber formations could defend themselves
against fighter attack by day. Attempts to bomb German naval bases soon suffered unsustainable
losses to fighter interception, however, and Bomber Command turned to night bombing.**

IN BOMBER COMMAND'S largest operation of the war
to date, on 14 December 1939, North Sea shipping
searches were flown by 23 Hampdens,
12 Wellingtons and seven Whitleys, while two
Blenheims made reconnaissance flights to Sylt. The
Wellingtons found a German convoy in the Schillig
Roads, north of the port of Wilhelmshaven, but low

ORGANIZATION

Bases of No. 3 (Wellington) Group, RAF Bomber Command
September 1939

Feltwell	Marham	Mildenhall (Group HQ)	Honington
	Bassingbourn	Stradishall	

cloud and poor visibility prevented them from
achieving the required bombing position. Even so,
the Wellingtons remained in the area for some
30 minutes, flying at low level as they sought to
achieve a viable position from which to unload their
bombs, and being engaged by flak and also by
fighters during this time, losing no fewer than five of
their number shot down.

But the RAF was not willing to admit that
German fighters had shot down almost half of a

BOMBER COMMAND, NO. 3 GROUP (SEPTEMBER 1939)		
Unit	Type	Base
No. 9 Sqn	Wellington	Honington
No. 37 Sqn	Wellington	Feltwell
No. 38 Sqn	Wellington	Marham
No. 99 Sqn	Wellington	Mildenhall
No. 115 Sqn	Wellington	Marham
No. 149 Sqn	Wellington	Mildenhall
No. 214 Sqn	Wellington	Feltwell
No. 215 Sqn	Wellington	Bassingbourn

formation of Bomber Command's best-armed warplanes, and it was officially claimed that the losses were the result of flak fire. The Germans claimed to the contrary, and admitted that one fighter had been lost. No German vessels were hit, and the other British aircraft saw no action.

Wilhelmshaven raid

On 18 December, 24 Wellingtons were dispatched in another shipping search in the region of Wilhelmshaven, but in this instance the crews were instructed not to attack at any altitude less than 3050m (10,000ft) to escape the worst effects of flak. Some 22 of the 24 aircraft reached the target area and, from an altitude of 3960m (13,000ft), bombed the German ships their crews spotted off Wilhelmshaven. There was no cloud, and the visibility was perfect for bombing.

For the first time in the war, however, German fighters were vectored to this bomber force by a ground controller, who was being given information from a German naval establishment on Heligoland and an experimental 'Freya' radar station of the *Luftwaffe* on the nearby island of Wangerooge. The latter had detected the Wellingtons when they were still 113km (70 miles) distant on their approach. Flak fire caused the bomber formation to spread out

slightly, and the twin-engined fighters of I *Gruppe*, *Zerstörergeschwader* 76 (I/ZG 76) and of II and III/ZG 77, as well as the single-engined fighters of 10. *Staffel*, *Jagdgeschwader* 26 (10./JG 26), shot down 12 of the Wellingtons, though they also lost two of their own number to the bombers' defensive armament.

The key elements in this action were the superior speed and agility of the fighters, which enabled them to achieve the right firing positions, and their armament, including at least one 20mm (0.79in) cannon, providing greater range than the machine guns with which the British bombers were armed, as well as an explosive shell causing much greater damage in the bombers than the ball ammunition of the British machine guns.

This celebrated action, coming so soon after that of 14 December, had a major impact on the thinking of the commanders of the British bomber arm. Exactly half of the 34 Wellingtons dispatched in the two missions had been shot down in these two actions, and the bombers had not even attempted to penetrate over the mainland of Germany, which was known to be more strongly defended. The conceptual validity of the bomber formation able to protect itself had now been seriously questioned, and thoughts immediately turned to night bombing.

Specifications

Crew: 6	length 18.54m (60ft 10in);
Powerplant: two 1119kW (1500hp) Bristol	height 5.31m (17ft 5in);
Hercules XI radial piston engines	Weight: 9527kg (21,000lb) loaded
Maximum speed: 378km/h (235mph)	Armament: 6 x 7.7mm (0.303in) Browning MGs
Range: 2478km (1540 miles)	in nose and tail and Frazer-Nash ventral
Service ceiling: 5791m (19,000ft)	positions; either 9 x 227kg (500lb) of bombs,
Dimensions: span 26.26m (86ft 2in);	or 2 x 907kg (2000lb) of bombs

▲ Vickers Wellington Mk I

No. 38 Squadron / RAF Bomber Command, Marham, Norfolk, 1940

No. 38 Squadron received its first Wellington twin-engined bombers in 1938, and operated the type in several marks until early in 1942. The Wellington proved very vulnerable to fighter interception in early daylight raids, and was then switched to the night bombing role.

Retaliatory raid on Mannheim
DECEMBER 1940

After the *Luftwaffe* had bombed British urban centres, RAF Bomber Command was instructed to retaliate against a German city, and the resulting raid on Mannheim set the pattern for area bombing attacks, which became the staple of Bomber Command for the following four years.

IN ALL PROBABILITY the most interesting British raid of the war to date, the attack made on Mannheim on 16/17 December 1940, resulted from the decision of the War Cabinet that an attack should be carried out on the centre of a German city in retaliation for the recent heavy bombing of English cities such as Coventry and Southampton. Mannheim was selected as the target, and a force of 200 bombers was readied. The threat of deteriorating weather then led to the trimming of the force to 134 twin-engined aircraft in the form of 61 Wellingtons, 35 Whitleys, 29

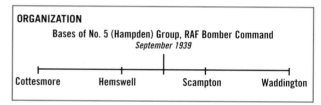

ORGANIZATION

Bases of No. 5 (Hampden) Group, RAF Bomber Command
September 1939

| Cottesmore | Hemswell | Scampton | Waddington |

Hampdens and nine Blenheims. Even so, this was still the British largest force despatched against a single target to date. The attack was started by eight Wellingtons. They used incendiary bombs in an

▲ **Night bomber**
This Whitley Mk V of No. 78 Squadron is painted in the overall black used by aircraft engaged in night raids over Germany in the early years of the war.

BOMBER COMMAND, NO. 5 GROUP (SEPTEMBER 1939)		
Unit	Type	Base
No. 44 Sqn	Hampden	Waddington
No. 49 Sqn	Hampden	Scampton
No. 50 Sqn	Hampden	Waddington
No. 61 Sqn	Hampden	Hemswell
No. 83 Sqn	Hampden	Scampton
No. 106 Sqn	Hampden	Cottesmore
No. 144 Sqn	Hampden	Hemswell
No. 185 Sqn	Hampden	Cottesmore

▲ **Blenheims on patrol**
Even in its definitive Mk IV form, the Blenheim was technically obsolete by 1942.

effort to start fires that would serve as the aiming points for the following crews. For the first time in more than 15 months of war, Bomber Command was attacking a target not primarily of military or industrial nature.

The weather over the target was generally clear, and there was also a full moon. Mannheim's defences were not strong, and Bomber Command's records suggest that anything between 82 and 102 aircraft claimed to have bombed Mannheim. But the attack was unsuccessful, for the 'pathfinder' Wellingtons bombed inaccurately and the largest fires were not in the centre of the city.

Most of the bombs fell in residential areas, 240 buildings being destroyed or damaged by the incendiaries and 236 by HE bombs. The German casualty list totalled 34 dead, 81 injured and 1266

rendered homeless. Of those bombed out, 223 were in the town of Ludwigshafen on the other side of the Rhine. During the raid, Bomber Command lost two Hampdens and one Blenheim, and another four aircraft crashed in England on return.

Specifications

Crew: 4

Powerplant: 746kW (1000hp) Bristol Pegasus
XVII radial piston engines

Maximum speed: 409km/h (254mph)

Range: 3034km (1885 miles)

Service ceiling: 5791m (19,000ft)

Dimensions: span 21.08m (69ft 2in);
length 16.33m (53ft 7in);
height 4.55m (14ft 11in)

Weight: 8508kg (18,756lb) loaded

Armament: 2 x forward-firing and twin 7.7mm
(0.303in) MGs; 1814kg (4000lb) bombs

▲ **Handley Page Hampden Mk I**

No. 106 Squadron / No. 5 Group / RAF Bomber Command, Finningley, Yorkshire, April 1940

The Hampden Mk I was operated by a four-man crew all located in the 'pod' section of the fuselage, which was so narrow that it was impossible for anyone to exchange seats. Thus a badly wounded pilot could not be replaced.

The campaign gathers pace
1941–42

In 1941–42 Bomber Command grew in size and capability, and its night area attacks on German cities began to have a real effect despite the problems associated with accurate navigation and bombing by night. With bomber production increasing steadily, the scene was set fair for 1943.

MANY UNITS and men from Commonwealth and other European countries were evident in the make-up of Bomber Command. Activated on the first day of 1943, No. 6 Group was unique inasmuch as it was not an RAF formation, but rather an element of the RCAF attached to Bomber Command. At maximum, No. 6 Group had 14 bomber squadrons, and in overall terms some 15 different squadrons served with the group. Apart from No. 6 Group, many Canadian personnel served with British and other commonwealth squadrons, and by May 1945 almost 25 per cent of Bomber Command's personnel was provided by the RCAF.

Night navigation

No. 8 Group was activated on 15 August 1942, and its aircraft and crews were instrumental in overcoming Bomber Command's night navigation problems. These problems were dealt with in two fashions: one was the development of an assortment of ever more sophisticated electronic aids to accurate navigation over steadily longer ranges, and the other was the use of the specialized air crews of the Pathfinder Force.

The technical aids were themselves of two types. One was external radio navigation aids such as Gee and the later and extremely accurate Oboe systems, and the other the internal H2S centimetric radar carried in the bombers and providing enough accuracy for bombing as well as navigation. The Pathfinders were a group of elite, specially trained and experienced crews who flew ahead of the main bombing forces, and marked the targets with flares and special marker bombs.

Specifications

Crew: 6

Powerplant: two x 1119kW (1500hp) Bristol Hercules XI radial piston engines

Maximum speed: 378km/h (235mph)

Range: 2478km (1540 miles)

Service ceiling: 5791m (19,000ft)

Dimensions: span 26.26m (86ft 2in);
length 18.54m (60ft 10in);
height 5.31m (17ft 5in);

Weight: 9527kg (21,000lb) loaded

Armament: 8 x 7.7mm (0.303in) Browning MGs in nose and tail and Frazer-Nash ventral positions; either 9 x 227kg (500lb) of bombs, or 2 x 907kg (2000lb) of bombs

▲ **Vickers Wellington Mk IA**

No. 37 Squadron / RAF Bomber Command, Feltwell, Norfolk, April 1941

The Wellington Mk IA switched from the Mk I's Vickers nose and tail turrets to Nash and Thompson turrets in these two positions. Production mounted to 183 aircraft before Vickers switched to the definitive Wellington Mk IC (2685 built).

Growing command

By the time these developments came about, Bomber Command was also increasing massively in size. In the early days of the war, it was common for raids to consist of a few tens of aircraft, which had a negligible target effect. By late in 1941, however, raids by hundreds of aircraft were being flown on a regular basis.

Specifications

Crew: 7

Powerplant: 4 x 954kW (1280hp) Rolls-Royce
  Merlin X inline engines

Maximum speed: 426km/h (265mph)

Range: 2993km (1860 miles)

Service ceiling: 6950m (22,800ft)

Dimensions: span 30.21m (98ft 10in);

length 21.36m (70ft 1in);
height 6.32m (20ft 9in)

Weight: 24,970kg (55,000lb) loaded

Armament: 2 x 7.7mm (0.303in) Browning
  MGs; 2 x Vickers 7.7mm (0.303in) K MGs;
  6 x 454kg (1000lb), 2 x 907kg (2000lb) and
  6 x 227kg (500lb) bombs

▲ Handley Page Halifax Mk I Series 1

No. 76 Squadron / RAF Bomber Command, Middleton St George, August 1941

The major partner of the Avro Lancaster in the UK's heavy night bomber forces of World War II, the Halifax was built to the extent of 6178 aircraft. Though generally associated with the air-cooled powerplant of four Bristol Hercules radial engines, the first marks had four liquid-cooled Rolls-Royce Merlin V-12 engines.

Specifications

Crew: 10

Powerplant: 4 x 895kW (1200hp) Wright R-
  1820-65 engines

Maximum speed: 524km/h (325mph)

Range: 5472km (3400 miles)

Service ceiling: 11,278m (37,000ft)

Dimensions: span 31.62m (103ft. 9in);

length 20.56m (67ft 11in);
height 4.7m (15ft 5in)

Weight: 21,999kg (48,500lb) loaded

Armament: 1 x 7.62mm (0.3in) and
  6 x 12.7mm (0.5in) MGs; 2177kg (4800lb)
  of bombs

▲ Boeing Fortress Mk I

No. 90 Squadron / RAF Bomber Command, Watton, Cambridgeshire, summer 1941

The Fortress Mk I was based on the USAAF's B-17C, and 20 such aircraft were delivered to the UK. After unsuccessful initial service in the bomber role, the aircraft were transferred to RAF Coastal Command for adaptation as long-range maritime reconnaissance machines.

▲ Short Stirling Mk I Series 1

No. 7 Squadron / No, 3 Group / RAF Bomber Command, Oakington,
1941

The Stirling was the UK's first four-engined heavy bomber of World War II, and this aeroplane remained on the strength of No. 7 Squadron until December 1941, when it passed to No. 26 Conversion Flight and later No. 1651 (Heavy) Conversion Unit.

Specifications

Crew: 7

Powerplant: 4 x 1030kW (1375hp) Bristol
  Hercules radial engines

Maximum speed: 410km/h (255mph)

Range: 3750km (2330 miles)

Service ceiling: 5030m (16,500ft)

Dimensions: span 30.2m (99ft 1in)

length 26.6m (87ft 3in);

height 8.8m (28ft 10in)

Weight: 31,750kg (70,000lb) loaded

Armament: 8 x 7.7mm (0.303in) Browning

  MGs: two in the nose, four in the tail, two

  dorsal; up to 8164 kg (18,000lb) of bombs

▲ Armstrong Whitworth Whitley Mk V

No. 78 Squadron / RAF Bomber Command, Croft, late 1941

This aeroplane is depicted in an overall black finish, not standard for Bomber Command, but alleviated by national, squadron, serial and personal markings.

Specifications

Crew: 5

Powerplant: 2 x 854kW (1145hp) Rolls-Royce
  Merlin X inline piston engines

Maximum speed: 370km/h (230mph)

Range: 2414km (1500 miles)

Service ceiling: 7925m (26,000ft)

Dimensions: span 25.6m (84ft);

  length 21.49m (70ft 6in); height 4.57m (15ft)

Weight: 15,195kg (33,500lb) loaded

Armament: 4 x 7.7mm (0.303in) MGs in

  powered tail turret and one similar gun in

  nose turret; up to 3175kg (7000lb) of bombs

▲ Handley Page Hampden Mk I

No. 420 'Snowy Owl' Squadron / No. 5 Group / RAF Bomber Command,
Waddington, Lincolnshire, 1941

This Canadian squadron flew the initial version of the Hampden in the night-bomber role until August 1942, and then transferred to the Vickers Wellington.

Specifications

Crew: 4

Powerplant: 2 x 746kW (1000hp) Bristol
  Pegasus XVII radial piston engines

Maximum speed: 409km/h (254mph)

Range: 3034km (1885 miles)

Service ceiling: 5791m (19,000ft)

Dimensions: span 21.08m (69ft 2in);

  length 16.330m (53ft 7in);

  height 4.55m (14ft 11in)

Weight: 5343kg (11,780lb) loaded

Armament: 2 x 7.7mm (0.303in) MGs, plus up

  to 1814kg (4000lb) bombs

Specifications

Mk IA Crew: 7

Powerplant: 2 x 1312kW (1760hp) Rolls-Royce
Vulture inline piston engines

Maximum speed: 426km/h (265mph)

Range: 2623km (1630 miles)

Service ceiling: 5850m (19,200ft)

Dimensions: span 27.46m (90ft 1in);

length 21.13m (69ft 4in);

height 5.94m (19ft 6in)

Weight: 25,401kg (56,000lb) loaded

Armament: 8 x 7.7mm (0.3i03n) MGs (two each
in nose and dorsal turrets, four in tail turret);
up to 4695kg (10,350lb) of bombs

▲ Avro Manchester Mk I

No. 83 Squadron / RAF Bomber Command, Scampton, Lincolnshire,
spring 1942

The mission symbols on the nose of this Manchester indicate it had completed 10
operational sorties by the spring of 1942. The aircraft was to fly a further four
mission before being lost on its fifteenth, a raid against the Blohm und Voss
shipyards in Hamburg.

Specifications

Crew: 2

Powerplant: 2 x 918kW (1230hp) Rolls-Royce
Merlin XX

Maximum speed: 612km/h (380mph)

Range: 1963km (1220 miles)

Service ceiling: 9449m (31,000ft)

Dimensions: span 16.51m (54ft 2in);

length 12.43m (40ft 10in);

height 4.65m (15ft 3in)

Weight: 5942kg (13,100lb) loaded

Armament: none

▲ de Havilland Mosquito PR.Mk I

No. 1 Photographic Unit / RAF, Benson, Oxfordshire, 1941

This was the ninth Mosquito Mk I to be completed, and served with No. 1 PRU
until 4 December 1941, when it was lost in the course of an operational mission.
The aeroplane was finished in photo-reconnaissance unit (PRU) blue overall with
pale grey unit code letters.

Dawn of the thousand-bomber raid
1942–43

An inability to bomb accurately with modest numbers of bombers forced the British to switch to the carpet bombing of industrial and urban areas, and the campaign gathered strength in numbers of aircraft and the capabilities of the new generation of heavy bombers.

PROFESSOR FREDERICK Lindemann, the chief scientific adviser to the British government, had the ear of Prime Minister Winston Churchill, who gave Lindemann a seat in the War Cabinet. During 1942, Lindemann presented to the Cabinet a paper that called for the 'aerial bombing of German cities by carpet bombing' as the tactical core of a strategic bombing campaign.

Lindemann advocated carpet, or area, bombing because of Bomber Command's proven inability to strike specific industrial targets or even whole towns and cities with real accuracy. Lindemann had thus decided that the area bombing of major industrial cities was the only way in which Bomber Command could strike effectively at the German war machine.

An inevitable side effect of area bombing would be the destruction of many industrial workers' homes clustered round the factory centres. The housing of the industrial working class was therefore to be targeted because it was more densely packed and was therefore more prone to major devastation, dislocating the German work force and adversely affecting industrial output.

Controversial policy

This scheme was very controversial within the British political and military leadership even before it was launched. In overall terms, though, it was considered to be implicit within the concept of 'total war' as begun by Germany with its 'terror' attacks on Warsaw, Rotterdam, London and Belgrade. The British Cabinet agreed that bombing was the only course by which the UK could strike directly at Germany in the period before the invasion of north-west Europe, which was still some time away even by the most optimistic assessments.

First thousand bomber raid

Once accepted by the Cabinet, the concept was passed to Harris for action. Harris decided to

Specifications

Mk IA Crew: 7

Powerplant: 2 x 1312kW (1760hp) Rolls-Royce Vulture inline piston engines

Maximum speed: 426km/h (265mph)

Range: 2623km (1630 miles)

Service ceiling: 5850m (19,200ft)

Dimensions: span 27.46m (90ft 1in);

length 21.13m (69ft 4in);

height 5.94m (19ft 6in)

Weight: 25,401kg (56,000lb) loaded

Armament: 8 x 7.7mm (0.3i03n) MGs (two each in nose and dorsal turrets, four in tail turret); up to 4695kg (10,350lb) of bombs

▲ **Avro Manchester Mk I**

No. 207 Squadron / RAF Bomber Command, Waddington, Lincolnshire, 1942

The Manchester heavy bomber was not successful in itself, largely as a result of the chronic unreliability of its two under-developed Rolls-Royce Vulture engines, but it paved the way for the Lancaster with four Rolls-Royce Merlin engines.

▲ **Avro Lancaster night-bomber**

Adequately armed for defence, the Lancaster could carry a heavy bomb load.

▲ **Handley Page Halifax B.Mk II**

No. 405 Squadron / RAF Bomber Command, Topcliffe, 1942

Nicknamed as the 'Ruhr Valley Express', this was a typical Halifax B.Mk II of
the first stages of the Halifax's development life with comparatively small
twin fin-and-rudder units characterized by swept leading edges above and
below the tailplane.

Specifications

Crew: 7	length 21.36m (70ft 1in);
Powerplant: 4 x 1037kW (1390hp) Rolls-Royce	height 6.32m (20ft 9in)
Merlin X inline engines	Weight: 27,215kg (60,000lb) loaded
Maximum speed: 426km/h (265mph)	Armament: 8 x 7.7mm (0.303in) Browning MGs
Range: 3058km (1900 miles)	in nose, dorsal turret and tail; 6 x 454kg
Service ceiling: 6706m (22,000ft)	(1000lb), 2 x 907kg (2000lb) and 6 x 227kg
Dimensions: span 30.21m (98ft 10in);	(500lb) bombs

mount a huge raid against Köln on 30 May 1942.
For this, the Command had to gather virtually
every airworthy aeroplane and crew within its
operational and advanced training unit, and so
assembled a force of slightly more than 1000

aircraft. Köln was very badly hit, only some 300
houses escaping damage. This first 'thousand-
bomber' raid was nonetheless not something
which could be repeated on a regular basis by the
RAF in 1942, and in the short term had an

▲ Handley Page Halifax B.Mk II Series 1A

No. 78 Squadron / RAF Bomber Command, Breighton, Yorkshire,
September 1943

Both the Halifax Mks I and II were powered by the Rolls-Royce Merlin liquid-cooled
V-12 engine rather than the Bristol Hercules air-cooled radial engine that became
standard on the considerably more numerous later variants.

Specifications

Crew: 7

Powerplant: 4 x 1036kW (1390hp) Rolls-Royce
  Merlin engines

Maximum speed: 454km/h (282mph)

Range: 3194km (1985 miles)

Service ceiling: 7315m (24,000ft)

Dimensions: span 30.12m (98ft 10in);
  length 21.74m (71ft 4in);
  height 6.12m (20ft 1in)

Weight: 29,484kg (65,000lb) loaded

Armament: 9 x 7.7mm (0.303in) MGs; internal
  bomb load of 6577kg (14,500lb)

▲ Short Stirling Mk I Series 2

No. 7 Squadron / No. 8 Group (Pathfinder Force) / RAF Bomber Command,
Oakington, summer 1943

Pathfinder Force aircraft marked targets for the Main Force bombers, and had
high-quality crews and aids such as H_2S navigation/bombing radar with its
antenna in a ventral radome.

Specifications

Crew: 7

Powerplant: 4 x 1186kW (1590hp) Bristol
  Hercules XI radial engines

Maximum speed: 410km/h (255mph)

Range: 3750km (2330 miles)

Service ceiling: 5030m (16,500ft)

Dimensions: span 30.2m (99ft 1in)

length 26.6m (87ft 3in);
  height 8.8m (28ft 10in)

Weight: 31,750kg (70,000lb) loaded

Armament: 8 x 7.7mm (0.303in) Browning
  MGs: two in the nose, four in the tail, two
  dorsal; up to 8164kg (18,000lb) of bombs

adverse effect on the strength of the period's
standard raids.

Even so, the raid was of great psychological
importance to the British, and served notice on the
Germans that Bomber Command was on its way
to becoming a formation that could achieve
genuinely strategic bombing results.

This period was notable not only for the major
expansion of Bomber Command in terms of its
strength in aircraft and personnel, but also in the
capability of its first-line aircraft. The year 1942

was that in which Bomber Command's most
important aircraft of the whole war came into
service. Twin-engined medium bombers were
replaced by large numbers of four-engined heavy
bombers such as the Handley Page Halifax and
Avro Lancaster. These offered longer range, greater
speed and heavier bomb loads. The one major
exception to this trend toward larger aircraft was
the superb multi-role de Havilland Mosquito, a
twin-engined fast bomber that became the major
mount of the Pathfinders.

▲ **Lockheed Ventura Mk II**

No. 21 Squadron / RAF Bomber Command, Methwold, mid-1943

A high-speed light bomber of US design and manufacture, the Ventura saw limited British service, primarily for daylight operations over German-occupied Europe. No. 21 Squadron received its first Ventura bombers in mid-1942.

Specifications

Crew: 5	Dimensions: span 19.96m (65ft 6in); length
Powerplant: 2 x 1491kW (2000hp) Pratt &	15.62m (51ft 3in); height 3.63m (11ft 11in)
Whitney GR-2800-S1A4-G Double Wasp radial	Weight: 11,793kg (26,000lb) loaded
piston engines	Armament: 4 x 12.7mm (0.5in) MGs;
Maximum speed: 483km/h (300mph)	2 x 7.62mm (0.3in) MGs; 1400kg (3000lb)
Range: 1529km (950 miles)	general ordnance or 6 x 147kg (325lb) depth
Service ceiling: 7620m (25,000ft)	charges or 1 x torpedo

Köln – first 'thousand-bomber' raid
MAY 1942

Though Bomber Command had to 'scrape the bottom of the barrel' to put together the required number, the 'thousand-bomber' attack on Köln marked a significant improvement in Bomber Command's ability to strike hard at major German cities.

ON 30/31 MAY 1942, Bomber Command flew its first 'thousand-bomber raid', its target the city of Köln on the Rhine. Some 1047 bombers were despatched in the form of 602 Wellingtons, 131 Halifaxes, 88 Stirlings, 79 Hampdens, 73 Lancasters, 46 Manchesters and 28 Whitleys. The number of aircraft claiming to have bombed Köln cannot be ascertained with total accuracy, the British official history claiming it was 898 aircraft, but Bomber Command records suggest that 868 aircraft bombed the main target and another 15 other targets. Some 1478 tonnes (1455 tons) of bombs, two-thirds of them incendiaries, were dropped.

German records indicate that 2500 separate fires were started, 1700 of them classified by the local fire brigade as large, but there was no firestorm, as there had been in earlier raids against Lubeck and Rostock, since Köln was essentially a modern city with wide

ORGANIZATION

Köln raid
30/31 May 1942

No. 1 Group (156 Wellingtons)	No. 3 Group (134 Wellingtons & 88 Stirlings)		No. 4 Group (131 Halifaxes, 9 Wellingtons & 7 Whitleys)
No. 5 Group (73 Lancasters, 46 Manchesters & 34 Hampdens)	Nos 91 & 92 OTUs (299 Wellingtons, 45 Hampdens & 21 Whitleys)		Flying Training Command (four Wellingtons)

streets and little wooden construction. Local records reveal that the damage included 3330 buildings destroyed, 2090 seriously damaged and 7420 lightly damaged, more than 90 per cent of the damage being the result of fire rather than blast. Included in these

12,840 buildings were 2560 industrial and commercial buildings. Many of these were small, but 36 large companies suffered a complete loss of production, 70 suffered 50–80 per cent loss and 222 up to 50 per cent loss. Among the buildings classed as totally destroyed were seven official administration buildings, 14 public buildings, seven banks, nine hospitals, 17 churches, 16 schools, four university buildings, 10 postal and railway buildings, 10 buildings of historic interest, two newspaper offices, four hotels, two cinemas and six department

◀ **Lancaster flight**

A formation of early-production Lancaster Mk Is of No. 44 Squadron form for the photographer some time in 1942.

Specifications

Crew: 7

Powerplant: 4 x 1030kW (1375hp) Bristol Hercules radial engines

Maximum speed: 410km/h (255mph)

Range: 3750km (2330 miles)

Service ceiling: 5030m (16,500ft)

Dimensions: span 30.2m (99ft 1in)

length 26.6m (87ft 3in); height 8.8m (28ft 10in)

Weight: 31,750kg (70,000lb) loaded

Armament: 8 x 7.7mm (0.303in) Browning MGs: two in the nose, four in the tail, two dorsal; up to 8164kg (18,000lb) of bombs

▲ **Short Stirling Mk III**

No. 149 Squadron / RAF Bomber Command, Mildenhall, Suffolk, 1942–43

The Stirling Mk III, of which 875 were built, was a simple development of the Stirling Mk I with a different dorsal turret reducing the drag burden faced by the powerplant of four 1189kW (1595hp) Bristol Hercules XI air-cooled radial engines.

▲ **Mosquito B.Mk IV**

No. 139 Squadron / RAF Bomber Command, Marham, Norfolk, 1942

The first bomber variant of the family to enter service, the Mosquito B.Mk IV (273 built) relied on speed rather than guns for defence, and carried a 907kg (2000lb) internal bomb load or, in 54 converted aircraft, one 1814kg (5000lb) bomb. The Mosquito proved itself superbly capable.

Specifications

Crew: 2

Powerplant: 2 x 918kW (1230hp) Rolls-Royce Merlin XX

Maximum speed: 612km/h (380mph)

Range: 1963km (1220 miles)

Service ceiling: 9449m (31,000ft)

Dimensions: span 16.51m (54ft 2in);

length 12.43m (40ft 10in); height 4.65m (15ft 3in)

Weight: 5942kg (13,100lb) loaded

Armament: normal internal bomb load 907kg (2000lb)

stores. Damage was also caused to 17 water mains, five gas mains, 32 main electricity cables and 12 main telephone routes. So far as the civilian housing stock was concerned, the list of dwelling units (primarily flats and apartments) included 13,010 destroyed, 6360 badly damaged and 22,270 lightly damaged.

The casualty figures for the Köln area are precise, with between 469 and 486 dead, the former comprising 411 civilian and 58 military casualties, the latter mostly members of flak units. Some 5027 were listed as injured and 45,132 were rendered homeless. The RAF casualties were also high, with 41 aircraft lost: 29 Wellingtons, four Manchesters, three Halifaxes, two Stirlings, one Hampden, one Lancaster and one Whitley. The loss rate of 3.9 per cent was thought acceptable in view of the perfect weather, which aided the German defence.

Specifications

Crew: 6

Powerplant: 2 x 1119kW (1500hp) Bristol
Hercules XI radial piston engines

Maximum speed: 378km/h (235mph)

Range: 2478km (1540 miles)

Service ceiling: 5791m (19,000ft)

Dimensions: span 26.26m (86ft 2in);
length 18.54m (60ft 10in);
height 5.31m (17ft 5in)

Weight: 13381kg (29,500lb) loaded

Armament: 8 x 7.7mm (0.303in) MGs, plus up
to 2041kg (4500lb) of bombs

▲ Vickers Wellington Mk III

No. 425 'Alouette' Squadron / No. 4 Group / RAF Bomber Command, Dishforth, Yorkshire, September 1942

This Canadian-manned unit flew the first definitive version of the Wellington, the Mk III with Bristol Hercules radial engines rather than Bristol Pegasus radial or Rolls-Royce Merlin V-12 engines (Mks I or II respectively), and introduced a four-rather than two-gun tail turret.

▲ Handley Page Halifax B.Mk II

No. 405 Squadron / RAF Bomber Command, Topcliffe, 1942

Nicknamed as the 'Ruhr Valley Express', this was a typical Halifax B.Mk II of the first stages of the Halifax's development life with comparatively small twin fin-and-rudder units characterized by swept leading edges above the below the tailplane.

Specifications

Crew: 7

Powerplant: 4 x 1037kW (1390hp) Rolls-Royce
Merlin X inline engines

Maximum speed: 426km/h (265mph)

Range: 3058km (1900 miles)

Service ceiling: 6706m (22,000ft)

Dimensions: span 30.21m (98ft 10in);

length 21.36m (70ft 1in);
height 6.32m (20ft 9in)

Weight: 27,215kg (60,000lb) loaded

Armament: 8 x 7.7mm (0.303in) Browning MGs
in nose, dorsal turret and tail; 6 x 454kg
(1000lb), 2 x 907kg (2000lb) and 6 x 227kg
(500lb) bombs

Specifications

Crew: 7

Powerplant: 4 x 1186kW (1590hp) Bristol
  Hercules XI radial engines

Maximum speed: 410km/h (255mph)

Range: 3750km (2330 miles)

Service ceiling: 5030m (16,500ft)

Dimensions: span 30.2m (99ft 1in)

length 26.6m (87ft 3in);

height 8.8m (28ft 10in)

Weight: 31,750kg (70,000lb) loaded

Armament: 8 x 7.7mm (0.303in) Browning

MGs: two in the nose, four in the tail, two

dorsal; up to 8164kg (18,000lb) of bombs

▲ **Short Stirling Mk I Series 2**

No. 149 Squadron / RAF Bomber Command, Mildenhall, Suffolk, early 1942
Entering service in August 1940 and built to the extent of 2374 aircraft, the
Stirling was the UK's first four-engined heavy bomber of World War II, and carried
the definitive night-bomber armament of eight machine guns in two-gun nose
and dorsal turrets, and a four-gun tail turret.

The dams raid
MAY 1943

The attack by modified Lancasters of No. 617 Squadron on a series of dams controlling the flow of water through the Ruhr was designed to inflict substantial damage and also cut electrical power generation. The raid was only partially successful, but remains an epic of its type.

IT WAS ON 21 MARCH 1943 that No. 617 Squadron was formed, under the command of Wing Commander Guy Gibson, on the basis of specially selected crews in No. 5 Group. The squadron then trained intensively for six weeks for a special operation, namely attacks using special spinning, cylindrical bombs on a number of dams controlling the flow of much of the water to the Ruhr industrial region.

Low level operation

On 16 May, the squadron despatched three waves of specially modified Lancaster bombers, 19 in total, each bomber carrying one of the 'bouncing bombs' developed by Dr Barnes Wallis of Vickers-Armstrong for attacks on dams. The entire operation was flown at low level to avoid radar detection and to escape attack by German night-fighters and so reach the reservoirs behind the dams, where the bombs were to be released at a precise air speed, and an exact and very low altitude above the water. One of the Lancasters was

compelled to turn back at an early stage of the operation after it struck the sea a glancing blow that tore off the bomb. Another five aircraft were shot down or crashed before reaching their targets, and one was so badly damaged by flak that it too was compelled to turn back.

This left 12 Lancasters to bomb the dams. The aircraft of Gibson's crew and four other crews attacked the Möhne dam and breached it, despite intense fire from the light flak guns defending the dam. Three aircraft went on to bomb the Eder dam, which was also breached. Two aircraft bombed the Sorpe dam and one the Schwelme dam, but without causing breaches in their walls. The twelfth aeroplane could not find its target in misty conditions and returned to England without dropping its bomb. Three of the Lancasters were shot down after they had released their bombs.

The British aircraft losses were thus eight out of the 19 that had been despatched: it is believed that four were shot down by light flak, one crashed after being damaged by the explosion of its own bomb, two hit electricity cables and crashed, and one went down after hitting a tree as its pilot was dazzled by a searchlight.

Successful operation

Of the 56 crew members in these aircraft, 53 were killed and only three (two of them badly injured) were taken prisoner. For his leadership of this amazing operation and for his courage in attacking the flak positions at the Mohne dam after he had completed his own bombing run, Gibson was awarded the Victoria Cross. Some 34 other men of the Lancaster crews were also decorated.

The breaching of the Mohne and Eder dams was a success. The Mohne reservoir was the major source for the Ruhr some 32km (20 miles) away. The water released caused widespread flooding as well as the disruption of rail, road and canal communications and the interruption of electricity and water supplies.

The Eder reservoir was larger than the Mohne reservoir, but it was 100km (62 miles) from the Ruhr. However, Kassel, which was only 40km (25 miles) distant, and the inland waterway system in the area of Kassel, suffered more than the Ruhr from the breach of the Eder dam. If the aircraft allocated to the Eder dam had instead been allocated to the Sorpe dam, the

Specifications

Crew: 7/8

Powerplant: 4 x 1089kW (1460hp) Packard (Rolls-Royce) Merlin piston engines

Maximum speed: 452km/h (281mph)

Range: 4313km (2680 miles)

Service ceiling: 7460m (24,500ft)

Dimensions: span 31.09m (102ft); length 20.98m (68ft 10in); height 6.19m (20ft 4in)

Weight: 18,598kg (41,000lb) loaded

Armament: 8 x 7.7mm (0.303in) MGs, up to 6350kg (14,000lb) bombs

▲ Avro Lancaster B.Mk III

No. 617 Squadron / RAF Bomber Command, Coningsby, Lincolnshire, May 1943

Modified to carry the special 'bouncing bomb', this aeroplane was used in No. 617's Squadron's celebrated 'dams raid' of 17 May 1943 against the Mohne, Eder and Sorpe dams. The aeroplane remained in first-line service to December 1943.

▲ Avro Lancaster B.Mk III

No. 617 Squadron / RAF Bomber Command, Coningsby, Lincolnshire, May 1943

Another of the specially adapted 'dams raid' aircraft, this machine was otherwise a standard Lancaster Mk III, of which 3020 were built to a standard differing from that of the Lancaster Mk I only in Packard rather than Roll-Royce Merlin engines.

Specifications

Crew: 7/8

Powerplant: 4 x 1089kW (1460hp) Packard (Rolls-Royce) Merlin piston engines

Maximum speed: 452km/h (281mph)

Range: 4313km (2680 miles)

Service ceiling: 7460m (24,500ft)

Dimensions: span 31.09m (102ft); length 20.98m (68ft 10in); height 6.19m (20ft 4in)

Weight: 18,598kg (41,000lb) loaded

Armament: 8 x 7.7mm (0.303in) MGs; up to 6350kg (14,000lb) bombs

Germans' believed that there would have been very serious consequences for the Ruhr's industrial production.

But the nature of the Sorpe dam made it a notably difficult target for the 'bouncing bomb', and for this reason it was placed lower down the list of attack priorities. The intact Sorpe reservoir managed to keep the Ruhr supplied with water until the Möhne dam had been repaired. The number of people drowned was some 1294, most of them near the Möhne dam. Neheim-Husten, 8km (5 miles) downstream of the Möhne dam, received the full weight of the flood and at least 859 people died there. It was unfortunate that 493 foreigners (most of them Ukrainian women working on the land), died in their camp at Neheim-Husten. It is believed that 58 or more of the dead were around the Eder dam.

The total number of dead was a new record for a raid on Germany, easily exceeding the 693 people killed at Dortmund in a 596-aircraft raid earlier in May.

▶ **Broken dam**
This aerial photograph shows the floodwater damage sustained by the Möhne dam just days after the attack.

The destruction of Hamburg
JULY–AUGUST 1943

As Germany's second-largest city, Hamburg was deemed worthy of RAF Bomber Command's maximum effort over a 10-day period. Aided by radar navigation and the first operational use of chaff, the four major raids burned the heart out of the ancient port.

HAMBURG WAS GERMANY'S most important port, and by July 1943 it had been attacked 98 times, though never in overwhelming force. This changed in the battle of Hamburg, a series of raids (four British and one US) between 24 July and 3 August 1943. Hamburg lay beyond the range of the 'Oboe' navigation aid, but was a good target for H_2S radar.

Harris directed four major raids on Hamburg over 10 nights: 791 aircraft on 24/25 July, 787 aircraft on 27/28 July, 777 aircraft on 29/30 July and 740 aircraft on 2/3 August, with almost 10,160 tonnes (10,000 tons) of bombs being dropped. As a firestorm started during the second raid, it has been claimed that the bombers carried an unusually high proportion of incendiaries with the specific purpose of starting such an event. In fact, slightly under 50 per cent of the tonnage dropped on Hamburg was incendiary, a proportion lower than that used on many of the recent raids against Ruhr targets.

Chaff

The major British tactical advance pioneered over Hamburg was the use of 'Window', or chaff. This was dropped by the bombers to drift towards the ground and saturate the screens of the German interception and flak-laying radars with false echoes. 'Window' had been ready since April 1942, but Bomber Command had not been allowed to use it for fear that the *Luftwaffe* would copy it and use it in raids against England. An understandable fear, but it was the wrong decision, for at this time the *Luftwaffe*'s preoccupation was with the Eastern Front and Bomber Command had lost some 2200 aircraft, many to Germany's radar-assisted defences. In the six major raids (including those on Essen and Remscheid) of the battle of Hamburg, 'Window' probably saved between 100 and 130 Bomber Command aircraft. The German defensive system was rendered obsolete at a stroke.

Specifications

Crew: 7

Powerplant: 4 x 1030kW (1375hp) Bristol Hercules radial engines

Maximum speed: 410km/h (255mph)

Range: 3750km (2330 miles)

Service ceiling: 5030m (16,500ft)

Dimensions: span 30.2m (99ft 1in)

length 26.6m (87ft 3in); height 8.8m (28ft 10in)

Weight: 31,750kg (70,000lb) loaded

Armament: 8 x 7.7mm (0.303in) Browning MGs: two in the nose, four in the tail, two dorsal; up to 8164 kg (18,000lb) of bombs

▲ Short Stirling B.Mk III

No. 622 Squadron / No. 3 Group / RAF Bomber Command, Mildenhall, Suffolk, 1943

The Stirling was a worthy rather than genuinely capable bomber, and throughout its first-line bomber career suffered from poor payload/range figures and a low service ceiling. By 1943, the type was being relegated to the transport role.

Specifications

Crew: 7

Powerplant: 4 x 1223kW (1640hp) Rolls-Royce Merlin XX1V inline piston engines

Maximum speed: 462km/h (287mph)

Range: 4072km (2530 miles)

Service ceiling: 7470m (24,500ft)

Dimensions: span 31.09m (102ft); length 21.18m (69ft 6in); height 6.10m (20ft)

Weight: 31,751kg (70,000lb) loaded

Armament: 8 x 7.7mm (0.303in) MGs; either one 9979kg (22,000lb) bomb or 6350kg (14,000lb) of smaller bombs

▲ Avro Lancaster B.Mk I

No. 514 Squadron / RAF Bomber Command, Waterbeach, Cambridgeshire, 1943

Production of the Lancaster Mk I totalled 3444 aircraft by five manufacturers, this aeroplane being one of 919 manufactured by Armstong Whitworth and fitted with H_2S navigation and bombing radar.

Target Peenemünde
AUGUST 1943

Although Bomber Command's everyday 'trade' was area bombing of German cities, every so often there emerged a specific target worthy of rapid destruction. Such a target was Peenemünde, an island off Germany's Baltic coast where much development of 'secret weapons' was undertaken.

ON 17/18 AUGUST 1943, Bomber Command despatched 596 aircraft (324 Lancasters, 218 Halifaxes and 54 Stirlings) against Peenemünde in a raid to destroy the German research establishment off the Baltic coast, at which V-2 rockets were being built and tested.

Master bomber
The raid was carried out in moonlight to improve bombing accuracy in what was the only occasion in the second half of the war when Bomber Command attempted a nocturnal precision raid by large forces against a small target.

For the first time, there was a master bomber to control a major raid. The pathfinder aircraft crews found the target without difficulty, and the master bomber controlled the raid successfully. A diversionary attack by Mosquito light bombers against the city of Berlin drew off most of the German night-fighters for the first two of the raid's three phases.

The initial marking and bombing fell on a camp for forced labourers 2.4km (1.5 miles) south of the first aiming point, but the master bomber and pathfinders quickly brought the bombing back to the main targets, which were bombed successfully. Some 560 aircraft dropped nearly 1829 tonnes (1800 tons) of bombs, of which 85 per cent were HE. This raid probably delayed the V-2 programme by some two months or more, and reduced the scale of the eventual rocket attack. About 180 Germans were killed. Some 500 to 600 foreign workers, mostly

Specifications

Crew: 2	Dimensions: span 16.51m (54ft 2in);
Powerplant: 2 x 918kW (1230hp) Rolls-Royce	length 12.43m (40ft 10in);
Merlin 21 inline piston engines	height 4.65m (15ft 3in)
Maximum speed: 612km/h (380mph)	Weight: 5942kg (13,00lb) loaded
Range: 1963km (1220 miles)	Armament: normal internal bomb load 907kg
Service ceiling: 9449m (31,000ft)	(2000lb)

▲ **de Havilland Mosquito B.Mk IV Series 2**

No. 105 Squadron / RAF Bomber Command, Marham, Norfolk, 1943

With No. 139 Squadron, No. 105 Squadron pioneered the service debut of the Mosquito B.Mk IV Series 2 during 1942, and used the type for high-speed bombing missions over Germany. During World War II, the Mosquito equipped 38 British light bomber squadrons.

▲ **Handley Page Halifax**

Though not as well known as the Avro Lancaster (its primary stablemate in the squadrons of RAF Bomber Command), the Halifax was nonetheless a very capable four-engine heavy bomber.

Polish, were also killed in the labourers' camp. Bomber Command lost 40 aircraft (23 Lancasters, 15 Halifaxes and two Stirlings), representing 6.7 per cent of the force despatched, but this was thought acceptable for so important a target.

Most of the losses were suffered by aircraft of the last wave, when the German night-fighters arrived in strength. This was the occasion on which the Germans employed the novel *schräge Musik* weapon: two forward/upward-firing cannon in the cockpit of Bf 110 night-fighters.

▲ **Handley Page Halifax B.Mk II Series 1 (Special)**

No. 10 Squadron / RAF Bomber Command, Melbourne, Yorkshire, April 1943

The Halifax B.Mk II was a development of the initial Halifax Mk I with more powerful engines and, in some of the 1977 such aircraft, a power-operated dorsal turret carrying four 7.7mm (0.303in) Browning machine guns. A single 7.7mm (0.303in) Vickers K machine gun could be fitted in the nose perspex.

Specifications

Crew: 7	length 21.36m (70ft 1in);
Powerplant: 4 x 1037kW (1390hp) Rolls-Royce	height 6.32m (20ft 9in)
Merlin X inline engines	Weight: 27,215kg (60,000lb) loaded
Maximum speed: 426km/h (265mph)	Armament: 8 x 7.7mm (0.303in) Browning MGs
Range: 3058km (1900 miles)	in nose, dorsal turret and tail; 6 x 454kg
Service ceiling: 6706m (22,000ft)	(1000lb), 2 x 907kg (2000lb) and 6 x 227kg
Dimensions: span 30.21m (98ft 10in);	(500lb) of bombs

Specifications

Crew: 7/8	Dimensions: span 31.09m (102ft);
Powerplant: 4 x 1089kW (1460hp) Packard	length 20.98m (68ft 10in);
(Rolls-Royce)Merlin piston engines	height 6.19m (20ft 4in)
Maximum speed: 452km/h (281mph)	Weight: 18,598kg (41,000lb) loaded
Range: 4313km (2680 miles)	Armament: 8 x 7.7mm (0.303in) MGs; up to
Service ceiling: 7468m (24,500ft)	6350kg (14,000lb) bombs

▲ **Avro Lancaster B.Mk III**

No. 61 Squadron / No. 5 Group / RAF Bomber Command, Skellingthorpe, mid-1944

The Lancaster was so 'right' from the beginning of its operational career that the two major marks, of which 6464 were built, were the Lancaster Mks I and III that differed from each other only in having British- and US-made Merlin engines.

The flames of victory?
1944–45

In spring 1944 and much against the wishes of its commander, Bomber Command was switched from strategic bombing, undertaken in concert with the USAAF, to tactical work in support of the Normandy campaign. Then it reverted to strategic bombing to the war's end.

B Y APRIL 1944, a mightily unwilling Harris had been compelled to bring his strategic offensive to a temporary close as Bomber Command was retasked to tactical targets and the German lines of communications in north-west Europe in the run-up to the Allied invasion of Normandy, launched in June 1944. The campaign against German transport and lines of communication was notably effective, and as the Allies streamed across northern France Bomber

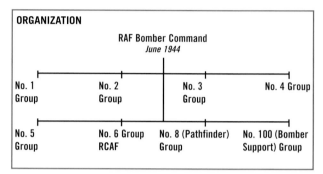

ORGANIZATION

RAF Bomber Command
June 1944

| No. 1 Group | No. 2 Group | No. 3 Group | No. 4 Group |
| No. 5 Group | No. 6 Group RCAF | No. 8 (Pathfinder) Group | No. 100 (Bomber Support) Group |

▼ **British heavy bomber night squadron (June 1944)**

The typical heavy bomber squadron of mid-1944 comprised between 12 and 24 four-engined heavy bombers of the Avro Lancaster or Handley Page Halifax types divided into three four- or eight-aircraft flights.

1st Flight   **2nd Flight**   **3rd Flight**

Specifications

Crew: 7

Powerplant: 4 x 1223kW (1640hp) Rolls-Royce
    Merlin XXIV inline piston engines

Maximum speed: 462km/h (287mph)

Range: 4072km (2530 miles)

Service ceiling: 7470m (24,500ft)

Dimensions: span 31.09m (102f); length
    21.18m (69ft 6in); height 6.10m (20ft)

Weight: 31,751kg (70,000lb) loaded

Armament: 8 x 7.7mm (0.303in) MGs; bomb
    load of one 9979kg (22,000lb) bomb or up to
    6350kg (14,000lb) of smaller bombs

▲ **Avro Lancaster B.Mk I**

No. 15 Squadron / RAF Bomber Command, Mildenhall, Suffolk, summer 1944

The Lancaster possessed good payload/range performance, and was the only British bomber of World War II large enough to carry the 5443kg (12,000lb) 'Tallboy' and 9979kg (22,000lb) 'Grand Slam' earthquake bombs designed to penetrate deep into the earth or through concrete before detonating.

Command was allowed to revert to its primary task.

From late in 1944, Bomber Command, now with still greater strength and overall capability, was well able to despatch 'thousand-bomber' raids without undue difficulty. Ironically, however, this capability became steadily less needed as the Allied land forces liberated France, Belgium and much of the Netherlands, and plunged into Germany.

Germany's war effort was now crumbling due to exhaustion, lack of adequate manpower, and the decimation of Germany's internal means of land communication (preventing newly made weapons from being delivered to the front), as well as an increasing scarcity of raw materials including, in particular, fuel.

By this time, the German night-fighter arm had ceased to be a significant factor, and the decline of the German day-fighter arm made it possible for Bomber Command to switch a major part of its effort from night bombing to precise, accurate day attacks.

BOMBER COMMAND, NO. 6 GROUP RCAF (JUNE 1944)		
Unit	Type	Base
No. 408 Sqn	Halifax	Linton-on-Ouse
No. 419 Sqn	Halifax	Middleton St George
No. 420 Sqn	Halifax	Tholthorpe
No. 424 Sqn	Halifax	Skipton-on-Swale
No. 425 Sqn	Halifax	Tholthorpe
No. 426 Sqn	Halifax	Linton-on-Ouse
No. 427 Sqn	Halifax	Leeming
No. 428 Sqn	Halifax	Middleton St George
No. 429 Sqn	Halifax	Leeming
No. 431 Sqn	Halifax	Croft
No. 432 Sqn	Halifax	East Moor
No. 433 Sqn	Halifax	Skipton-on-Swale
No. 434 Sqn	Halifax	Croft

BOMBER COMMAND, NO. 100 (BOMBER SUPPORT) GROUP (JUNE 1944)		
Unit	Type	Base
No. 23 Sqn	Mosquito	Little Snoring
No. 85 Sqn	Mosquito	Swannington
No. 141 Sqn	Mosquito	West Raynham
No. 157 Sqn	Mosquito	Swannington
No. 169 Sqn	Mosquito	Great Massingham
No. 192 Sqn	Wellington, Halifax & Mosquito	Foulsham
No. 199 Sqn	Stirling	North Creake
No. 214 Sqn	Fortress	Oulton
No. 239 Sqn	Mosquito	West Raynham
No. 515 Sqn	Mosquito	Little Snoring
No. 1692 Flt	Beaufighter	Great Massingham
No. 1699 Flt	Fortress	Oulton

Specifications

Crew: 7

Powerplant: 4 x 1223kW (1640hp) Rolls-Royce
  Merlin XXIV V-12 piston engines

Maximum speed: 462km/h (287mph)

Range: 4070km (2530 miles)

Service ceiling: 7470m (24,500ft)

Dimensions: span 31.09m (102ft);
  length 21.18m (69ft 6in); height 6.10m (20ft)

Weight: 16738kg (36,900lb) loaded

Armament: 8 x 7.7mm (0.303in) MGs; bomb
  load of either one 9979kg (22,000lb) or up to
  6350kg (14,000lb) of smaller bombs

▲ Avro Lancaster B.Mk I

*No. 101 Squadron / No. 1 Group / RAF Bomber Command, Ludford Magna,
Lincolnshire, 1944*

This aeroplane carried the 'Airborne Cigar' radio
equipment, allowing its operators to pass
disinformation to German night-fighters.

Specifications

Crew: 2

Powerplant: 2 x 1253kW (1680hp) Merlin 72
  engines

Maximum speed: 668km/h (415mph)

Range: 2888km (1795 miles)

Service ceiling: 10,975m (36,000ft)

Dimensions: span 16.51m (54ft 2in);
  length 12.43m (40ft 10in);
  height 4.65m (15ft 3in)

Weight: 11,238kg (24,753lb) loaded

Armament: 4 x 227kg (500lb) bombs internally
  and one under each wing.

▲ de Havilland Mosquito B.Mk IX

*No. 105 Squadron / No. 8 Group / RAF Bomber Command, Marham, Norfolk,
March 1944*

The Mosquito B.Mk IX was a development of the initial Mosquito B.Mk IV with more
powerful engines, and this machine carries the 'Oboe' navigation system for
accurate long-range navigation in the pathfinder role.

Specifications

Crew: 8

Powerplant: 4 x 895kW (1200hp) Pratt &
  Whitney Twin Wasp radial piston engines

Maximum speed: 435km/h (270mph)

Range: 2366km (1470 miles)

Service ceiling: 8534m (28,000ft)

Dimensions: span 17.63m (57ft 10in);

length 12.7m (41ft 8in);

height 4.83m (15ft 10in)

Weight: 11,431kg (25,200lb) loaded

Armament: 4 x 20mm (0.79in) cannon,
  7 x 7.7mm (0.303in) MGs; 1 x torpedo and
  2 x 113kg (250lb) bombs or 8 x 41kg (90lb)
  rocket projectiles

▲ Consolidated Liberator B.Mk VI

*No. 223 Squadron / No. 100 Group / RAF Bomber Command, Oulton,
August 1944*

With its long range, the Liberator was mostly used in the maritime reconnaissance
bomber role by RAF Coastal Command, but its speed and large fuselage also led
to its use by Bomber Command's No. 100 Group in the special duties support role.

de Havilland Mosquito B.Mk IV Series 2

No. 105 Squadron / RAF Bomber Command, Horsham St Faith, 1944

Nos 105 and 139 Squadrons were the units that introduced the Mosquito B.Mk IV series 2 into operational service and, with this type, unescorted high-speed missions over Germany.

Specifications

Mk IV Series II Crew: 2

Powerplant: 2 x 918kW (1230hp) Rolls-Royce
  Merlin XX engines

Maximum speed: 612km/h (380mph)

Range: 1963km (1220 miles)

Service ceiling: 9449m (31,000ft)

Dimensions: span 16.51m (54ft 2in);
  length 12.43m (40ft 10in);
  height 4.65m (15ft 3in)

Weight: 5942kg (13,100lb) loaded

Armament: normal internal bomb load
  907kg (2000lb)

BOMBER COMMAND, NO. 1 GROUP (JUNE 1944)

Unit	Type	Base
No. 12 Sqn	Lancaster	Wickenby
No. 100 Sqn	Lancaster	Grimsby
No. 101 Sqn	Lancaster	Ludford Magna
No. 103 Sqn	Lancaster	Kirmington
No. 300 (Pol) Sqn	Lancaster	Faldingworth
No. 460 (Aus) Sqn	Lancaster	Binbrook
No. 550 Sqn	Lancaster	North Killingholme
No. 576 Sqn	Lancaster	Elsham Wolds
No. 625 Sqn	Lancaster	Kelstern
No. 626 Sqn	Lancaster	Wickenby

BOMBER COMMAND, NO. 1 GROUP (MARCH 1945)

Unit	Type	Base	Strength
No. 12 Sqn	Lancaster	Wickenby	20
No. 100 Sqn	Lancaster	Grimsby	19
No. 101 Sqn	Lancaster	Ludford Magna	32
No. 103 Sqn	Lancaster	Elsham Wolds	19
No. 150 Sqn	Lancaster	Hemswell	16
No. 153 Sqn	Lancaster	Scampton	21
No. 166 Sqn	Lancaster	Kirmington	27
No. 170 Sqn	Lancaster	Hemswell	18
No. 300 Sqn (Pol)	Lancaster	Faldingworth	20
No. 460 Sqn, RAAF	Lancaster	Binbrook	27
No. 550 Sqn	Lancaster	North Killingholme	27
No. 576 Sqn	Lancaster	Fiskerton	19
No. 625 Sqn	Lancaster	Kelstern	29
No. 626 Sqn	Lancaster	Wickenby	21

BOMBER COMMAND, NO. 3 GROUP (JUNE 1944)

Unit	Type	Base
No. 15 Sqn	Lancaster	Mildenhall
No. 75 Sqn (NZ)	Lancaster	Mepal
No. 90 Sqn	Stirling & Lancaster	Tuddenham
No. 115 Sqn	Lancaster	Witchford
No. 138 (SD) Sqn	Halifax & Stirling	Tempsford
No. 149 Sqn	Stirling	Methwold
No. 161 (SD) Sqn	Lysander, Hudson & Stirling	Tempsford
No. 218 Sqn	Stirling	Woolfox Lodge
No. 514 Sqn	Lancaster	Waterbeach
No. 622 Sqn	Lancaster	Mildenhall

BOMBER COMMAND, NO. 8 (PATHFINDER) GROUP (1944)

Unit	Type	Base
No. 7 Sqn	Lancaster	Oakington
No. 35 Sqn	Lancaster	Graveley
No. 105 Sqn	Mosquito	Bourn
No. 109 Sqn	Mosquito	Little Staughton
No. 139 Sqn	Mosquito	Upwood
No. 156 Sqn	Lancaster	Upwood
No. 405 Sqn RCAF	Lancaster	Gransden Lodge
No. 571 Sqn	Mosquito	Oakington
No. 582 Sqn	Lancaster	Little Staughton
No. 635 Sqn	Lancaster	Downham Market
No. 692 Sqn	Mosquito	Graveley

Specifications

▲ de Havilland Mosquito B.Mk XVI

No. 571 Squadron / No. 8 (Pathfinder) Group / Light Night Striking Force / RAF Bomber Command, Oakington, 1944

Crew: 2

Powerplant: 2 x 1253kW (1680hp) Rolls-Royce
  Merlin 72 V-12 piston engines

Maximum speed: 656km/h (408mph)

Range: 2389km (1485 miles)

Service ceiling: 11,280m (37,000ft)

Dimensions: span 16.51m (54ft 2in); length
  12.47m (40ft 11in); height 3.81m (12ft 6in)

Weight: 10,433kg (23,000lb) loaded

Armament: 4 x 227kg (500lb) bombs internally
  and two more under wings or 1 x 1814kg
  (4000lb) bomb

The Mosquito B.Mk XVI, of which 1200 were delivered as the most important Mosquito light bomber variant, was a development of the limited-production Mosquito B.Mk IX with a pressurized cockpit for better high-altitude capability.

Specifications

▲ Handley Page Halifax B.Mk III

No. 466 Squadron / Royal Australian Air Force / No.4 Group / RAF Bomber Command, Driffield, Yorkshire, 1944

Crew: 7

Powerplant: 4 x 1204kW (1615hp) Bristol
  Hercules XVI radial piston engines

Maximum speed: 454km/h (282mph)

Range: 3194km (1985 miles)

Service ceiling: 7315m (24,000ft)

Dimensions: span 30.12m (98ft 10in); length
  21.74m (71ft 4in); height 6.12m (20ft 1in)

Weight: 29,484kg (65,000lb) loaded

Armament: 9 x 7.7mm (0.303in) machine
  guns; internal bomb load of 6577kg
  (14,500lb)

The yellow-striped fin-and-rudder units were identifying marks of No. 4 Group's aircraft in 1944.

Taking the war to Berlin
MARCH 1944

The capital of Germany, Berlin had long possessed a fascination for Bomber Command's leadership, and the city had been bombed on many occasions. The last major night raid on the city occurred in March 1944.

ALTHOUGH MOSQUITOES CONTINUED to attack the city until 20th April 1945, the last major British raid on Berlin was delivered on 24/25 March

1944, when 811 aircraft attacked, and in the process lost 72 aircraft. A strong northerly wind drove the bombers south and scattered them, especially during the homeward flight, when radar-laid flak batteries achieved considerable success – some 50 of the aircraft lost succumbed to the flak. The wind also caused difficulties in marking the target; thus 126 small towns and villages outside Berlin were hit.

Most of the damage occurred in Berlin's southwest area. Much housing was destroyed, about 20,000 people lost their homes, and about 150 people were killed.

No industrial concerns were classed as destroyed, but several important ones were damaged. Although this was the last major raid on Berlin, the city was later bombed by small forces of Mosquitos to keep the Germans off balance.

▲ **Avro Lancaster B.Mk III**

No. 626 Squadron / No. 1 Group / RAF Bomber Command, Wickenby, 1944

The Lancaster Mks I and III were fitted defensively with power-operated nose and dorsal turrets, each carrying two 7.7mm (0.303in) machine guns, and a power-operated tail turret carrying four 7.7mm (0.303in) machine guns.

Specifications

Crew: 7/8	Dimensions: span 31.09m (102ft);
Powerplant: 4 x 1089kW (1460hp) Packard	length 20.98m (68ft 10in);
(Rolls-Royce) Merlin piston engines	height 6.19m (20ft 4in)
Maximum speed: 452km/h (281mph)	Weight: 18,598kg (41,000lb) loaded
Range: 4313km (2680 miles)	Armament: 8 x 7.7mm (0.303in) MGs; up to
Service ceiling: 7460m (24,500ft)	6350kg (14,000lb) of bombs

Specifications

Crew: 7	Dimensions: span 31.09m (102ft);
Powerplant: 4 x 1223kW (1640hp) Rolls-Royce	length 21.18m (69ft 6in); height 6.10m (20ft)
Merlin XX1V inline piston engines	Weight: 31,751kg (70,000lb) loaded
Maximum speed: 462km/h (287mph)	Armament: 8 x 7.7mm (0.303in) MGs; either
Range: 4072km (2530 miles)	one 9979kg (22,000lb) bomb or 6350kg
Service ceiling: 7470m (24,500ft)	(14,000lb) of smaller bombs

▲ **Avro Lancaster B. Mk I**

No. 101 Squadron / RAF Bomber Command, Ludford Magna, Lincolnshire, 1944

This aeroplane carries over its fuselage the aerials for the 'Airborne Cigar' electronic warfare system, in which misleading information was radioed to the crews of German night-fighters to divert them from the British bomber streams.

2nd Tactical Air Force
1944–45

Together with the US Ninth Air force, the British 2nd Tactical Air Force (TAF) was vital to the success of the Allied armies during and after the D-Day landings. The 2nd TAF provided the Anglo-Canadian 21st Army Group with decisive tactical air support until the end of the war.

COMMANDED BY Air Marshal Sir Arthur Coningham, who had developed and honed his concept of tactical air support in the North African campaign, the 2nd TAF was a balanced formation with its own three squadrons of reconnaissance aircraft as well as four groups of tactical warplanes, one airborne forces group and one transport group. The most important of these groups were No. 2 Bomber Group with five wings of tactical bombers (13 squadrons), and Nos 83, 84 and 85 Groups with fighters and fighter-bombers. The first two of these groups each had its own three-squadron reconnaissance wing for tactical reconnaissance, and also its own air observation post wing (four and five squadrons respectively) for battlefield reconnaissance and artillery spotting.

In the face of steadily declining German fighter capability, the squadrons of Nos 83 and 84 Groups were used increasingly in the fighter-bomber role with the fixed forward-firing armament of their Spitfire, Typhoon and Tempest warplanes complemented by loads of bombs and rockets. So while the twin-engined Mitchell and Mosquito medium bombers of No. 2 Group struck close

2ND TACTICAL AIR FORCE, NO. 2 BOMBER GROUP (JUNE 1944)		
Unit	Type	Base
No. 21 Sqn	Mosquito	Gravesend
No. 88 Sqn	Boston	Hartford Bridge
No. 98 Sqn	Mitchell	Dunsfold
No. 107 Sqn	Mosquito	Lasham
No. 180 Sqn	Mitchell	Dunsfold
No. 226 Sqn	Mitchell	Hartford Bridge
No. 305 Sqn (Pol)	Mosquito	Lasham
No. 320 Sqn (Dutch)	Mitchell	Dunsfold
No. 342 Sqn (Fr)	Boston	Hartford Bridge
No. 464 Sqn (Aus)	Mosquito	Gravesend
No. 487 Sqn (NZ)	Mosquito	Gravesend
No. 613 Sqn	Mosquito	Lasham

Specifications
Crew: 5
Powerplant: 2 x 1268kW (1700hp) Wright Double Row Cyclone radial piston engines
Maximum speed: 470km/h (292mph)
Range: 1979km (1230 miles)
Service ceiling: 8138m (26,700ft)
Dimensions: span 20.57m (67ft 7in); length 16.48m (54ft 1in); height 4.83m (15ft 10in)
Weight: 11,793kg (26,000lb) loaded
Armament: 2 x 12.7mm (0.5in) and 1 x 7.62mm (0.3in) MGs; bomb load of 1814kg (4000lb)

▲ **North American Mitchell Mk II**
No. 320 (Dutch) Squadron / No. 2 Group / 2nd Tactical Air Force / RAF, Dunsfold, April 1944
The medium bombers of the 2nd TAF's 2nd Bomber Group, including this Mitchell of No. 139 Wing, saw intense employment in the period leading up to the *Overlord* invasion of Normandy in June 1944, and in the following campaign.

Specifications

Crew: 5	Dimensions: span 20.57m (67ft 7in);
Powerplant: 2 x 1268kW (1700hp) Wright	length 16.48m (54ft 1in);
Double Row Cyclone radial piston engines	height 4.83m (15ft 10in)
Maximum speed: 470km/h (292mph)	Weight: 11,793kg (26,000lb) loaded
Range: 1979km (1230 miles)	Armament: 2 x 12.7mm (0.5in) and 1 x 7.62mm
Service ceiling: 8138m (26,700ft)	(0.3in) MGs; bomb load of 1814kg (4000lb)

▲ **North American Mitchell Mk II**

No. 226 Squadron / 2nd Tactical Air Force, Gilze Rijen, the Netherlands, 1944

The Mitchell medium bomber was of US origins, but used by the RAF in tactical support of the ground forces of the 21st Army Group. By this time the 'invasion stripes' should have been removed, but the pace of operations was too hectic to allow time for this to be done.

behind the German front lines to isolate the ground forces from reinforcement and resupply, the single-engined fighter-bombers loitered over the battlefield to attack targets of opportunity. Thus the 2nd TAF was able to play a hugely important part in the success of the Canadian First and British Second Armies as they pushed through northwest Europe between June 1944 and May 1945.

Transport conversions
1944–45

As the Lancaster and late-mark Halifax came to predominate in Bomber Command's strength, older aircraft and obsolescent types such as the Stirling were converted for the transport role and, in some cases, further developed specifically for this task late in World War II.

At THE TIME OF THE ALLIED INVASION of Normandy in June 1944, the British tactical air transport capability was vested in the five squadrons of Transport Command's No. 46 Group with the Douglas Dakota twin-engined transport and Airspeed Horsa assault glider, and with No. 38 Airborne Forces Group of the 2nd Tactical Air Force (TAF) with 10 squadrons of two- and four-engined aircraft towing Horsa assault and Hamilcar logistical transport gliders.

This organization was enlarged and rationalized to meet the requirements of the Arnhem operation of September 1944, and in preparation for the Rhine-crossing operations of 1945 had become Transport Command's Nos 44 to 47 Groups.

By this time, older four-engined bombers, most notably the Handley Page Halifax and Short Stirling, had become available in some numbers for

▲ **Vickers Wellington**

The Wellington was a British mainstay throughout the war, first as a bomber and then in the maritime reconnaissance, transport and training roles.

conversion as transports and heavy glider tugs, and late-production aircraft were completed as the Halifax C.Mk VIII and A.Mk IX, and Stirling A.Mk V, all of which saw useful post-war transport service.

Specifications

Crew: 5

Powerplant: 2 x 854kW (1145hp) Rolls-Royce
Merlin X inline piston engines

Maximum speed: 370km/h (230mph)

Range: 2414km (1500 miles)

Service ceiling: 7925m (26,000ft)

Dimensions: span 25.6m (84ft);
length 21.49m (70ft 6in); height 4.57m (15ft)

Weight: 15,195kg (33,500lb) loaded

Armament: 4 x 7.7mm (0.303in) MGs in
powered tail turret and one similar gun in
nose turret; up to 3175kg (7000lb) of bombs`

▲ Armstrong Whitworth Whitley Mk V

Royal Air Force, 1944

Seen in the standard day-bomber camouflage and markings of the period, this
Whitley Mk V was used for glider-towing, as revealed by the yoke on the rear of the
fuselage and the removal of the guns from the tail turret.

Specifications

Mk VI Crew: 4

Powerplant: 2 x 1186kW (1590hp) Bristol
Hercules XI radial piston engines

Maximum speed: 426km/h (265mph)

Range: 2092km (1300 miles)

Service ceiling: 5485m (18,000ft)

Dimensions: span 23.47m (77ft 0in);
length 18.26m (59ft 11in);
height 4.75m (15ft 7in)

Weight: 10,251kg (22,600lb) loaded

Armament: 2 x 7.7mm (0.303in) Vickers K MGs
in dorsal position

▲ Armstrong Whitworth Albemarle Mk V

*No. 297 Squadron / No. 38 Airborne Forces Group / 2nd Tactical Air Force /
RAF, Brize Norton, Oxfordshire, June 1944*

Some 24 Albemarle aircraft delivered British airborne forces to Normandy in
Airspeed Horsa gliders during the very first stage of the *Overlord* invasion of
France on 6 June 1944.

Specifications

Crew: 7

Powerplant: 4 x 1230kW (1650hp) Bristol
Hercules XV 14-cylinder air-cooled radial
piston engines

Maximum speed: 451km/h (280mph)

Range: 4828km (3000 miles)

Service ceiling: 5182m (17,000t)

Dimensions: span 30.2m (99ft 1in);
length 26.59m (87ft 3in);
height 6.93m (22ft 9in)

Weight: 31,751kg (70,000lb) loaded

Armament: 4 x 7.7mm (0.303in) Browning MGs
in turret

▲ Short Stirling Mk V

*No. 46 Squadron / No. 47 Group / RAF Transport Command, Stoney Cross,
early 1945*

The Stirling Mk V was a purpose-built airborne forces variant, the last to be
manufactured, of the Stirling series. These 160 aircraft had no armament, and
had provision for freight as well as 40 conventional or 20 airborne troops.

Bomber Command: Dresden
JANUARY–MARCH 1945

In the absence of effective enemy flak and fighter opposition, Bomber Command was able to operate by day as well as night in the last months of the war, and to concentrate its power on smaller targets of immediate importance to Germany's continued war effort.

THE SINGLE MOST controversial attack of Bomber Command's history took place in the early morning of 14 February 1945, and was the bombing of Dresden, essentially a non-military target, in which a huge firestorm erupted. This killed a huge but unquantified number of civilians, most of them refugees fleeing from the Soviets' westward advances.

City targets

The apogee of Bomber Command's effort was March 1945, when it dropped the greatest weight of bombs of any month in the entire war. The major targets, often supplemented by smaller raids on lesser targets, included Mannheim by 478 aircraft on 1 March; Köln by 858 aircraft on 2 March; Kamen and the Dortmund-Ems Canal by 234 and 220 aircraft respectively on 3 March; Chemnitz by 760 aircraft on 5/6 March; Dessau, Hemmingstedt and

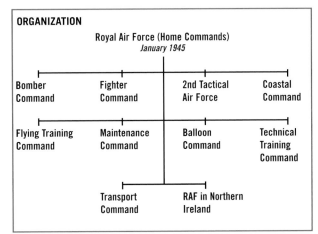

ORGANIZATION

Royal Air Force (Home Commands)
January 1945

Bomber Command	Fighter Command	2nd Tactical Air Force	Coastal Command
Flying Training Command	Maintenance Command	Balloon Command	Technical Training Command
	Transport Command	RAF in Northern Ireland	

Harburg by 526, 256 and 234 aircraft on 6/7 March; Hamburg and Kassel by 312 and 262 aircraft on 8/9 March; Essen by 1079 aircraft on 11 March;

Specifications

Crew: 7

Powerplant: 4 x 1204kW (1615hp) Bristol Hercules XVI radial piston engines

Maximum speed: 454km/h (282mph)

Range: 3194km (1985 miles)

Service ceiling: 7315m (24,000ft)

Dimensions: span 30.12m (98ft 10in);
length 21.74m (71ft 4in);
height 6.12m (20ft 1in)

Weight: 29,484kg (65,000lb) loaded

Armament: 9 x 7.7mm (0.303in) MGs; internal bomb load of 6577kg (14,500lb)

▲ **Handley Page Halifax B.Mk III**

No. 462 (Special Duties) Squadron / Royal Australian Air Force / RAF Bomber Command, Foulsham, Norfolk, early 1945

This aeroplane carries the antennae for the 'Airborne Cigar' radio transmission jamming and disinformation system.

BOMBER COMMAND, NO. 5 GROUP (MARCH 1945)		
Unit	Type	Base
No. 9 Sqn	Lancaster	Bardney
No. 44 Sqn	Lancaster	Dunholme Lodge
No. 49 Sqn	Lancaster	Fiskerton
No. 50 Sqn	Lancaster	Skellingthorpe
No. 57 Sqn	Lancaster	East Kirkby
No. 61 Sqn	Lancaster	Skellingthorpe
No. 83 Sqn	Lancaster	Coningsby
No. 97 Sqn	Lancaster	Coningsby
No. 106 Sqn	Lancaster	Metheringham
No. 207 Sqn	Lancaster	Spilsby
No. 463 Sqn (RAAF)	Lancaster	Waddington
No. 467 Sqn (RCAF)	Lancaster	Waddington
No. 617 Sqn	Lancaster	Woodhall Spa
No. 619 Sqn	Lancaster	Dunholme Lodge
No. 627 Sqn	Lancaster	Woodhall Spa
No. 630 Sqn	Lancaster	East Kirkby

BOMBER COMMAND, NO. 4 GROUP (MARCH 1945)			
Unit	Type	Base	Strength
No. 10 Sqn	Halifax	Melbourne	25
No. 51 Sqn	Halifax	Snaith	31
No. 76 Sqn	Halifax	Holme	40
No. 77 Sqn	Halifax	Full Sutton	47
No. 78 Sqn	Halifax	Breighton	29
No. 102 Sqn	Halifax	Pocklington	20
No. 158 Sqn	Halifax	Lissett	29
No. 346 Sqn (Fr)	Halifax	Elvington	24
No. 347 Sqn (Fr)	Halifax	Elvington	23
No. 466 Sqn (RAAF)	Halifax	Driffield	19
No. 640 Sqn	Halifax	Leconfield	15

▲ **Avro Lancaster B.Mk I**

No. 463 Squadron / Royal Australian Air Force / No. 5 Group / RAF Bomber Command, Waddington, Lincolnshire, spring 1945

This aeroplane carries the yellow-outlined unit code typical of No. 5 Group late in World War II, and was shot down by a German night-fighter in the last Lancaster night raid of the war, on the Tonsberg oil refinery in Norway, on 25/26 April 1945.

Specifications

Crew: 7

Powerplant: 4 x 1223kW (1640hp) Rolls-Royce Merlin XXIV inline piston engines

Maximum speed: 462km/h (287mph)

Range: 4072km (2530 miles)

Service ceiling: 7470m (24,500ft)

Dimensions: span 31.09m (102f); length 21.18m (69ft 6in); height 6.10m (20ft)

Weight: 31,751kg (70,000lb) loaded

Armament: 8 x 7.7mm (0.303in) MGs; bomb load of one 9979kg (22,000lb) bomb or up to 6350kg (14,000lb) of smaller bombs

Dortmund by 1079 aircraft on 12 March; Wuppertal and Barmen by 354 aircraft on 13 March; Herne and Gelsenkirchen by 195 and Datteln and Hattingen by 169 aircraft on 14 March; Lützkendorf and Zweibrücken by 244 and 230 aircraft on 14/15 March; Hagen and Misburg by 267 and 257 aircraft on 15/16 March; Nürnberg and Würzburg by 231 and 225 aircraft on 16/17 March; Witten and Hanau by 324 and 277 aircraft on 18/19 March; and Böhlen and Hemmingstedt by 224 and 166 aircraft on 20/21 March. The total of sorties by day on 21 March was 497 aircraft, while the total of sorties by night on 21/22 March amounted to 536 aircraft. Germany's destruction was all but complete.

Bomber Command: final raids
MARCH–MAY 1945

By the last three months of the European campaign, Bomber Command had in effect exhausted its supply of useful targets. Roaming by day as well as night, the command's aircraft completed their destruction of Germany's industries with pinpoint attacks on the last surviving targets.

BOMBER COMMAND, NO. 3 GROUP (MARCH 1945)

Unit	Type	Base	Strength
No. 15 Sqn	Lancaster	Mildenhall	22
No. 75 Sqn	Lancaster	Mepal	26
No. 90 Sqn	Lancaster	Tuddenham	21
No. 115 Sqn	Lancaster	Witchford	32
No. 138 Sqn	Lancaster	Tuddenham	20
No. 149 Sqn	Lancaster	Methwold	30
No. 186 Sqn	Lancaster	Stradishall	31
No. 195 Sqn	Lancaster	Wratting Common	30
No. 218 Sqn	Lancaster	Chedburgh	29
No. 514 Sqn	Lancaster	Waterbeach	32
No. 622 Sqn	Lancaster	Mildenhall	22

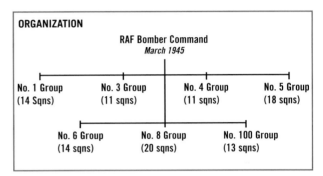

ORGANIZATION

RAF Bomber Command
March 1945

No. 1 Group (14 Sqns)	No. 3 Group (11 sqns)	No. 4 Group (11 sqns)	No. 5 Group (18 sqns)

No. 6 Group (14 sqns)	No. 8 Group (20 sqns)	No. 100 Group (13 sqns)

ON THE NIGHT OF 22/23 MARCH and during the day of 23 March 1945, some 300 Bomber Command aircraft flew small raids. Then, on the night of 23/24 March, 195 Lancaster and 23 Mosquito aircraft of Nos

5 and 8 Groups carried out the last British bombing raid on Wesel, losing no aircraft in the process. It is believed that, for its size, Wesel was by this time the most intensively bombed town in Germany: 97 per cent of the buildings in the town's main area had been destroyed, and the population had fallen to just 1900 persons in May 1945 from a figure of almost 25,000 in September 1939. This attack was part of 537 sorties flown in tactical support of the British land forces' crossing of the Rhine on 24 March.

Specifications

Crew: 7

Powerplant: 4 x 1223kW (1640hp) Rolls-Royce Merlin XXIV inline piston engines

Maximum speed: 462km/h (287mph)

Range: 4072km (2530 miles)

Service ceiling: 7470m (24,500ft)

Dimensions: span 31.09m (102f);

length 21.18m (69ft 6in);

height 6.10m (20ft)

Weight: 31,751kg (70,000lb) loaded

Armament: 8 x 7.7mm (0.303in) MGs, bomb load of one 9979kg (22,000lb) bomb or up to 6350kg (14,000lb) of smaller bombs

▲ **Avro Lancaster Mk I**

No. 149 Squadron / No. 3 Group / RAF Bomber Command, Methwold, Norfolk, 1945

The deepened bomb bay and the yellow stripes on the fins indicated that the aeroplane had G-H radar and was the machine of a flight leader.

BOMBER COMMAND, NO. 5 GROUP (MAY 1945)			
Unit	Type	Base	Strength
No. 9 Sqn	Lancaster	Bardney	22
No. 44 Sqn (Rhod)	Lancaster	Spilsby	16
No. 49 Sqn	Lancaster	Fulbeck	19
No. 50 Sqn	Lancaster	Skellingthorpe	17
No. 57 Sqn	Lancaster	East Kirkby	16
No. 61 Sqn	Lancaster	Skellingthorpe	19
No. 106 Sqn	Lancaster	Metheringham	16
No. 189 Sqn	Lancaster	Fulbeck	17
No. 207 Sqn	Lancaster	Spilsby	21
No. 227 Sqn	Lancaster	Balderton	18
No. 463 Sqn (RAAF)	Lancaster	Waddington	21
No. 467 Sqn (RAAF)	Lancaster	Waddington	19
No. 617	Lancaster & Mosquito	Woodhall Spa	42
No. 619	Lancaster	Strubby	17
No. 630 Sqn	Lancaster	East Kirkby	21
No. 83 Sqn (PFF)	Lancaster	Coningsby	22
No. 97 Sqn (PFF)	Lancaster	Coningsby	19
No. 627 Sqn (PFF)	Lancaster & Mosquito	Woodhall Spa	29

BOMBER COMMAND, NO. 6 GROUP (MARCH 1945)			
Unit	Type	Base	Strength
No. 408 Sqn	Halifax	Linton	24
No. 415 Sqn	Halifax	East Moor	24
No. 419 Sqn	Lancaster	Middleton St George	23
No. 420 Sqn	Halifax	Tholthorpe	20
No. 424 Sqn	Lancaster	Skipton-on-Swale	20
No. 425 Sqn	Halifax	Tholthorpe	22
No. 426 Sqn	Halifax	Linton	25
No. 427 Sqn	Lancaster & Halifax	Leeming	28
No. 428 Sqn	Lancaster	Middleton St George	25
No. 429 Sqn	Lancaster & Halifax	Leeming	24
No. 431 Sqn	Lancaster	Croft	20
No. 432 Sqn	Halifax	East Moor	24
No. 433 Sqn	Lancaster & Halifax	Skipton-on-Swale	21
No. 434 Sqn	Lancaster	Croft	24

Specifications

Crew: 7

Powerplant: 1204kW (1615hp) Bristol Hercules XVI radial piston engines

Maximum speed: 454km/h (282mph)

Range: 1658km (1030 miles)

Service ceiling: 7315m (24,000ft)

Dimensions: span 31.75m (104ft 2in); length 21.36m (70ft 1in); height 6.32m (20ft 9in)

Weight: 29,484kg (65,000lb) loaded

Armament: 9 x 7.7mm (0.303in) MGs; up to 5897kg (13,000lb) bomb load

▲ Handley Page Halifax B.Mk III

No. 158 Squadron / RAF Bomber Command, Lissett, 1945

Carrying the nickname *Friday the 13th*, this was the first Halifax to complete 100 operational sorties, and survived World War II with a total of 128 sorties, the largest number recorded by any Halifax bomber.

Razing towns

On the following day, there were attacks on towns from which the Germans might be able to reinforce the Rhine front: Hanover was visited by 267 aircraft, Munster by 175, and Osnabruck by

156. On 27 March, attacks were flown against Paderborn by 268 aircraft, Hamm by 150 and other smaller areas by 541. On the last day of March, Hamburg was attacked by 469 aircraft.

The last raid on Berlin was delivered on the night of 21/22 April, when 76 Mosquitoes flew six separate raids just before Soviet forces entered the city centre. After this, Bomber Command limited

Specifications

Crew: 7

Powerplant: 4 x 1223kW (1640hp) Rolls-Royce
Merlin XXIV V-12 piston engines

Maximum speed: 462km/h (287mph)

Range: 4070km (2530 miles)

Service ceiling: 7470m (24,500ft)

Dimensions: span 31.09m (102ft);
length 21.18m (69ft 6in); height 6.10m (20ft)

Weight: 16738kg (36,900lb) loaded

Armament: 8 x 7.7mm (0.303in) MGs; bomb
load of either one 9979kg (22,000lb) or up to
6350kg (4000lb) of smaller bombs

▲ **Avro Lancaster B.Mk I**

No. 467 Squadron / Royal Australian Air Force / RAF Bomber Command, 1945

No. 467 Squadron was one of four bomber squadrons of the RAAF to serve with RAF Bomber Command, the others being Nos 460, 463 and 466 Squadrons. However, there were insufficient squadrons to allow the creation of an Australian group like the Canadian No. 6 Group.

Specifications

Crew: 7

Powerplant: 4 x 1204kW (1615hp) Bristol
Hercules XVI radial piston engines

Maximum speed: 454km/h (282mph)

Range: 1658km (1030 miles)

Service ceiling: 7315m (24,000ft)

Dimensions: span 31.75m (104ft 2in);
length 21.36m (70ft 1in);
height 6.32m (20ft 9in)

Weight: 29,484kg (65,000lb) loaded

Armament: 9 x 7.7mm (0.303in) MGs; up to
5897kg (13,000lb) of bombs

▲ **Handley Page Halifax Mk III**

No. 171 (Special Duties) Squadron / No. 100 Group / RAF Bomber Command, North Creake, 1945

This aeroplane was operated in the 'Mandrel', or radio countermeasures, role in the later stages of World War II.

itself primarily to raids in tactical support of the army, but the last major strategic raid was the destruction of the oil refinery at Tonsberg in southern Norway by 107 Lancasters during the night of 25/26 April. Another controversial RAF raid occurred on 3 May, when the *Cap Arcona*, *Thielbek* and *Deutschland* were bombed, killing between 7000 and 8000 refugees.

With the surrender of Germany, the Allies could concentrate on Japan. Bomber Command was a significant resource for the proposed invasion of Japan, and plans were prepared to send 30 bomber squadrons to bases on Okinawa, but the nuclear attacks on Hiroshima and Nagasaki occurred before any of the force had been transferred to the Pacific.

Germany's losses
1940–45

The British night bombing campaign against German cities remains one of the most debated aspects of World War II. But Germany had initiated the bombing of civilian centres, and Bomber Command merely responded with the only means the British had to strike directly at Germany.

IN OVERALL TERMS, IT IS ESTIMATED THAT the British and US bombing of Germany killed between 305,000 and 600,000 civilians, some 67 per cent of them succumbing to British attacks, and it was Bomber Command's area bombing campaign that became one of the most controversial aspects of World War II.

Devastated cities

Up to 1942, navigational capability could provide for nothing better than the targeting of an urban area by night bombing. Germany's cities invariably had major industrial districts, and were therefore seen as legitimate targets by the Allies, and especially Bomber Command.

The most destructive single raids in casualty terms were those that caused appalling firestorms in Hamburg (45,000 dead) in 1943 and Dresden (25,000–35,000 dead) in March 1945. Other major raids on German cities that resulted in notably large civilian casualties were those on Darmstadt (12,300 dead), Pforzheim (17,600 dead) and Kassel (10,000 dead).

▲ **Rail yard attack**

This aerial photograph shows the devastation caused by Bomber Command's attack on the Juvisy rail yard on the southern outskirts of Paris, 18–19 April 1944. Led by Mosquito pathfinders, 184 Lancasters from No. 5 Group demolished almost the entire track complex.

Specifications

Crew: 7	Dimensions: span 30.12m (98ft 10in);
Powerplant: 4 x 1204kW (1615hp) Bristol	length 21.74m (71ft 4in);
Hercules XVI radial piston engines	height 6.12m (20ft 1in)
Maximum speed: 454km/h (282mph)	Weight: 29,484kg (65,000lb) loaded
Range: 3194km (1985 miles)	Armament: 9 x 7.7mm (0.303in) MGs; internal
Service ceiling: 7315m (24,000ft)	bomb load of 6577kg (14,500lb)

▲ **Handley Page Halifax B.Mk III**

No. 640 Squadron / RAF Bomber Command, Leconfield, Yorkshire, 1945

No. 640 Squadron was the highest-numbered of the 36 home-based units to fly the Halifax in the ranks of RAF Bomber Command. This aeroplane has four-gun power-operated dorsal and tail turrets, as well as H$_2$S navigation/bombing radar.

Bomber Command: casualties

1939–45

Bomber Command carried the war to Germany in a manner that no other element of the British armed forces could attempt. The industrial cost was enormous, but so too was the price that Bomber Command's crews had to pay in men killed, wounded and maimed.

WITH REGARD TO the legality of the campaign, an article in the *International Review of the Red Cross* stated 'In examining [aerial area bombardment] in the light of international humanitarian law, it should be borne in mind that during the Second World War there was no agreement, treaty, convention or any other instrument governing the protection of the civilian population or civilian property, as the conventions then in force dealt only with the protection of the wounded and the sick on the battlefield and in naval warfare, hospital ships, the laws and customs of war and the protection of prisoners of war.'

The butcher's bill

For its efforts Bomber Command paid a very high price, in the form of 55,573 dead, some 4000 wounded and 9784 taken prisoner. The dead included more than 38,000 RAF aircrew of all nationalities, 9900 men of the RCAF, and more than 1500 men of European countries occupied by the Germans. The manpower strength of the Australian squadrons in Bomber Command represented just 2 per cent of Royal Australian Air Force (RAAF) strength, but the 4050 men killed were 23 per cent of

the total number of RAAF personnel lost in action during World War II: No. 460 Squadron of the RAAF, with an establishment of some 200 men, in fact suffered 1018 deaths in combat during 1942–45 and so was in effect 'destroyed' five times.

On average, of every 100 aircrew serving with Bomber Command, 55 were killed or died of their wounds, three were injured on operations or active service, 12 (some injured) were taken prisoner, two were shot down and were not captured, and 27 survived a complete tour of operations.

In overall terms, Bomber Command flew 364,514 operational sorties and dropped 1.046 million tonnes (1.0305 million tons) of bombs for the loss in action of 8325 aircraft.

The very high casualty figures suffered by the squadrons of Bomber Command, combined with the command's high levels of morale and operational capability, provide very compelling evidence of both the determination and the courage displayed by all

▲ **Boeing Fortress Mk III**

No. 223 (Special Duties) Squadron / No. 100 Group / RAF Bomber Command, Oulton, Norfolk, 1944–45

This aeroplane was operated in the electronic jamming and intelligence-gathering roles in the later stages of World War II.

Specifications

Crew: 8

Powerplant: 4 x 895kW (1200hp) Wright Cyclone GR-1820 radial piston engines

Maximum speed: 451km/h (280mph)

Range: 4410km (2740 miles)

Service ceiling: 9601m (31,500ft)

Dimensions: span 31.62m (103ft 9in); length 22.25m (73ft); height 4.72m (15ft 6in)

Weight: 29,030kg (64,000lb) loaded

Armament: 13 x 12.7mm (0.5in) MGs in nose, turrets, waist and tail; up to 5806kg (12,800lb) bomb load aircrew. They took the war to a Germany increasingly better defended by radar-equipped night-fighters and radar-directed anti-aircraft guns.

In statistical terms all aircrew were aware that there was little chance that they would survive through a full tour of 30 operations without being killed, wounded or taken prisoner. This fact was derived from the appreciation that, for much of the war, the loss rate on each mission was in the order of 5 per cent: on average, therefore, one of every 20 aircraft on a mission would be shot down. However, on some missions the loss rate could exceed 10 per cent.

Specifications

Crew: 7

Powerplant: 4 x 1223kW (1640hp) Rolls-Royce
  Merlin XXIV inline piston engines

Maximum speed: 462km/h (287mph)

Range: 4072km (2530 miles)

Service ceiling: 7470m (24,500ft)

Dimensions: span 31.09m (102f);
  length 21.18m (69ft 6in);
  height 6.10m (20ft)

Weight: 31,751kg (70,000lb) loaded

Armament: 8 x 7.7mm (0.303in) MGs;
  1 x 'Grand Slam' 9979kg (22,000lb) bomb

▲ Avro Lancaster B.Mk I (Special)

No. 617 Squadron / RAF Bomber Command, Woodhall Spa, Lincolnshire, early 1945

This aeroplane of the celebrated 'Dambusters squadron' has the cutaway lower fuselage, without bomb bay doors, to carry the 9979kg (22,000lb) 'Grand Slam' earth-penetrating bomb used for the destruction of canals, bridges and viaducts.

▲ Avro Lancaster

The Lancaster was the most important British heavy bomber of World War II, and this No. 635 Squadron aeroplane was used to repatriate POWs at the war's end.

Objectives missed and achieved
1940–45

Bomber Command patently failed in its objective of destroying German civilian morale, and its real strategic successes, while tangible, are very difficult to quantity in any objective fashion. However, the command was certainly of major importance in the last 12 months of the war.

THE NOTIONAL OBJECT of Bomber Command's effort was to break German civilian morale, and this was not achieved. The bombing was a constant trial to the German people, but the apparently indiscriminate targeting, heavy civilian casualties and widespread damage helped to stiffen German resolve, just as the German Blitz had served to bolster British morale.

In himself, Harris believed that there was a direct relationship between the tonnage of bombs dropped, the areas of city wiped out and military production lost, but in fact the overall effect of Bomber Command's efforts on industrial production is not easy to quantify. The British Bombing Survey at the end of the war was purposefully under-resourced to put matters firmly in the past without due consideration.

The USAAF was concerned with precision attacks, and its analysis highlighted the huge success of US attacks on German synthetic oil production from the spring of 1944 in crippling German transport and military operations. And in attacking targets the

▲ **Bomb bursts**

On 27 December 1944 Bomber Command atacked the Rheydt rail marshalling yard. This photograph shows the target area marked out in a dotted line, with the concentration of bomb bursts over the target.

Germans had to defend, the USAAF knew that its fighters would inflict crippling losses on the Luftwaffe's fighter force. The RAF also contributed to this daylight effort from mid-1944.

▲ **de Havilland Mosquito PR.Mk XVI**

No. 100 Squadron / RAF, Melsbroek, Belgium, 1944–45

The Mosquito PR.Mk XVI was the photo-reconnaissance counterpart of the Mosquito B.Mk XVI bomber, and as such was the RAF's standard high-altitude reconnaissance aeroplane in the later stages of World War II.

Specifications

Crew: 2

Powerplant: 2 x 1275kW (1710hp) Rolls-Royce
Merlin 76 or 77 V-type engines

Maximum speed: 667km/h (415mph)

Range: 3942km (2450 miles)

Service ceiling: 11,742m (38,500ft)

Dimensions: span 16.53m (54ft 2in);
length 13.57m (44ft 6in);
height 3.8m (12ft 5in)

Weight: 10,419kg (23,000lb) loaded

Armament: none

Specifications

Crew: 8

Powerplant: 4 x 895kW (1200hp) Wright Cyclone GR-1820 radial piston engines

Maximum speed: 451km/h (280mph)

Range: 4410km (2740 miles)

Service ceiling: 9601m (31,500ft)

Dimensions: span 31.62m (103ft 9in); length 22.25m (73ft); height 4.72m (15ft 6in)

Weight: 29,030kg (64,000lb) loaded

Armament: 13 x 12.7mm (0.5in) MGs in nose, turrets, waist and tail; up to 5806kg (12,800lb) of bombs

▲ **Boeing Fortress Mk III**

No. 214 Squadron / No. 100 (Bomber Support) Group / RAF Bomber Command, Sculthorpe, Norfolk, 1944–45

The Fortress Mk III was the British version of the USAAF's B-17G, the variant that introduced a chin turret for defence against head-on fighter attacks. The UK took 85 such aircraft for use in the countermeasures, clandestine and decoy roles.

Bomber Command's contribution
1940–45

The increasing scale and capability of Bomber Command's night offensive played a huge part in forcing the Germans to retain substantial numbers of weapons and personnel for the defence of Germany, to the detriment of the frontline and industrial production.

THOUGH IMPOSSIBLE to quantify in any comprehensive fashion, the British night-bomber did achieve real results, but was made difficult by the fact that Germany's industrial base was very strong, and also widely scattered even before a policy of deliberate dispersal was launched. This made complete destruction by area bombing effectively impossible. Moreover, right into 1943 Germany was not even on a full war basis so far as industrial effort was concerned, giving industry considerable leeway in restoring lost production.

A case has been argued for Bomber Command's success in limiting German production of weapons. Whether this is true or not, the German armed forces ultimately did not run out of weapons and ammunition so much as out of useful manpower and transport capability (trucks, locomotives, rolling stock and fuel) with which to move arms and ammunition from the factories to the front.

▲ **Lancaster production**

Undertaken by five British companies and, to a limited extent, the Canadian Victory Aircraft Ltd, manufacture of the Lancaster was aided by the fact that there were comparatively few major variants. Overall production was 7378 aircraft, some of these seeing post-war service with other nations.

Bomber Command's greatest contribution to winning the war derived from the huge diversion of German material and manpower resources into the defence of the *Reich*. By January 1943, for example, some 1000 night-fighters, most of them twin-engined Bf 110 and Ju 88 aircraft, were involved in the defence of Germany.

Perhaps more importantly, by September 1943 the AA defence of Germany involved no fewer than 8875 88mm (3.465in) guns, together with smaller numbers of heavier weapons and about 25,000 20mm (0.79in) and 37mm (1.46in) light flak guns. The '88' was arguably the war's best piece of artillery, and was both an effective AA weapon and a potent battlefield tank destroyer. These weapons would otherwise have been available for service on both the Eastern and Western Fronts.

Manning these guns, the flak regiments in Germany required some 900,000 personnel, and another one million people were committed to clearing wreckage and repairing bomb damage. The military personnel would have been useful at the front, and the civilians were lost to the industrial work force. This diversion of weapons and manpower to the defence of Germany was Bomber Command's greatest contribution to Allied victory. By 1944, defence against the bomber required 30 per cent of German artillery, 20 per cent of heavy shell, 33 per cent of sight and 50 per cent of electro-technical manufacture.

Specifications

Crew: 7/8

Powerplant: 4 x 1089kW (1460hp) Packard
(Rolls-Royce) Merlin piston engines

Maximum speed: 452km/h (281mph)

Range: 4313km (2680 miles)

Service ceiling: 7460m (24,500ft)

Dimensions: span 31.09m (102ft);
length 20.98m (68ft 10in);
height 6.19m (20ft 4in)

Weight: 18,598kg (41,000lb) loaded

Armament: 8 x 7.7mm (0.303in) MGs; up to
6350kg (14,000lb) of bombs

▲ **Avro Lancaster B.Mk X**

No. 431 'Iroquois' Squadron / Royal Canadian Air Force / No. 6 Group / RAF Bomber Command, Croft, County Durham, early 1945

The Lancaster B.Mk X was the counterpart of the Lancaster B.Mk III manufactured in Canada by Victory Aircraft Ltd. Production totalled 430 aircraft.

Specifications

Crew: 7

Powerplant: 4 x 1249kW (1675hp) Bristol
Hercules 100 engines

Maximum speed: 502km/h (312mph)

Range: 2027km (1260 miles)

Service ceiling: 7315m (24,000ft)

Dimensions: span 31.75m (104ft 2in);
length 21.46m (70ft 5in);
height 6.32m (20ft 9in)

Weight: 30,872kg (68,000lb) loaded

Armament: 8 x 7.7mm (0.303in) Browning
MGs; 5897kg (13,000lb) of bombs

▲ **Handley Page Halifax B.Mk VI**

No. 158 Squadron / No. 4 Group / RAF Bomber Command, Lissett, April 1945

This was a perfectly standard Halifax night-bomber of the late-war period with H2S navigation and bombing radar, as well as the yellow-striped vertical tail surfaces of No. 4 Group's units (the stripes were used from a time later in 1944).

Mediterranean Theatre
1940–45

British interest in the Mediterranean extended from the Straits of Gibraltar to the coast of Palestine, and from the coast of North Africa to northern Italy. Throughout the war Britain covered this vast region with flying boats and land-based reconnaissance aircraft.

WHEN ITALY ENTERED WORLD WAR II in June 1940, the British had to watch for activities not only in Italy itself and North Africa, but also in the Italian-held Dodecanese islands in the Aegean Sea and the progress of Italy's land campaign against Greece. Other factors that had to be monitored on a constant basis were the dispositions and strengths of the Italian fleet's various components, for these could pose a very real threat to British maritime communications in the Mediterranean, especially the resupply of troops in Egypt.

Battling the *Luftwaffe*

Despite the success of the British carrierborne air attack on the Italian fleet in Taranto during November 1940, which gave the Royal Navy effective command of the Mediterranean, Italian air power remained a major threat, and one that was supplemented, from a time early in 1941, by substantial German air strength directed against the British base at Malta as well as British maritime strength and operations.

Gradually, however, the British got the upper hand in the combined sea and air war over the Mediterranean through their combination of astute reconnaissance and well-planned bomber operations. Reconnaissance played a key role on the North African campaign through the discovery of Axis preparations for offensive undertakings, allowing the ground forces to be supported accordingly and the Axis supply dumps and lines of communication to be bombed. The nature of the British air effort changed after the defeat of the Axis in North Africa in May 1943. Major air efforts were required as part of the campaigns in Sicily and Italy, and constant watches still had to be maintained over the western Mediterranean until the autumn of 1944 and then over the Balkans right to the end of the war.

▲ **Bristol Blenheim Mk I**

No. 113 Squadron / RAF, Middle East, Egypt and Greece, 1940–41

No. 113 Squadron switched from the Hawker Hind to the Blenheim in May 1939 at Heliopolis in Egypt, and thereafter flew the type in the first stages of the North African desert campaign after Italy's declaration of war in June 1940. In February 1941, the squadron moved to Greece, where it lost all its aircraft in a devastating German ground attack on 15 April.

Specifications

Crew: 3	Dimensions: span 17.17m (56ft 4in);
Powerplant: 627kW (840hp) Bristol Mercury VIII	length 12.12m (39ft 9in);
9-cylinder single-row radial engines	height 3m (9ft 10in)
Maximum speed: 459km/h (285mph)	Weight: 4031kg (8839lb) loaded
Range: 1810km (1125 miles)	Armament: 2 x 7.7mm (0.303in) MGs and
Service ceiling: 8315m (27,280ft)	454kg (1000lb) bomb load

Specifications

Crew: 4

Powerplant: 2 x 895kW (1200hp) Pratt &
    Whitney twin Wasp radial piston engines

Maximum speed: 447km/h (278mph)

Range: 2897km (1800 miles)

Service ceiling: 9449m (31,000ft)

Dimensions: span 18.69m (61ft 4in);
    length 14.22m (46ft 8in); height 4.57m (15ft)

Weight: 7624kg (16,809lb) loaded

Armament: 4 x 7.7mm (0.303in) Browning
    MGs; 2 x single Vickers K MGs; up to 907kg
    (2000lb) of bombs

▲ Martin Maryland Mk II

No. 24 Squadron / South African Air Force, Fuka, Egypt, May 1941

The SAAF was a primary operator of the Maryland, and No. 24 Squadron was one
of three detailed for operations over Crete from 23 May. In November 1941, the
squadron transitioned to the more capable Douglas Boston.

Specifications

Crew: 4

Powerplant: 2 x 895kW (1200hp) Pratt &
    Whitney twin Wasp radial piston engines

Maximum speed: 447km/h (278mph)

Range: 2897km (1800 miles)

Service ceiling: 9449m (31,000ft)

Dimensions: span 18.69m (61ft 4in);
    length 14.22m (46ft 8in); height 4.57m (15ft)

Weight: 7624kg (16,809lb) loaded

Armament: 4 x 7.7mm (0.303in) Browning
    MGs; 2 x single Vickers K MGs; up to 907kg
    (2000lb) of bombs

▲ Martin Maryland Mk I

No. 431 Flight / RAF, Malta, 1941

Delivered to US standard but fitted with an Armstong Whitworth dorsal turret,
the Maryland Mk I was operated from Malta primarily in the long-range
reconnaissance role deep into the Mediterranean and around Italy's coast.

Specifications Mk III

Crew: 4

Powerplant: 2 x 1238kW (1660hp) Wright
    Cyclone radial piston engines

Maximum speed: 486km/h (302mph)

Range: 1529km (950 miles)

Service ceiling: 7315m (24,000ft)

Dimensions: span 18.59m (61ft 4in);
    length 14.78m (48ft 6in);
    height 5.41m (17ft 9in)

Weight: 6895kg (15,200lb) loaded

Armament: 14 x 7.7mm (0.303in) machine
    guns; bomb load of 907kg (2000lb)

▲ Martin Baltimore Mk V

No. 232 Wing / RAF, Mediterranean theatre, 1944

A development of the concept embodied in the Maryland, the Baltimore was
designed to European standards. Production totalled 1575 aircraft used mostly in
the Mediterranean theatre with a 907kg (2000lb) bomb load and up to 14 7.7mm
(0.303in) fixed and trainable machine guns.

Coastal Command
1936–45

Given the UK's reliance on the Royal Navy as its first line of defence and on the merchant navy for the trade on which the survival of the UK was dependent, Coastal Command was a vital asset, but nonetheless seldom received the priority it deserved.

COASTAL COMMAND came into existence in July 1936 as part of the major reorganization of the RAF's structure, a reorganization based on the latest official thinking about the probable nature of future war. Coastal Command was created out of the Coastal Area command, which had been established in 1919, and was the organization within the RAF that provided aerial protection for the United Kingdom's maritime interests against submarine, surface warship and aerial threats, and also to visit an aerial threat to any enemy's vessels.

Coastal Command's first commander-in-chief was Air Marshal Sir Arthur Longmore, who was succeeded on 1 September 1936 by Air Marshal Sir Philip Joubert de la Ferte, himself succeeded on 18 August 1937 by Air Marshal Sir Frederick Bowhill. Later commanders were Air Chief Marshal Sir Philip Joubert de la Ferte, once again, from 14 June 1941, Air Marshal Sir John Slessor from 5 February 1943 and, finally in the European context of World War II, Air Chief Marshal Sir William

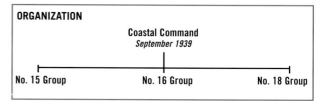

ORGANIZATION		
	Coastal Command *September 1939*	
No. 15 Group	No. 16 Group	No. 18 Group

COASTAL COMMAND, NO. 15 GROUP (1939)		
Unit	**Type**	**Base**
No. 204 Sqn	Sunderland & London	Mount Batten
No. 210 Sqn	Sunderland & London	Pembroke Dock
No. 217 Sqn	Anson & Tiger Moth	Warmwell
No. 228 Sqn	Sunderland	Pembroke Dock
No. 502 Sqn	Anson	Aldergrove

Sholto Douglas from 20 January 1944. As with the RAF's other major commands, Coastal Command was structured internally into regionally based groups, each comprising a number of squadrons

▲ **Avro Anson GR.Mk I**

No. 220 Squadron / RAF Coastal Command, 1938

This Anson is seen in Coastal Command's standard finish and markings of the period immediately before World War II, namely an overall silver dope finish with yellow-outlined roundels, black serials and yellow squadron markings.

Specifications

Crew: 3

Powerplant: 2 x 261kW (350hp) Armstrong
  Siddeley Cheetah IX radial piston engines

Maximum speed: 303km/h (188mph)

Range: 1271km (790 miles)

Service ceiling: 5791m (19,000ft)

Dimensions: span 17.22m (56ft 6in);
  length 12.88m (56ft 6in);
  height 3.99m (13ft 1in)

Weight: 3629kg (8000lb) loaded

Armament: 2 x 7.7mm (0.303in) MGs; provision
  to carry up to 163kg (360lb) of bombs

operating from bases close to the UK's long coast. In Coastal Command's youth, other commands had priority for men and equipment, so Coastal Command had to do the best it could with obsolescent aircraft and weapons. The delivery of aircraft was often so limited, indeed, that many units were 'borrowed' from the Fleet Air Arm (FAA) of the Royal Navy, one of the major beneficiaries of the command's existence, and the command's most important weapon was a small bomb that had to strike a submarine rather than detonate close to it. This bomb also possessed an alarming tendency to 'skip' off the water like a skimmed stone, and in one case even hit and destroyed the aeroplane that had

Specifications

Crew: 3/5	Dimensions: span 17.2m (56ft 5in);
Powerplant: 2 x 261kW (350hp) Armstrong	length 12.88m (42ft 3in);
Siddeley Cheetah IX radial piston engines	height 3.99m (13ft 1in)
Maximum speed: 303km/h (188mph)	Weight: 3629kg (8000lb) loaded
Range: 1271km (790 miles)	Armament: 2 x 7.7mm (0.303in) MGs; up to
Service ceiling: 5790m (19,000ft)	163kg (360lb) of bombs

▲ **Avro Anson GR.Mk I**

No. 206 Squadron / RAF Coastal Command, Bircham Newton, 1939–40

No. 206 Squadron received this Anson in 1937, and flew it over the North Sea until 1940 before passing the aeroplane to No. 1 Operational Training Unit. The machine crashed and was lost on 29 August 1940.

Specifications

Crew: 6	Dimensions: span 24.38m (80ft);
Powerplant: 2 x 682kW (915hp) Bristol	length 17.32m (56ft 10in);
Pegasus X radial piston engines	height 5.72m (18ft 9in)
Maximum speed: 249km/h (155mph)	Weight: 8346kg (18,400lb) loaded
Range: 1770km (1100 miles)	Armament: 3 x 7.7mm (0.303in) Lewis MGs;
Service ceiling: 6066m (19,900ft)	up to 907kg (2000lb) of bombs

▲ **Saro London Mk II**

No. 240 Squadron / RAF Coastal Command, Sullom Voe, Shetland, late 1939

This flying boat was built as a London Mk I, but later upgraded to Mk II standard with more powerful engines driving four- rather than two-bladed propellers. The last London biplane flying boats were retired from British service in 1941, some of the machines being passed to the RCAF.

dropped it. Had they not been so tragic, many early operations would have been amusing. Nevertheless, on several occasions German submarines were forced to fight off the attentions of Coastal Command aircraft, although the number of times the aircraft found any U-boat was limited.

In 1941 there began experiments of a depth charge that could be dropped from the air, and after successful trials this weapon (soon adapted for shallow detonation after this had been shown to be more useful) rapidly superseded the original bomb. In the same year, the introduction of several types of newer warplane to Bomber Command allowed the command to pass some of its older bomber types, including the Vickers Wellington, to Coastal Command. These acquisitions offered much longer range, making them much more effective. Then the introduction of the Leigh Light in 1942 allowed accurate night attacks, denying U-boats the freedom to recharge their batteries under cover of dark.

▸ **Bristol Blenheim**

The Blenheim Mk IV flew with 11 Coastal Command fighter squadrons, and also with four Coastal Command bomber squadrons in the early part of World War II.

Specifications

Crew: 10

Powerplant: 4x 753kW (1010hp) Bristol
  Pegasus XXII 9 cylinder single-row radial
  engines

Maximum speed: 336km/h (209mph)

Range: 4023km (2500 miles)

Service ceiling: 4570m (15,000ft)

Dimensions: span 34.38m (11ft 9.5in);
  length 26m (85ft 3.5in);
  height 10.52m (34ft 6in)

Weight: 22,226kg (49,000lb) loaded

Armament: 8 x 7.7mm (0.303in) MGs; internal
  bomb, depth charge and mine load of 907kg
  (2000lb)

▲ **Short Sunderland Mk II**

No. 201 Squadron / RAF Coastal Command, Castle Archdale, Co. Fermanagh, Northern Ireland, 1941

Remaining in service to 1944, this flying boat carries the early type of over-fuselage antennae associated with air-to-surface search radar. Operating from Northern Ireland, the squadron's aircraft could range deep into the Atlantic Ocean.

Specifications

Crew: 10

Powerplant: 4x 753kW (1010hp) Bristol
Pegasus XXII 9 cylinder single-row radial
engines

Maximum speed: 336km/h (209mph)

Range: 4023km (2500 miles)

Service ceiling: 4570m (15,000ft)

Dimensions: span 34.38m (11ft 9.5in);
length 26m (85ft 3.5in);
height 10.52m (34ft 6in)

Weight: 22,226kg (49,000lb) loaded

Armament: 8 x 7.7mm (0.303in) MGs; internal
bomb, depth charge and mine load of 907kg
(2000lb)

▲ **Short Sunderland Mk I**

No. 230 Squadron / RAF Coastal Command, Mediterranean, 1941

No. 230 Squadron was the first unit to receive the formidable Sunderland general reconnaissance flying boat, taking its first machines during the summer of 1938 before moving to the Mediterranean, where the unit operated for a time from Soudha Bay on the north coast of Crete before the island's fall to the Germans in May 1941.

Coastal Command – the first shots
1939–40

The advent of World War II found Coastal Command in a very difficult position, for the Command had huge responsibilities but only very meagre resources. Moreover, Bomber Command was very jealous of its own resources, thus denying Coastal Command many aircraft it could have used.

COASTAL COMMAND tried without much success to improve its capabilities in the first months of the war, but was aided by the fact that the German naval offensive in the North Atlantic was also slow to gather momentum.

Anti-U-boat operations

From the middle of 1940, however, the Command was faced by a host of often conflicting demands: anti-invasion patrols over the North Sea and English Channel, long-range fighter protection over the South-West Approaches, surveillance of the vast length of coast controlled by the Germans, escort

COASTAL COMMAND, NO. 16 GROUP (1939)		
Unit	Type	Base
No. 22 Sqn	Vildebeest	Thorney Island
No. 42 Sqn	Vildebeest	Bircham Newton
No. 48 Sqn	Anson	Thorney Island
No. 206 Sqn	Anson	Bircham Newton
No. 500 Sqn	Anson, Hind & Tutor	Detling

patrol for convoys, and offensive patrols against U-boats. As the war continued, all of these had to be extended in scope and range, but Coastal Command had a mere 500 operational aircraft. Most unfortunate of all, given the growing threat of the U-boat, was the fact that of these aircraft a mere 34 were Short Sunderland flying boats able to range more than 800km (500 miles) out into the ocean.

So successful did the U-boat attacks become in the South-West Approaches that convoys were re-routed via the North-West Approaches around the northern tip of Ireland to the ports of Liverpool and Glasgow.

Specifications

Crew: 7

Powerplant: 2 x 686kW (920p) Bristol Pegasus
X 9 cylinder air-cooled radial engines

Maximum speed: 241km/h (150mph)

Range: 1609km (1000 miles)

Service ceiling: 5640m (18,500ft)

Dimensions: span 25.91m (85ft 0in); length
16.71m (54ft 10in); height 6.63m (21ft 9in)

Weight: 8618kg (19,000lb) loaded

Armament: 3 x 7.7mm (0.303in) MGs; up to
454kg (1000lb) of bombs, mines or depth
charges

▲ Supermarine Stranraer

No. 240 Squadron / RAF Coastal Command, Pembroke Dock, South Wales, 1940

This squadron operated from Pembroke Dock and Stranraer, with the Stranraer flying boat in the general reconnaissance role until 1941.

Specifications

Crew: 3

Powerplant: 2 x 261kW (350hp) Armstrong
Siddeley Cheetah IX radial piston engines

Maximum speed: 303km/h (188mph)

Range: 1271km (790 miles)

Service ceiling: 5791m (19,000ft)

Dimensions: span 17.22m (56ft 6in);
length 12.88m (56ft 6in);
height 3.99m (13ft 1in)

Weight: 3629kg (8000lb) loaded

Armament: 2 x 7.7mm (0.303in) MGs; provision
to carry up to 163kg (360lb) of bombs

▲ Avro Anson GR.Mk I

No. 217 Squadron / RAF Coastal Command, 1939–40

Armed with two 7.7mm (0.303in) machine guns, one in the nose and the other in the manually operated Armstrong Whitworth dorsal turret, the Anson was indifferently armed for defensive purposes, and was replaced in Coastal Command by the Bristol Beaufort from a time late in 1940.

Convoy protection
1940

The Germans soon discovered that the British had switched many convoys further to the north and shifted the focus of their efforts to the new area. Here Coastal Command's task was made all the more difficult by the relative shortage of airfields and flying boat bases.

THE NEW CONVOY lane was soon discovered and the Germans switched their attention to the waters west and north of Ireland. Coastal Command lacked the airfields and flying boat bases to relocate large numbers of aircraft, so this placed a further burden on the already overextended command. Compounding the problem was the fact that in August 1940 the Germans introduced new U-boat tactics, following the target convoy out of the range of its escorts by day, and closing at night for a surface attack undetected by the convoy escorts' sonars.

Radar search

Coastal Command had no immediate answer, as night operations were still tricky, and except in bright moonlight visual detection of a U-boat was difficult. The only real hope lay with air-to-surface search radar, but only about one in six aircraft carried this electronic aid, which was next to useless against all

COASTAL COMMAND, NO. 18 GROUP (1940)		
Unit	Type	Base
No. 201 Sqn	London	Calshot
No. 209 Sqn	Stranraer	Invergordon
No. 220 Sqn	Hudson & Anson	Bircham Newton
No. 224 Sqn	Hudson & Anson	Leuchars
No. 233 Sqn	Hudson & Anson	Leuchars
No. 240 Sqn	London & Lerwick	Invergordon
No. 269 Sqn	Anson	Montrose
No. 608 Sqn	Anson	Thornaby
No. 612 Sqn	Anson, Hector & Hind	Dyce

but a fully surfaced U-boat at a range of less than 4.8km (3 miles).

And even anti-surface vessel (ASV) radar was limited; last-minute visual sighting was still required, as there was no illumination system, and the required

▲ **Bristol Blenheim Mk IVF**

No. 248 Squadron / RAF Coastal Command, North Coates, 1940–41

Used by Fighter Command in small numbers as well as by Coastal Command, the Blenheim Mk IVF was an extemporized fighter created by adapting the standard Mk IV light bomber with a ventral pack carrying four 7.7mm (0.303in) Browning fixed forward-firing machine guns.

Specifications

Crew: 3

Powerplant: 2 x 675kW (905hp) Bristol Mercury
  XV radial piston engines

Maximum speed: 428km/h (266mph)

Range: 2350km (1460 miles)

Service ceiling: 8310m (27,260ft)

Dimensions: span 17.17m (56ft 4in);

length 12.98m (42ft 7in); height 3m (9ft 10in)

Weight: 6532kg (14,400lb) loaded

Armament: 5 x 7.7mm (0.303in) MGs;
  4 x 7.7mm (0.303in) Browning MGs under
  the hull, up to 434kg (1000lb) of bombs
  internally and 145kg (320lb) of bombs
  externally

low-altitude release of the depth charge was dangerous under all but perfect conditions for lack of a reliable low-reading altimeter.

Thus convoys had to rely for safety on evasive routing on the basis of intercepted German radio signals, which also made it possible for the British to concentrate air patrols in the areas in which the U-boats were planning to operate. But radio intercepts were not always available or reliable, and shipping losses were often heavy. Between the beginning of

June and the end of 1940, more than 3.04 million tonnes (3 million tons) of British, Allied and neutral merchant shipping were sunk. Some 59 per cent of the total fell victim to U-boats, 12 per cent to Focke-Wulf Fw 200 Condor and other aircraft, and the rest to mines and surface raiders.

During this time, the British losses were more than 2.54 million tonnes (2.5 million tons) greater than replacements. There was an acute need for more and better weapons, aircraft and equipment.

Tipping the balance
1941–42

While 1941 was a year of crisis without much visible hope on the horizon for Coastal Command, there were some notable success and the beginnings of greater capability and a more effective concentration of effort. These changes were to start bearing fruit in the course of 1942.

THE NEEDS OF COASTAL COMMAND also included depth charges designed for air dropping, more radios allowing aircraft/ship communication, longer-range radar and the means (slow-dropping flares or searchlights) to illuminate U-boats at night so that they could be attacked visually. Progress was slow, but progress was nevertheless made.

The start of 1941 was marked by dreadful weather, which was as much a hindrance to German U-boats

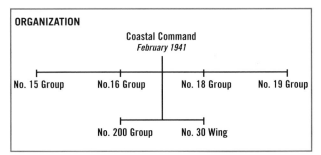

ORGANIZATION

Coastal Command
February 1941

No. 15 Group   No.16 Group   No. 18 Group   No. 19 Group

No. 200 Group   No. 30 Wing

▲ **Bristol Beaufort Mk I**

No. 22 Squadron / RAF Coastal Command, 1941–42

Initially based in the UK, No. 22 Squadron and its Beaufort aircraft were shipped to Ceylon during March 1942. The squadron remained in the Far East for the rest of World War II, but transitioned to the Bristol Beaufighter during June 1944.

Specifications

Crew: 4	height 13.59m (44ft 7in)
Powerplant: 2 x 843kW (1130hp) Bristol Taurus	Weight: 9630kg (21,230lb) loaded
VI, XII or XVI radial piston engines	Armament: 4 x 7.7mm (0.303in) MGs (two each
Maximum speed: 418km/h (260mph)	in nose and dorsal turrets) and, in some
Range: 1666km (1035 miles)	aircraft, three additional 7.7mm (0.303in) MGs
Service ceiling: 5030m (16,500ft)	(one in blister beneath the nose and two in
Dimensions: span 17.63m (57ft 10in);	beam positions); up to 1680kg (1500lb) of
length 13.59m (44ft 7in);	bombs or mines, or 1 x 728kg (1605lb) torpedo

and aircraft as Coastal Command. Convoy losses declined, and Coastal Command was afforded a little more breathing space, but from mid-February the weather improved and British losses increased as Germany committed more U-boats and aircraft, as well as four major surface raiding warships. In April 1941, losses amounted to 654,304 tonnes (644,000

tons), almost half of them to aircraft. Prime Minister Churchill demanded action, and at last Bomber Command released some obsolete squadrons whose Bristol Blenheims could cover the North Sea and so release Coastal Command squadrons for farther-reaching service. The U-boats moved deeper into the Atlantic to find respite from aircraft based in the UK

▲ **Lockheed Hudson GR.Mk IIIA**

No. 59 Squadron / RAF Coastal Command, UK, mid-1942

The Hudson Mk IIIA was the first Hudson model earmarked for RAF service under the terms of the USA's Lend-Lease Act. But of the 800 such aircraft expected only 382 were delivered, the others going to Commonwealth air forces and to the US Army Air Forces (USAAF), in which the type was known as the A-29.

Specifications

Crew: 6	length 13.50m (44ft 4in);
Powerplant: 2 x 890kW (1200hp) Wright	height 3.62m (11ft 10in)
Cyclone 9-cylinder radial engines	Weight: 7930kg (17,500lb) loaded
Maximum speed: 397km/h (246mph)	Armament: 7 x 7.7mm (0.303in) Browning MGs
Range: 3150km (1960 miles)	(two in nose, two in dorsal turret, two in
Service ceiling: 7470m (24,500ft)	beam and one ventral); 340kg (750lb) of
Dimensions: span 19.96m (65ft 4in);	bombs or depth charges

▲ **Lockheed Hudson GR.Mk IIIA**

No. 48 Squadron / RAF Coastal Command, UK, 1941–42

With its good speed and comparatively long endurance, the Hudson Mk III had decent defensive as well as offensive armament, and was popular with the men who flew the type.

Specifications

Crew: 6	length 13.50m (44ft 4in);
Powerplant: 2 x 890kW (1200hp) Wright	height 3.62m (11ft 10in)
Cyclone 9-cylinder radial engines	Weight: 7930kg (17,500lb) loaded
Maximum speed: 397km/h (246mph)	Armament: 7 x 7.7mm (0.303in) Browning MGs
Range: 3150km (1960 miles)	(two in nose, two in dorsal turret, two in
Service ceiling: 7470m (24,500ft)	beam and one ventral); 340kg (750lb) of
Dimensions: span 19.96m (65ft 4in);	bombs or depth charges

and West Africa, and this was reflected in a decline in losses to an average of 127,000 tonnes (125,000 tons) per month in July and August 1941, and a rise in U-boat sinkings as indicated by the loss of five such boats in March.

In June, Joubert returned as leader of Coastal Command, whose situation was improving as better radar was introduced and an aerial searchlight was in its final development. Joubert's first task was to develop the tactics that would make the best use of the new 'weapons'. Over this same period, Coastal Command's offensive capability, centred on the Bristol Beaufort torpedo-bomber and Bristol Beaufighter heavy fighter, was starting to exercise a significant effect on Germany's coastal shipping. The Beauforts' and Beaufighters' torpedoes supplemented the success of air- and sea-laid mines and the efforts of Bomber Command on German bases and the FAA on German shipping.

▲ **Consolidated Liberator GR.Mk I**

No. 120 Squadron / RAF Coastal Command, Aldergrove, Northern Ireland, late 1942

The Liberator's long range made it a natural choice for the maritime role, and this machine carries ASV.Mk II air-to-surface search radar as well as a ventral pack with four 20mm (0.79in) cannon for additional anti-submarine punch.

Specifications

Crew: 10	length 20.22m (66ft 4in);
Powerplant: 4 x 895kW (1200hp) Pratt &	height 5.49m (18ft)
Whitney Twin wasp radial piston engines	Weight: 32,296kg (71,200lb) loaded
Maximum speed: 488km/h (303mph)	Armament: 4 x 20mm (0.79in) in ventral
Range: 1730km (1080 miles)	position, plus 2 x 12.7mm (0.5in) guns each
Service ceiling: 8540m (28,000ft)	in dorsal, tail and retractable ball turrets; up
Dimensions: span 33.53m (110ft);	to 3629kg (8000lb) bombs

Specifications

Crew: 4	length 16.33m (53ft 7in);
Powerplant: 2 x 746kW (1000hp) Bristol	height 4.55m (14ft 11in)
Pegasus XVII radial piston engines	Weight: 8508kg (18,756lb) loaded
Maximum speed: 409km/h (254mph)	Armament: 2 x 7.7mm (0.303in) forward-firing
Range: 3034km (1885 miles)	twin MGs in dorsal and ventral positions; up
Service ceiling: 5791m (19,000ft)	to 1814kg (4000lb) of bombs
Dimensions: span 21.08m (69ft 2in);	

▲ **Handley Page Hampden TB.Mk I**

No. 489 Squadron / Royal New Zealand Air Force / RAF Coastal Command, Wick, 1942

A machine manufactured in Canada and operated in the torpedo-bomber role, this aeroplane flew anti-ship operations over the northern North Sea and Norwegian Sea in Coastal Command's standard finish of sea-grey upper surfaces and sky-blue under surfaces.

Coastal Command
1942–43

Improvements in aircraft, weapons, electronics and tactics implemented in 1942 made Coastal Command increasingly capable in 1943, and with the advent of the escort carrier to work in the central Atlantic 'black hole' the U-boat was harried day and night right across the Atlantic.

T HE ADVENT of the de Havilland Mosquito freed the Bristol Beaufighter for service with Coastal Command, in which the type became a highly useful short-range type using rocket and depth charge armament against German U-boats in the Bay of Biscay. The Beaufighter was also used in attacks on German surface vessels, including the formidable flak vessels used as escorts.

But of greater significance to Coastal Command was the entry to service, to supplement the Short Sunderland flying boat, of the Consolidated Liberator landplane in the very-long-range role. Bomber Command pressure meant that it was 1942 before even a few dozen Liberators were released, and much later still before a single squadron could be allocated to Gander, in Newfoundland, to reach the critical central Atlantic region and allow Coastal Command to cover all the North Atlantic zones. In

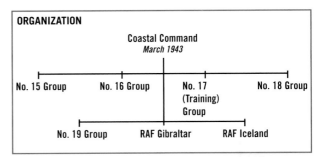

ORGANIZATION

Coastal Command
March 1943

No. 15 Group — No. 16 Group — No. 17 (Training) Group — No. 18 Group

No. 19 Group — RAF Gibraltar — RAF Iceland

the middle of 1942, 45 Boeing B-17Es were transferred to the RAF, by which they were designated Fortress Mk IIs. Probably as a result of the limitations of the Fortress Mk I (B-17C), the RAF decided not to use the Fortress Mk II in its intended high-altitude day bomber role, but to allocate them to Coastal Command for long-range maritime reconnaissance and anti-submarine work.

▲ **Lockheed Hudson GR.Mk III**

No. 233 Squadron / RAF Coastal Command, Aldergrove and St Eval, 1942

Developed from an American civil transport (the Lockheed Model 14) to meet a British requirement for a successor to the Avro Anson, the Hudson proved notably successful in the shorter-range coastal and maritime reconnaissance roles.

Specifications

Crew: 6	length 13.50m (44ft 4in);
Powerplant: 2 x 890kW (1200hp) Wright	height 3.62m (11ft 10in)
Cyclone 9-cylinder radial engines	Weight: 7930kg (17,500lb) loaded
Maximum speed: 397km/h (246mph)	Armament: 7 x 7.7mm (0.303in) Browning MGs
Range: 3150km (1960 miles)	(two in nose, two in dorsal turret, two in
Service ceiling: 7470m (24,500ft)	beam and one ventral); 340kg (750lb) of
Dimensions: span 19.96m (65ft 4in);	bombs or depth charges

COASTAL COMMAND, NO. 18 GROUP (JULY 1942)		
Unit	Type	Base
No. 42 Sqn	Beaufort	Leuchars
No. 48 Sqn	Hudson	Wick
No. 86 Sqn	Beaufort	Wick
No. 144 Sqn	Hampden	Leuchars
No. 210 Sqn	Catalina	Sullom Voe
No. 248 Sqn	Beaufighter	Sumburgh
No. 254 Sqn	Hurricane	Dyce
No. 404 Sqn, RCAF	Blenheim	Dyce
No. 455 Sqn, RAAF	Hampden	Leuchars
No. 608 Sqn	Hudson	Wick

By the start of 1943, the improvement in aircraft and tactics, combined with the debut of electronic aids such as centimetric radar and radio direction finding, resulted in a huge improvement in Coastal Command's efficiency: shipping losses fell and U-boat sinkings rose.

However, it was not so much in sinking as steady harassment of the boats that Coastal Command was so effective, for U-boats could no approach their targets by day. This meant that many more convoys remained unmolested.

Specifications

Crew: 7–10

Powerplant: 4 x 895kW (1200hp) Twin Wasp R
  14 cylinder radial engines

Maximum speed: 467km/h (290mph)

Range: 3540km (2200 miles)

Service ceiling: 85,340m (28,000ft)

Dimensions: span 33.5m (110ft);

length 20.47m (67ft 2in);

height 5.94m (18ft)

Weight: 29,484kg (65,000lb) loaded

Armament: 10 x 12.7mm (0.5in) Browning MGs
  in four turrets and two waist gun positions;
  two bomb bays for up to 3629kg (8000lbs)
  of bombs

▲ **Consolidated Liberator GR.Mk V**

No. 224 Squadron / RAF Coastal Command, St Eval, November 1942

Finished in sea-grey and white, with standard national markings and grey serials and squadron codes, this Liberator GR.Mk V has the later type of air-to-surface radar with its antenna in a chin radome.

Specifications

Crew: 8

Powerplant: 4 x 894kW (1200hp) Wright
  Cyclone air-cooled radial piston engines

Maximum speed: 480km/h (298mph)

Range: 1835km (1140 miles)

Service ceiling: 10,363m (34,000ft)

Dimensions: span 31.62m (103ft 9in);

length 22.5m (73ft 10in);

height 5.84m (19ft 2in)

Weight: 12,542kg (27,650lb) loaded

Armament: 10 x 12.7mm (0.5in) MGs in nose,
  dorsal, ventral, tail and beam; normal bomb
  load of up to 2722kg (6000lb) of bombs
  and/or depth charges

▲ **Boeing Fortress Mk IIA**

No. 220 Squadron / RAF Coastal Command, Ballykelly, Northern Ireland, late 1942

A development of the USAAF's B-17F Flying Fortress heavy bomber for British service, the Fortress Mk II was deemed unsuitable for RAF Bomber Command and passed to RAF Coastal Command for the very-long-range maritime role.

▲ Lockheed Hudson GR.Mk VI

RAF Coastal Command, UK, late 1942

During August 1941, RAF Coastal Command introduced a revised colour scheme for its aircraft: the upper surfaces remained dark green and ocean grey, but the undersurfaces were gloss white and the vertical surface matt white.

Specifications

Crew: 5	height 3.63m (11ft 11in)
Powerplant: 2 x 895kW (1200hp) Pratt &	Weight: 8391kg (18,500lb) loaded
Whitney Twin Wasp radial piston engines	Armament: 2 x 7.7mm (0.303in) MGs in fixed
Maximum speed: 420km/h (261mph)	forward and dorsal turret; 1 x 7.7mm
Range: 3476km (2160 miles)	(0.303n) MG in ventral position,; option of 2 x
Service ceiling: 8230m (27,000ft)	7.7mm (0.303in) MGs in beam positions; up
Dimensions: span 19.96m (65ft 6in);	to 454kg (1000lb) of bombs or underwing
length 13.51m (44ft 4in);	rockets

Specifications

Crew: 8-11	Armament: 1 x 7.7mm (0.303in) Vickers GO MG
Powerplant: 4 x 794kW (1066hp) Bristol	in nose turret; 2 x 7.7mm (0.303in) Browning
Pegasus XVII 9-cylinder radial piston engines	MGs in mid upper turret; 4 x Browning MGs in
Maximum speed: 341km/h (212mph)	tail turret; optional second nose turret gun;
Range: 4828km (3000 miles)	4 x fixed Browning MGs firing ahead;
Service ceiling: 4567m (15,000ft)	2 x 12.7mm (0.5in) Browning MGs firing
Dimensions: span 34.39m (112ft 10in); length	ahead; 2 x 12.7mm (0.5in) Browning MGs
26.01m (85ft 4in); height 9.79m (32ft 2in)	firing from waist hatches; assorted ordnance
Weight: 26,308kg (58,0000lb) loaded	up to 2250kg (4960lb)

▲ Short Sunderland GR.Mk II

No. 10 Squadron / Royal Australian Air Force / RAF Coastal Command, Mount Batten, April 1942

The primary difference between the Sunderland GR.Mk I and II was the replacement of the former's pair of manually operated 7.7mm (0.303in) Vickers K beam guns by two 7.7mm (0.303in) Browning machine guns in a power-operated dorsal turret. The ammunition supply for the four-gun tail turret was also doubled to 1000 rounds per gun.

Specifications

Crew: 9

Powerplant: 4 x 895kW (1200hp) Pratt &
  Whitney Twin Wasp radial piston engines

Maximum speed: 359km/h (223mph)

Range: 3814km (2370 miles)

Service ceiling: 6250m (20,500ft)

Dimensions: span 35.05m (115ft); length

24.16m (79ft 3in); height 8.38m (27ft 6in)

Weight: 30,844kg (68,000lb) loaded

Armament: 2 x 12.7mm (0.5in) MGs in bow,
  dorsal and tail turrets, and 1 x 12.7mm
  (0.5in) machine gun in two beam positions;
  up to 5443kg (12,000lb) of bombs, depth
  charges or torpedoes

▲ Consolidated Coronado GR.Mk I

RAF Coastal Command, Beaumaris, 1943

The RAF received 10 examples of the Coronado flying boat but, finding the type
unsuitable for the long-range reconnaissance/anti-submarine role, passed the
aircraft to No. 231 Squadron of No. 45 Group, based at Boucherville, Toronto,
Canada, as transports with accommodation for VIPs and 44 other passengers.

▲ Short Sunderland GR.Mk III

RAF Coastal Command, UK, 1943

Evident on the rear fuselage are the antennae associated with the ASV.Mk II air-
to-surface search radar, comprising vertical dipole masts (four above the
fuselage) and 16 transmitting loops (eight on each side of the fuselage).

Specifications

Crew: 8–11

Powerplant: 4 x 794kW (1066hp) Bristol
  Pegasus XVII 9-cylinder radial piston engines

Maximum speed: 341km/h (212mph)

Range: 4828km (3000 miles)

Service ceiling: 4567m (15,000ft)

Dimensions: span 34.39m (112ft 10in); length
  26.01m (85ft 4in); height 9.79m (32ft 2in)

Weight: 26,308kg (58,0000lb) loaded

Armament: 1 x 7.7mm (0.303in) Vickers GO MG
  in nose turret; 2 x 7.7mm (0.303in) Browning
  MGs in mid upper turret; 4 x Browning MGs in
  tail turret; optional second nose turret
  gun; 4 x fixed Browning MGs firing ahead,
  2 x 12.7mm (0.5in) Browning MGs firing
  ahead and twin 12.7mm (0.5in) Browning
  MGs firing from waist hatches; assorted
  ordnance up to 2250kg (4960lb)

Specifications

Crew: 10

Powerplant: 4 x 895kW (1200hp) Pratt &
Whitney Twin wasp radial piston engines

Maximum speed: 488km/h (303mph)

Range: 1730km (1080 miles)

Service ceiling: 8540m (28,000ft)

Dimensions: span 33.53m (110ft);

length 20.22m (66ft 4in);

height 5.49m (18ft)

Weight: 32,296kg (71,200lb) loaded

Armament: 1 x 12.7mm (0.5in) MG in nose,
2 x 12.7mm (0.5in) MG in beam position,
4 x 7.6mm (0.303in) MGs in rear turret; also
5 x 120kg (250lb) depth charges

▲ **Consolidated Liberator GR.Mk V**

RAF Coastal Command, UK, 1943

A maritime reconnaissance version of the USAAF's B-24G heavy bomber, the
Liberator GR.Mk V was used on the very-long-range role, and some of the aircraft
were later fitted with the Leigh Light installation below the wing for nocturnal
location and attack of submarines.

Zones of responsibility
1941–45

**The Coastal Command of the period late in World War II was hardly recognizable as the linear
descendant of the Coastal Command of 1939. It had expanded enormously in size and overall
capabilities, and its advanced aircraft were the dread of every surviving U-boat crew.**

DURING THE COURSE of World War II, Coastal
Command controlled many subordinate
formations. In September 1939, it comprised four
groups, of which No. 17 Group was responsible only
for the training of Coastal Command aircrews. The
other three groups were each allocated the
responsibility for coastal operations off a particular
part of the British coast: No. 16 Group was
responsible for the eastern half of the English
Channel and the southern half of the North Sea;
No. 18 Group covered the remainder of the North
Sea and areas around Scotland, north of a line
running north west from the Mull of Kintyre; and
No. 15 Group covered the rest of the UK's coast.

New group

In February 1941, the system was changed to allow
the introduction of No. 19 Group, the dividing line
between Nos 18 and 15 Groups being moved north

COASTAL COMMAND, NO. 16 GROUP (JUNE 1944)		
Unit	Type	Base
No. 143 Sqn	Beaufighter	Manston
No. 236 Sqn	Beaufighter	North Coates
No. 254 Sqn	Beaufighter	North Coates
No. 279 Sqn	Hudson	Strubby
No. 280 Sqn	Warwick	Strubby & Thornaby
No. 415 Sqn, RCAF	Wellington	Bircham Newton
No. 455 Sqn, RAAF	Beaufighter	Langham
No. 489, RNZAF	Beaufighter	Langham
No. 521 Sqn	Ventura & Gladiator	Docking
No. 819 Sqn, FAA	Swordfish	Manston
No. 848 Sqn, FAA	Avenger	Manston
No. 854 Sqn, FAA	Avenger	Hawkinge
No. 855 Sqn, FAA	Avenger	Hawkinge

to a position north-west from Cape Wrath, No. 19 Group then receiving responsibility for the southern part of the area previously allocated to No. 15 Group. In the Irish Sea, No. 19 Group's extended south of a line in about the middle of Cardigan Bay and, in the eastern Atlantic, slightly north of that line.

Coastal Command began to spread its wings further afield with the absorption of elements operating outside the UK. As early as November 1940, the Gibraltar-based No. 200 Group was absorbed into Coastal Command after having been a component of the RAF Mediterranean. The group's squadrons passed temporarily to the operational command of the Allied Forces Headquarters for the November 1942 Allied landing in French northwest, but otherwise remained under Coastal Command control for the rest of the war. No. 200 Group became RAF Gibraltar within Coastal Command during December 1941.

Iceland occupied

RAF units also arrived as British forces occupied Iceland, and given that Iceland's most important air use was as a base for maritime operations, Coastal Command was the lead command organization for what started as No. 30 Wing, but became RAF Iceland in July 1941. Coastal Command reached its maximum extent in mid-1943 after Portugal had granted the UK basing rights in the Azores Islands, which became the home of No. 247 Group, which was entrusted with the task of flying anti-submarine missions over the Atlantic.

In the later stages of World War II, Coastal Command's primary assets in the 'bomber', or long-range anti-submarine, role were the Consolidated Catalina and Short Sunderland flying boats, and the Consolidated Liberator and the Vickers Wellington and Warwick landplanes, all in later variants with more capable electronics and weapons.

The crews of these and other aircraft established close and effective links with the FAA's squadrons operating from escort carriers, especially in the mid-Atlantic area.

COASTAL COMMAND, NO. 18 GROUP (JUNE 1944)

Unit	Type	Base
No. 86 Sqn	Liberator	Tain
No. 210 Sqn	Catalina	Sullom Voe
No. 281 Sqn	Warwick	Sumburgh, Wick & Leuchars
No. 330 Sqn (Nor)	Sunderland	Sullom Voe
No. 333 Sqn (Nor)	Catalina & Mosquito	Woodhaven, Sumburgh & Leuchars
No. 519 Sqn	Ventura & Spitfire	Skitten
No. 544 Sqn	Mosquito	Leuchars
No. 618 Sqn	Mosquito	Turnberry

COASTAL COMMAND, NO. 19 GROUP (JUNE 1944)

Unit	Type	Base
No. 10 Sqn, RAAF	Sunderland	Mount Batten
No. 53 Sqn	Liberator	St Eval
No. 58 Sqn	Halifax	St Davids
No. 144 Sqn	Beaufighter	Davidstowe Moor
No. 172 Sqn	Wellington	Davidstowe Moor & Chivenor
No. 179 Sqn	Wellington	Predannack
No. 201 Sqn	Sunderland	Pembroke Dock
No. 206 Sqn	Liberator	St Eval
No. 224 Sqn	Liberator	St Eval
No. 228 Sqn	Sunderland	Pembroke Dock
No. 235 Sqn	Beaufighter	Portreath
No. 248 Sqn	Beaufighter	Portreath
No. 282 Sqn	Warwick	Davidstowe Moor
No. 304 Sqn (Pol)	Wellington	Chivenor
No. 311 Sqn (Cz)	Liberator	Predannack
No. 404 Sqn, RCAF	Beaufighter	Davidstowe Moor
No. 407 Sqn, RCAF	Wellington	Chivenor
No. 415 Sqn, RCAF	Albacore	Winkleigh
No. 461 Sqn, RAAF	Sunderland	Pembroke Dock
No. 502 Sqn	Halifax	St Davids
No. 517 Sqn	Halifax	Brawdy
No. 524 Sqn	Wellington	Davidstowe Moor
No. 541 Sqn	Spitfire	St Eval
No. 547 Sqn	Liberator	St Eval
No. 612 Sqn	Wellington	Chivenor
No. 616 Sqn, FAA	Swordfish	Perranporth
No. 838 Sqn, FAA	Swordfish	Harrowbeer
No. 849 Sqn, FAA	Avenger	Perranporth
No. 850 Sqn, FAA	Avenger	Perranporth

▲ Short Sunderland GR. Mk III

RAF Coastal Command, UK, 1943

This was a Blackburn-built aeroplane. The offensive armament was four 227kg (500lb) or eight 113kg (250lb) bombs carried on racks in the upper part of the fuselage below the wing. In combat the racks were winched out through windowed hatches in the sides of the fuselage to positions inboard of the inner engines.

Specifications

Crew: 8-11

Powerplant: 4 x 794kW (1066hp) Bristol Pegasus XVII 9-cylinder radial piston engines

Maximum speed: 341km/h (212mph)

Range: 4828km (3000 miles)

Service ceiling: 4567m (15,000ft)

Dimensions: span 34.39m (112ft 10in); length 26.01m (85ft 4in); height 9.79m (32ft 2in)

Weight: 26,308kg (58,0000lb) loaded

Armament: 1 x 7.7mm (0.303in) Vickers GO MG in nose turret; 2 x 7.7mm (0.303in) Browning MGs in mid upper turret; 4 x Browning MGs in tail turret; optional second nose turret gun; 4 x fixed Browning MGs firing ahead, 2 x 12.7mm (0.5in) Browning MGs firing ahead and twin 12.7mm (0.5in) Browning MGs firing from waist hatches; assorted ordnance up to 2250kg (4960lb)

▲ Vickers Wellington GR.Mk XIV

No. 304 (Polish) Squadron / RAF Coastal Command, Chivenor, late 1944

Operated over the English Channel and eastern part of the Atlantic Ocean, this aeroplane has ASV.Mk III radar (with its antenna in the chin radome), and a Leigh Light installation in an retractable installation that could be lowered from its location in the fuselage just to the rear of the weapons bay.

Specifications

Crew: 5

Powerplant: 2 x 1294kW (1735hp) Hercules XVII engines

Maximum speed: 402km/h (250mph)

Range: 2816km (1750 miles)

Service ceiling: 4875m (16,0000ft)

Dimensions: span 26.26m (0ft 0in); length 19.68m (64ft 7in); height 5.31m (17ft 5in)

Weight: 14,062kg√(31,000lb) loaded

Armament: 2 x 7.7mm (0.303in) Browning trainable forward-firing MGs in a power-operated Frazer-Nash F.N.7A nose turret; 2 x 7.7mm (0.303in) Browning trainable rearward-firing in a power-operated Frazer-Nash F.N.7A tail turret; 9 x 227kg (500lb) or 113kg (250lb) bombs, or 2 or 4 x 191kg (420lb) depth charges, or 2 x torpedoes

In World War II, Coastal Command flew more than 240,000 sorties, sank 212 U-boats and caused the loss of 485,648 tonnes (478,000 tons) of enemy shipping. In exchange, it lost a total of 1777 aircraft and, according to various sources, between 5865 and 10,875 men killed in action, the lower figure possibly not including Commonwealth and Allied aircrew, and men missing and only later declared dead.

Victory in sight
1943–45

Enlarged, equipped with modern aircraft and drawing on the experience of several years of hard operations, Coastal Command's flying boats and landplanes proved the scourge of Germany's U-boat arm and coastal shipping in the later years of the war.

THE STEADILY GROWING capability of Coastal Command started to become evident in August 1942 as the command at last felt itself in a position to divert some of its assets from the UK to points such as northern Russia, which for a time became home to one squadron of Consolidated Catalina twin-engined flying boats and two squadrons of Handley Page Hampden twin-engined torpedo-bombers. These aided the efforts of the Royal Navy in the extremely

ORGANIZATION

Coastal Command
June 1944

No. 15 Group   No. 16 Group   No. 18 Group   No. 19 Group

No. 247 Group   RAF Gibraltar   RAF Iceland

▲ **Short Sunderland GR. Mk III**

No. 330 (Norwegian) Squadron / RAF Coastal Command, Sullom Voe, Shetland, late 1944

This Norwegian-manned unit was formed in Iceland in April 1941, and transferred to the Norwegian Air Force shortly before it was disbanded in November 1945. The squadron flew several types of aircraft, of which the last was the Sunderland.

Specifications

Crew: 8–11

Powerplant: 4 x 794kW (1066hp) Bristol Pegasus XVII 9-cylinder radial piston engines

Maximum speed: 341km/h (212mph)

Range: 4828km (3000 miles)

Service ceiling: 4567m (15,000ft)

Dimensions: span 34.39m (112ft 10in); length 26.01m (85ft 4in); height 9.79m (32ft 2in)

Weight: 26,308kg (58,0000lb) loaded

Armament: 1 x 7.7mm (0.303in) Vickers GO MG in nose turret; 2 x 7.7mm (0.303in) Browning MGs in mid upper turret; 4 x Browning MGs in tail turret; optional second nose turret gun; 4 x fixed Browning MGs firing ahead, 2 x 12.7mm (0.5in) Browning MGs firing ahead and twin 12.7mm (0.5in) Browning MGs firing from waist hatches; assorted ordnance up to 2250kg (4960lb) difficult task of getting supply-laden convoys through Arctic waters and past the attentions of German warplanes, warships and U-boats to reach Murmansk and Archangel. It was an almost impossible task, and the convoys were suspended from September, being resumed only in the dark of the period between December 1942 and spring 1943, and the same period in 1943–44. Closer to home, Coastal Command's attack aircraft were taking the war ever more capably and effectively to German coastal shipping and installations, but the decisive theatre remained the convoy routes across the Atlantic.

The advent of longer-range aircraft with more effective equipment, such as a larger number of Sunderland and Catalina flying boats, complemented by land-based aircraft such as the twin-engined Vickers Wellington, had driven the U-boats deeper into the Atlantic for their operations, but the boats were harried to and from their operational areas by shorter-range aircraft to the extent that they had to operate under the water even during their transits, thus increasing their losses and reducing the time they could remain on station. Then the advent of still longer-ranged aircraft, such as the four-engined Boeing Fortress and Consolidated Liberator, further strengthened Coastal Command and weakened the U-boat arm.

The Germans initially tried to fight it out by installing ever stronger light flak armament on their boats, but Coastal Command responded by the addition of fixed forward-firing batteries of cannon or machine guns to kill the flak gunners. They also added centrimetric radar, which the Germans could not initially detect, to close the range at low level until the U-boat crews, on seeing the oncoming aeroplane, had too little time to submerge their boats before the attack was upon them.

U-boat responses

The Germans then had recourse to expedients, such as the fitting of snorkels to allow extended underwater running, but while this enhanced survivability it further degraded the time the boats could spend on station in the central Atlantic.

Here, too, they were increasingly threatened as the Allies introduced larger numbers of small and

▲ Consolidated Catalina Mk IVA

No. 210 Squadron / RAF Coastal Command, Sullom Voe, Shetland, 1944

No. 210 Squadron operated the Catalina flying boat from April 1941 to the end of World War II, and is credited with the sinking of eight U-boats. This Catalina Mk IVa carries air-to-surface search radar with its antenna under the port wing, and a Leigh Light nocturnal illumination device in a pod under the starboard wing.

Specifications

Crew: 8/9
Powerplant: 895kW (1200hp) Pratt & Whitney
  radial piston engines
Maximum speed: 306km/h (190mph)
Range: 6437km (4000 miles)
Service ceiling: 7315m (24,000ft)
Dimensions: span 31.7m (104ft); length

19.86m (65ft 2in); height 5.46m (17ft 11in)
Weight: 12,283kg (27,038lb) loaded
Armament: 1 x 7.7mm (0.303in) MG in bow
  and 2 x 7.7mm (0.303in) MGs in each side
  blister and in ventral position; up to 907kg
  (2000lb) of bombs or depth charges.

comparatively cheap escort carriers carrying specialized anti-submarine aircraft and a few fighters. Despite the dedication of the U-boat crews, the introduction of advanced torpedoes, and the final debut of a new generation of submarines capable of far higher sustained underwater speeds, the tide of battle swayed against the U-boats from mid-1943.

There were still months when the relative fortunes of the two sides moved, but Coastal Command nonetheless had the technical edge over its adversary and, in combination with larger numbers of more effective aircraft, was able finally to crush the real threat which had been posed by the previously dominant U-boats.

Specifications

Crew: 8

Powerplant: 4 x 895kW (1200hp) Pratt & Whitney Twin Wasp radial piston engines

Maximum speed: 435km/h (270mph)

Range: 2366km (1470 miles)

Service ceiling: 8534m (28,000ft)

Dimensions: span 17.63m (57ft 10in);
length 12.7m (41ft 8in);

height 4.83m (15ft 10in)

Weight: 11,431kg (25,200lb) loaded

Armament: 4 x 20mm (0.79in) forward-firing cannon; 6 x 7.7mm (0.303in) forward-firing MGs and 1 x 7.7mm (0.303in) Vickers K MG in dorsal position; 1 x torpedo and 2 x 113kg (250lb) bombs or 8 x 41kg (90lb) rocket projectiles

▲ Consolidated Liberator GR.Mk VI

No. 547 Squadron / RAF Coastal Command, Leuchars, Fife, 1944–45

Carrying radar and a retractable Leigh Light, and fitted with six 12.7mm (0.5in) machine guns in three power-operated turrets, the Liberator GR.Mk VI had an anti-submarine endurance of 12 hours 30 minutes with a 907kg (2000lb) load of depth charges.

Specifications

Crew: 7

Powerplant: 2 x 1864kW (2500hp) Bristol Centaurus VI radial piston engines

Maximum speed: 422km/h (262mph)

Range: 4908km (5791 miles)

Service ceiling: 5791m (19,000ft)

Dimensions: span 29.49m (96ft 9in);

length 20.88m (68ft 6in);

height 5.64m (18ft 6in)

Weight: 23,247kg (51,250lb) loaded

Armament: 6 x 7.7mm (0.303in) machine guns (one each in nose, dorsal turrets, four in tail turret); up to 5557kg (12,250lb) of bombs

▲ Vickers Warwick GR.Mk V

No. 179 Squadron / RAF Coastal Command, Benbecula and St Eval, 1944–45

No. 179 Squadron, which had flown the Vickers Wellington up to that time, in November 1944 became the first unit to receive the Warwick GR.Mk V. The variant had a modified nose with the antenna for the air-to-surface search in a radome below it, and also carried a retractable Leigh Light installation in the lower fuselage to the rear of the bomb bay.

Specifications

Crew: 7/8

Powerplant: 4 x 1089kW (1460hp) Packard

(Rolls-Royce) Merlin piston engines

Maximum speed: 452km/h (281mph)

Range: 4313km (2680 miles)

Service ceiling: 7460m (24,500ft)

Dimensions: span 31.09m (102ft);

length 20.98m (68ft 10in);

height 6.19m (20ft 4in)

Weight: 18,598kg (41,000lb) loaded

Armament: 8 x 7.7mm (0.303in) MGs; up to

6350kg (14,000lb) bombs

▲ **Avro Lancaster GR.Mk III**

School of Maritime Reconnaissance / RAF Coastal Command, St Mawgan,

1945

This aeroplane was not withdrawn from service until October 1956; up to that time it had been the last operational Lancaster remaining in RAF service.

Fleet Air Arm
1939–45

From very humble beginnings in 1939, when its carrierborne aircraft operated from just six ships, the Fleet Air Arm grew enormously in size and capability through World War II, and by August 1945 flew some 3700 aircraft from shore bases and operated no fewer than 59 carriers.

THE ROYAL NAVAL AIR SERVICE, which had been established in 1914 as the Royal Navy's own air arm, lost its independence in April 1918 when it was merged with its British Army equivalent, the Royal Flying Corps, to create the Royal Air Force.

This was the world's first independent air force, and as such controlled the air units and their equipment allocated to shore bases and Royal Navy warships, on which they came under operational control of the ships' captains. Through the 1920s and 1930s this became a patently inadequate system, and in 1937 the Naval Air Branch was returned to Admiralty control and was soon renamed as the Fleet Air Arm (FAA).

Carrier force

At the start of World War II, the Royal Navy had six aircraft carriers with another six being built, and the FAA comprised just 20 squadrons with a mere 232

ORGANIZATION

British Carrierborne Strength
September 1939

Ark Royal (1938) with 60 aircraft	Courageous (1928–30) with 48 aircraft	Glorious (1928–30) with 48 aircraft
Furious (1921–25) with 33 aircraft	Eagle (1924) with 21 aircraft	Hermes (1924) with 15 aircraft

almost universally obsolete aircraft. By the end of the war, the strength of the Royal Navy and FAA had grown to 59 aircraft carriers, 3700 aircraft, 72,000 officers and men, and 56 air stations. The carrier had replaced the battleship as the navy's capital ship, and carrierborne aircraft were now decisive offensive and defensive weapons of naval warfare.

◀ **Diving Swordfish**

The Fairey Swordfish's primary weapon was a single 730kg (1610lb) torpedo slung beneath the fuselage. Although slow and unmanoeuvrable, the biplane proved very stable during the crucial torpedo run.

The loss of the *Courageous* in the war's first few weeks highlighted the vulnerability of the carrier when working independently, a factor confirmed by the loss of the *Glorious* in June 1940. Tactics and weapons were improved, and carriers now operated at the heart of destroyer, cruiser and even battleship escort. The role of the carrier became ever more important as aircraft started to mature as one of the decisive weapons in defeating the U-boat, surface

warships and aircraft. The U-boat threat was a particular concern, as it threatened to sever the maritime supply of materiel across the Atlantic on which the UK so relied.

The same threat faced British transport and supply convoys operating in the Mediterranean and Arctic. The fall of France in June 1940 gave the Germans bases from which their attackers could roam further out into the Atlantic with aircraft as well as warships and U-boats. Only a few ships currently possessed adequate anti-aircraft weapons, and the optimum manner of beating the air threat was the fighter, but

FAA SQUADRONS WITH BLACKBURN SKUA AIRCRAFT (1939)

Unit	Type	Base
No. 800 Sqn	Skua	*Ark Royal*
No. 801 Sqn	Skua	*Ark Royal & Furious*
No. 803 Sqn	Skua	*Ark Royal*
No. 806 Sqn	Skua	Eastleigh

▲ **Blackburn Skua Mk II**

No. 5 Maintenance Unit, Kemble, 1939

The Skua Mk II was the production variant of the Skua Mk I prototype. Through designed as a carrierborne dive-bomber, the Skua doubled as a naval fighter, but was ineffective in each role and withdrawn from first-line service in 1941.

Specifications

Crew: 2

Powerplant: 664kW (890hp) Bristol Perseus XII radial engine

Maximum speed: 362km/h (225mph)

Range: 1223km (760 miles)

Service ceiling: 6160m (20,200ft)

Dimensions: span 14.07m (46ft 2in); length 10.85m (35ft 7in); height 3.81m (12ft 6in)

Weight: 3732kg (8228lb) loaded

Armament: 4 x 7.7mm (0.303in) MGs in wings; Lewis rear gun; 1 x 227kg (500lb) bomb beneath fusilage there were no carriers available. An interim measure was the Catapult Aircraft Merchant (CAM) ship with a catapult-launched fighter, which had to ditch at the end of its flight. In the event, only 35 CAM ships conversions were completed.

In 1942, there was an urgent demand for a small carrier that could be created swiftly and cheaply as a convoy escort type, and the Admiralty looked to conversions of merchant vessels with their cargo capacities left unaffected.

This became the Merchant Aircraft Carrier (MAC), which by mid-1943 was serving in the Atlantic with aircraft parked on their exposed flightdecks. The MAC ships helped turn the tide against the U-boats, and also paved the way for escort carriers with limited hangar volumes.

▲ Fairey Swordfish Mk I

No. 820 Squadron / Fleet Air Arm, HMS Ark Royal, 1939

Though slow and not agile when carrying its external torpedo armament, the Swordfish Mk I was very sturdy and had a high level of carrier compatibility.

Specifications

Crew: 3
Powerplant: 1 x 559.3kW (750hp) Bristol Pegasus XXX radial piston engine
Maximum speed: 222km/h (138mph)
Range: 879km (546 miles)
Service ceiling: 5867m (19,250ft)
Dimensions: span 12.87m (45ft 6in); length 10.87m (35ft 8in); height 3.76m (12ft 4in)
Weight: 3406kg (7510lb) loaded
Armament: 2 x 7.7mm (0.303in) MGs; load of 1 x 457mm (18in) torpedo or 8 x 27.2kg (60lb) rocket projectiles

▲ Fairey Swordfish Mk I

No. 824 Squadron / Fleet Air Arm, HMS Eagle, 1939

This aeroplane is depicted in the standard camouflage and markings of the Fleet Air Arm for this period of the war.

Specifications

Crew: 3
Powerplant: 1 x 559.3kW (750hp) Bristol Pegasus XXX radial piston engine
Maximum speed: 222km/h (138mph)
Range: 879km (546 miles)
Service ceiling: 5867m (19,250ft)
Dimensions: span 12.87m (45ft 6in); length 10.87m (35ft 8in); height 3.76m (12ft 4in)
Weight: 3406kg (7510lb) loaded
Armament: 2 x 7.7mm (0.303in) MGs; load of 1 x 457mm (18in) torpedo or 8 x 27.2kg (60lb) rocket projectiles

▲ Fairey Albacore Mk I

No. 826 Squadron / Fleet Air Arm, 1941–43

A more modern iteration of the Swordfish's concept, the Albacore was not as successful. No. 826 Squadron flew convoy escorts from HMS *Formidable* between November 1940 and April 1941, and was then shore-based in North Africa.

Specifications

Crew: 3	length 12.13m (39ft 9.5in);
Powerplant: 1 x 794kW (1065hp) Bristol Taurus	height 4.65m (15ft 3in)
II radial piston engine	Weight: 5715kg (12,600lb) loaded
Maximum speed: 259km/h (161mph)	Armament: 1 x 7.7mm (0.303in) Vickers MG
Range: 1320km (820 miles)	and 2 x 7.7mm (0.303in) Vickers K MGs in the
Service ceiling: 6309m (20,700ft)	rear cockpit; 1 x 457mm (18in) torpedo or up
Dimensions: span 15.24m (50ft);	to 907kg (2000lb) of bombs

Fleet Air Arm: operations
1941–45

From 1941, the Fleet Air Arm grew steadily in strength and capability to become a formidable force later in World War II. There were many more carriers, and also large numbers of advanced warplanes, most of them from the United States.

THROUGHOUT THE first part of the war, the FAA's primary strike warplane was the Fairey Swordfish, a technically obsolete biplane that nonetheless proved very successful. It outlasted its Fairey Albacore successor, and was much preferred to the Fairey Barracuda monoplane which, it was hoped, would finally replace the Swordfish.

Attack at Taranto

The Swordfish played a major role in slowing the German battleship *Bismarck* so that she could be caught and sunk in May 1941, but achieved its greatest single success in November 1940, when 21 Swordfishes launched from HMS *Illustrious* attacked the Italian fleet in Taranto, sinking one battleship and severely damaging another two as well as one cruiser.

The Swordfish remained in service to the end of the war, even though it was replaced by warplanes of

▲ Hunting Swordfish

With its slow speed and steady handling at low altitude, the Swordfish was an ideal platform for the carriage of air-launched torpedoes.

US origin on larger carriers, for it could operate without difficulty from escort carriers and, armed with eight rockets under its lower wing, remained a potent threat to U-boats.

Torch landings

The FAA participated in all the significant European-theatre joint operations of World War II, including the Allied landings in northwest Africa, Sicily, Italy and Normandy, although in the last operation the FAA's contribution was only small as the invasion area could be covered by aircraft operating from the south of England.

During most of the landings, the FAA flew in tactical support of the troops, spotted for the heavy guns of the battleships, undertook general

Specifications

Crew: 3	length 12.12m (39ft 9in);
Powerplant: 1 x 1222.9kW (1640hp) Rolls-	height 4.6m (15ft 1in)
Royce Merlin 32 V-12 piston engine	Weight: 6396kg (14,100lb) loaded
Maximum speed: 367km/h (228mph)	Armament: 2 x 7.7mm (0.3in) Vickers K MGs
Range: 1851km (1150 miles)	in the rear cockpit; 1 x 735kg (1620lb)
Service ceiling: 5060m (16,600ft)	torpedo, or 4 x 204kg (450lb) depth charges,
Dimensions: span 14.99m (49ft 2in);	or 6 x 113kg (250lb) of bombs

▲ **Fairey Barracuda Mk II**

No. 785 Squadron / Fleet Air Arm, Crail, 1943

No. 785 Squadron flew the Barracuda in the torpedo-bomber and reconnaissance training roles from April 1943 until after the end of World War II.

▲ **Fairey Swordfish Mk II**

No. 1 Naval Air Gunnery School, Yarmouth, Nova Scotia, Canada, 1943

Swordfish aircraft operating in Canada, such as this Swordfish Mk II, generally had the aeroplane's squadron code letter, painted in black on a yellow square, on the side of the rear fuselage.

Specifications

Crew: 2/3	height 4.44m (14ft 7in)
Powerplant: 1 x 559kW (750hp) Bristol	Weight: 3679kg (8110lb) loaded
Pegasus XXX radial piston engine	Armament: 1 x 7.7mm (0.303in) MG in forward
Maximum speed: 128km/h (128mph)	fuselage; 1 x 7.7mm (0.303in) Lewis MG on
Range: 1658km (1030 miles)	Fairey mounting in aft cockpit; 1 x 730kg
Service ceiling: 3260m (10,700ft)	(1610lb) torpedo or depth charges, mines or
Dimensions: span 13.87m (45ft 6in);	bombs up to 680kg (1500lb), or up to 8 x
length 12.34m (40ft 6in)	rocket projectiles on underwing racks

Specifications

Crew: 3

Powerplant: 1 x 1380kW (1850hp) Wright
  Cyclone radial piston engine

Maximum speed: 417km/h (259mph)

Range: 1642km (1020 miles)

Service ceiling: 7010m (23,000ft)

Dimensions: span 16.51m (54ft 2in);
  length 12.19m (40ft);

height 4.78m (15ft 8in)

Weight: 7394kg (16,300lb) loaded

Armament: 2 x 12.7mm (0.5) forward-firing
  MGs in wings, one similar weapon in dorsal
  turret and 1 x 7.62mm (0.3in) MG in ventral
  position; one 871kg (1921lb) torpedo or up to
  907kg (2000lb) of bombs

▲ Grumman Avenger Mk I

NO. 846 Squadron/ Fleet Air Arm, Macrihanish, 1943

The FAA's version of the US Navy's TBF-1B, the Avenger Mk I was flown in the
carrierborne and shore-based roles. The British received 408 examples of this
excellent torpedo bomber and anti-submarine aeroplane.

▲ Fairey Swordfish Mk II

No. 811 Squadron / Fleet Air Arm, HMS Biter, mid-1944

Despite its technical obsolescence, the Swordfish outlived the Albacore, created
as its successor, and was still effective in a number of roles in 1944.

Specifications

Crew: 3

Powerplant: 559kW (750hp) Bristol Pegasus
  XXX radial piston engine

Maximum speed: 222km/h (138mph)

Range: 879km (546 miles)

Service ceiling: 5867m (19,250ft)

Dimensions: span 12.87m (45ft 6in);

length 10.87m (35ft 8in);

height 3.76m (12ft 4in)

Weight: 3406kg (7510lb) loaded

Armament: 1 x 7.7mm (0.303in) fixed forward-
  firing MG; 1 x trainable 7.7mm (0.303in) MG
  in rear cockpit; 1 x 457mm (18in) torpedo or
  8 x 27.2kg (60lb) rocket projectiles

reconnaissance and provided fighter cover against
potential attacks by Vichy aircraft.

Further afield, the carrierborne assets of the FAA
was involved in the British capture of Madagascar
from the Vichy French in the Indian Ocean, and the
carriers of the British Pacific fleet, serving with the
US Navy's Fast Carrier Task Force as Task Force 57,
proved very useful in the later amphibious operations
of the Pacific theatre, especially the bloody campaign
that wrested Okinawa from the Japanese. Here the
armoured flightdecks of the British carriers proved
invulnerable to the attentions of *kamikaze* aircraft,
unlike those of their US counterparts with
unarmoured flightdecks.

▾ British Mediterranean Fleet carrier air wing, mid-1943

This is the air group embarked in the fleet carrier HMS *Illustrious* in the autumn of 1943, when she served in the Mediterranean Fleet for operations off Italy.

1 x fighter squadron Supermarine Seafire Mk IICs

2 x fighter squadrons Grumman Martlet Mk Vs

1 x fighter squadron Fairey Barracuda torpedo/divebombers

▲ Barracuda's take off

Fairey Barracuda's take-off from an unidentified aircraft carrier in the North Atlantic, probably preparing for the raid against the German battleship *Tirpitz* in 1944.

Chapter 3

United States

The established doctrine of the US armed forces has long been to strike at an enemy's main concentrations of strength as soon as possible and as directly as possible. For the US Army, this meant the maximum effort to destroy the enemy's ground forces by direct assault. For the US Army Air Forces (USAAF), it meant tactical attacks on the enemy's ground and sea forces, plus the lines of communication nourishing them, and strategic attacks on the enemy's sources and stocks of raw materials, war-making industries, and both internal and external transport systems. The USAAF became notably adept at both types of bombing during World War II, in the Pacific as well as European theatres, and also pioneered the use of nuclear weapons to bring about the surrender of the Japanese in 1945.

◀ **Boeing B-17 Flying Fortress**
This B-17 has had its port tailplane hit by bombs dropped from other aircraft in its squadron, caught by the camera over Europe, 1944.

US Eighth Army Air Force
1942–43

The US Eighth Army Air Force (AAF) reached England in the summer of 1942 as the US began to build up its military capability against Germany. Equipped with long-range heavy bombers, the Eighth AAF was to destroy key elements of German industry with precision daylight attacks.

THE HEADQUARTERS OF THE US Eighth AAF came into existence at Savannah, Georgia, on 28 January 1942, and the new air force's bomber formation, the VIII Bomber Command, was then established in England on 22 February 1942, initially at RAF Bomber Command's headquarters at High Wycombe. The Eighth AAF's other commands were the VIII Air Support Command and VIII Fighter Command. During World War II, the headquarters of the Eighth AAF were located at the Wycombe Abbey School for Girls, Buckinghamshire, and this air force was commanded successively by Major-General Carl A. Spaatz, Brigadier-General (soon Major-General) Ira C. Eaker, and Lieutenant-General 'Jimmy' Doolittle. Doolittle was the officer who had led the 'Doolittle raid' of April 1942, when USAAF North American B-25 Mitchell twin-engined

ORGANIZATION

Eighth Army Air Force
August 1942

VIII Bomber Command	VIII Fighter Command	VIII Air Support Command

medium bombers had taken off from a US Navy aircraft carrier to make the first air attacks on targets in Japan. The US Eighth AAF finally became the US Air Forces in Europe (USAFE).

First daylight sweep

On 4 July 1942, six crews from the US 15th Bombardment Group (Light), operating with six RAF crews, departed Swanton Morley, Norfolk, on a

▲ **Boeing B-17E Flying Fortress**
414th Bomb Squadron / 97th Bomb Group / Eighth Army Air Force, Grafton Underwood, September 1942

This has an early pattern of national markings without lateral bars, and early camouflage based on medium-green and earth upper surfaces, and azure blue under surfaces. General Ira C. Eaker, commanding the Eighth AAF, flew in this aeroplane for the first US raid on German-occupied Europe on 17 August 1942.

Specifications
Crew: 8–10
Powerplant: 4 x 895kW (1200hp) Wright turbo-
supercharged engines
Maximum speed: 510km/h (317mph)
Range: 5150km (3200 miles)
Service ceiling: 10,973m (36,000ft)
Dimensions: span 31.6m (103ft 9in);

length 22.50m (73ft 10in);
height 6.3m (19ft 2in)
Weight: 23,133kg (51,000lb) loaded
Armament: 1 x 7.62mm (0.3in) MG in nose;
2 x 12.7mm (0.5in) waist MGs; nose, ventral
and tail turrets each with 2 x 12.7mm (0.5in)
MGs; 1905kg (4200lb) of bombs

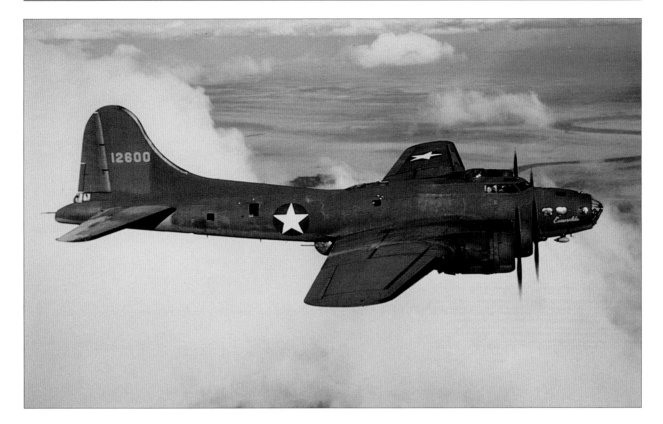

VIII BOMBER COMMAND GROUPS (AUGUST 1942)			
Group	Squadrons	Base	Aircraft
92nd Bomb Group	325th, 326th, 327th, 407th BSs	Bovingdon	B-17E/F
301st Bomb Group	32nd, 352nd, 353rd, 419th BSs	Chelveston	B-17F

▲ **Boeing B-17E Flying Fortress**
The B-17E bore the brunt of the US Eighth AAF's early operations over northwest Europe. The first such aircraft arrived with 97th Bomber Group in July 1942.

daylight sweep against four German airfields in the Netherlands. This was the first occasion on which US airmen had flown in American-built bombers against a German target but, despite being a historical milestone, the raid was not wholly successful, two US-manned aircraft being shot down.

92nd Bomb Group

In August 1942, the 92nd and 301st Bomb Groups arrived to join the swiftly expanding Eighth AAF. The 92nd Bomb Group was the first heavy bombardment group to complete the non-stop deployment flight from Newfoundland to Scotland.

It took some time for the new groups to be made ready for combat, and training in many areas was woefully deficient. As internal argument continued about whether or not to stop the daylight bombing of strongly defended targets in Europe, and also whether or not the bomb loads and defensive armament of the Boeing B-17 Flying Fortress and Consolidated B-24 Liberator were adequate to their tasks, the first B-17 raid of the European war was scheduled for 17 August 1942.

Six B-17E bombers lifted off from Polebrook to undertake a diversionary raid on St Omer, while at Grafton Underwood Colonel Frank A. Armstrong, commanding the 97th Bomb Group, boarded *Butcher Shop*, piloted by Major Paul Tibbets, and led 11 B-17s to the marshalling yards at Rouen Sotteville in north-western France.

Spaatz had felt confident enough to allow Brigadier-General Eaker to join the crew of *Yankee Doodle*, lead aeroplane of the second flight of six. Over the Channel, the B-17s were joined by their escort of British Supermarine Spitfire Mk V fighters.

The US aircraft bombed from 7010m (23,000ft): a few bombs fell wide, but the majority landed in the assigned area. Several repair and maintenance workshops were badly damaged. From this very limited start, the Eighth AAF steadily increased the number of its combat groups and its range of targets. The Eighth AAF thus attacked naval targets in France, and worked with RAF Bomber Command for missions into Germany.

Specifications

Crew: 8–10

Powerplant: 4 x 895kW (1200hp) Wright turbo-
supercharged engines

Maximum speed: 510km/h (317mph)

Range: 5150km (3200 miles)

Service ceiling: 10,973m (36,000ft)

Dimensions: span 31.6m (103ft 9in);

length 22.5m (73ft 10in);

height 6.3m (19ft 2in)

Weight: 23,133kg (51,000lb) loaded

Armament: 1 x 7.62mm (0.3in) MG in nose;
2 x 12.7mm (0.5in) waist MGs; ventral and
tail turrets each with 2 x 12.7mm (0.5in)
MGs; 1905kg (4200lb) of bombs

▲ Boeing B-17E Flying Fortress

68th Bomb Goup / US Eighth Army Air Force, UK, autumn 1942

The B-17E introduced the definitive rear fuselage and redesigned vertical tail surfaces of the Flying Fortress family. There were twin 12.7mm (0.5in) machine guns in the dorsal and ventral turrets, and also in the tail position. The other positions carried single guns. Production totalled 512 aircraft.

▲ Consolidated B-24D bombers in flight

The first Liberator variant built in large numbers (2738 aircraft), the B-24D had a framed plexiglas nose without the power-operated turret introduced on the B-24G.

Target Germany
SUMMER 1942 – SPRING 1943

The US Eighth AAF cut its operational teeth with shorter-range missions against targets in occupied France, and encountered strengthening German opposition. From January 1943, the Americans switched their focus to north German targets, and initially met only limited defences.

IT HAD ENJOYED a relatively auspicious start, but by the winter of 1942–43 the US Eighth AAF seemed to be suffering from a measure of official neglect as North Africa and the Pacific took priority for aircraft and reinforcements.

The VIII Bomber Command started with raids against short-range targets in northern France, and from 20 October launched an offensive on the U-boat bases at Lorient, St Nazaire and La Rochelle in western France.

These efforts were escorted up to 65km (40 miles) inland by Supermarine Spitfire Mk VB fighters, but thereafter the bombers had to fight it out alone with the German fighters and radar-directed 88mm

▲ **Loading up**
US ground crew on an English air base prepare a bomb load for a B-17E Flying Fortress before a mission in October 1942.

VIII BOMBER COMMAND GROUPS (DECEMBER 1942)			
Group	Squadrons	Base	Aircraft
44th Bomb Group	66th, 67th, 68th, 506th BSs	Shipdham	B-24D
91st Bomb Group	322nd, 323rd, 324th, 401st BSs	Bassingbourn	B-17F
93rd Bomb Group	328th, 329th, 330th, 409th BSs	Alconbury, Hardwick	B-24D
303rd Bomb Group	358th, 359th, 360th, 427th BSs	Molesworth	B-17F
305th Bomb Group	364th, 365th, 366th, 422nd BSs	Grafton Underwood, Chelveston	B-17F
306th Bomb Group	367th, 368th, 369th, 423d BSs	Thurleigh	B-17F

▲ **Ball turret**
Installed in the ventral position on this B-17E, the ball turret carried two 12.7mm (0.5in) Browning machine guns for lower-hemisphere defence.

(3.465in) and 105mm (4.13in) flak artillery over the often heavily defended targets.

Early operations

At first the US losses were small, but the German fighter pilots were quickly beginning to get to grips with the tactics required for effective attacks on the well-armed US bombers, with special emphasis on high-speed head-on attacks. US losses thus rose from 3.7 per cent in November to 8.8 per cent in December 1942. The VIII Bomber Command was also affected by low aircraft strengths: of the 140 B-17F and B-24D machines on the establishment of the 91st, 93rd, 44th, 305th, 306th and 303rd Bomb Groups (Heavy), only about half were available.

This situation lasted to May 1943, and further degradation of strength resulted from the detachment of many of the 44th Bomb Group's Liberators and the posting of the 93rd Bomb Group to North Africa. At this time, the VIII Fighter Command comprised only the Debden-based 4th Fighter Group (334th, 335th and 336th Fighter Squadrons) with the Spitfire Mk VB. The 56th and 78th Fighter Groups were training in England with the new Republic P-47 Thunderbolt, but would not become available until April 1943.

Shipyard attack

On 27 January 1943, the VIII Bomber Command made its first raid on Germany. The primary target for the 91 B-17s and B-24s of the 91st, 303rd, 305th, 306th and 44th Bomb Groups was the Bremer-

Vulkan Vegesack shipyard, just to the north-west of Bremen, but adverse conditions persuaded the leader to divert to the alternate target, the Germania yard at Wilhelmshaven. Given the intensity of the German fighter reaction to their raids over France, the Americans were surprised by the limited response they encountered on this pioneering attack on Germany.

New armaments, new tactics

However, the increasing capability of German fighter attacks, in particular in head-on attacks, forced the VIII Bomber Command to react: by a time early in spring 1943, more armour was being carried in the B-17F and B-24D, and an additional pair of 12.7mm (0.5in) machine guns was installed around the plexiglas noses.

Since the winter of 1942–43, the tactics had also been changed, and the bombers now flew in tight combat boxes (basic 18/21-aircraft group formation made up of three-aircraft 'vics') with squadrons echeloned vertically to improve the dorsal and ventral turrets' fields of fire.

Already two or more groups were formatting in vertically spaced combat wings (up to 54 bombers), but numbers on operations at present precluded the extensive use of this formation. Thus the German fighters were receiving more concentrated fire as they attacked.

Over the next six weeks, the US VIII Bomber Command flew six missions over Germany: 524 aircraft were despatched, but as a result largely of

▲ **Forward fire power**

This nose-on view of the B-17G shows the firepower the Flying Fortress could bring to bear in frontal defence, with two x 12.7mm (0.5in) Browning trainable machine guns in the chin turret and two in the dorsal turret.

aborted sorties resulting from adverse weather and technical difficulties, only 241 actually attacked and 19 were lost. The VIII Bomber Command's effort to attack Hamm on 2 February 1943 failed because of cloud cover.

Two days later, Emden was attacked by 39 B-17s out of 86 despatched, with five downed. The Wilhelmshaven raid on 26 February saw the loss of seven US aircraft; and on 4 March, 42 out of 85 attacked Hamm, seven of the bombers being lost. The Bremer yard at Vegesack was attacked on 18 March by 76 B-17Fs of the 1st Bomb Wing and 27 Liberators of the 2nd Wing: 97 bombers released 536 454kg (1000lb) bombs from 7315m (24,000ft)

and achieved good concentration, and only two bombers were shot down.

In April 1943, the US 4th, 56th and 78th Fighter Groups became operational with the P-47C and P-47D, but these had a radius of only 280km (175 miles) and were thus limited to escorts over France. Meanwhile, the forces of VIII Bomber Command were increased after the alleviation of pressure in the Mediterranean.

The B-17s of the new 95th, 96th and 351st Bomb Groups became operational on 13 May, and the 94th Bomb Group on the following day, while the 92nd Bomb Group was at last released from its training commitment.

Specifications

Crew: 8–10	Dimensions: span 31.6m (103ft 9in);
Powerplant: 4 x 895kW (1200hp) Wright	length 22.8m (74ft 9in);
Cyclone radial piston engines	height 5.85m (19ft 2in)
Maximum speed: 475km/h (295mph)	Weight: 25400kg (56,000lb) loaded
Range: 2071km (1287 miles)	Armament: 12 x 12.7mm (0.5in) guns; 7983kg
Service ceiling: 10,975m (36,000ft)	(17,600) bomb load

▲ **Boeing B-17F Flying Fortress**

360th Bomb Squadron / 303rd Bomb Group / US Eighth Army Air Force, Molesworth, Cambridgeshire, late 1942

This aeroplane force-landed in France on 12 December 1942 after a raid on the Rouen-Satteville marshalling yards, and was repaired by the Germans (as seen here) to be demonstrated to fighter units.

The pace hots up
SPRING–SUMMER 1943

As the pace and weight of the US Eighth AAF's campaign against German war industries increased, so too did its losses, especially as the bombers started to roam deeper inland with longer time spent over Germany. The long-range fighter escort was needed.

THE FOCKE-WULF factory at Bremen was attacked on 17 April 1943 by 106 out of 115 B-17s and B-24s, 16 being lost. There followed further raids on Bremen, and also on Antwerp, Wevelghem, Kiel, Emden, Flensburg, Wilhelmshaven and Cuxhaven. The attack of 13 June on Kiel marked the beginning of sustained German fighter opposition to the VIII Bomber Command's activities over Germany, and also on their route back to the UK: the VIII Bomber Command lost 26 bombers out of 182 that attacked Kiel and Bremen on this day.

On 22 June, the VIII Bomber Command flew deeper into Germany to attack the synthetic rubber factory at Hüls near Hannover: 235 aircraft were despatched, and 16 of these were brought down by flak and fighters, while 66 other US aircraft were damaged in fighter attacks. The increasing threat of US bombing was reflected on this day by the appearance of another *Jagdgruppe*, the first unit withdrawn from the Eastern Front to fight the VIII Bomber Command. At last, the acute nature of the Allies' round-the-clock bombing was coming home to the Germans, but more was to come.

ORGANIZATION		
	VIII Bomber Command	
	Summer 1943	
1st Bomb Division	**2nd Bomb Division**	**3rd Bomb Division**
(1st, 40th, 41st & 94th	(2nd, 14th & 20th	(4th, 13th & 45th
Combat Bomb Wings)	Combat Bomb Wings)	Combat Bomb Wings)

First, though, the Eighth AAF had problems to solve: the inadequacy of its Norden bomb sight under European conditions, the limited utility of its 227kg (500lb) and 454kg (1000lb) bombs, and lack of adequate fighter escort. On 12 April, Eaker listed the destruction of U-boat and aircraft manufacture as his command's highest priorities, and the Combined chiefs of staff agreed on 10 June. But first Eaker needed greater bomber strength as well as fighters with the range to escort bombers out and back.

▲ **Boeing B-17F Flying Fortress**
322nd Bomb Squadron / 91st Bomb Group / US Eighth Army Air Force, Bassingbourn, 1943
'The Ragged Irregulars' arrived at Kimbolton in September 1942, but moved to Bassingbourn in the following month and remained there for the rest of the war. The group suffered the heaviest losses of any Eighth AAF unit, with 197 aircraft lost in action, but also claimed the highest number of 'kills' – 420 aircraft.

Specifications

Crew: 8–10	Dimensions: span 31.6m (103ft 9in);
Powerplant: 4 x 895kW (1200hp) Wright	length 22.8m (74ft 9in);
Cyclone radial piston engines	height 5.85m (19ft 2in)
Maximum speed: 475km/h (295mph)	Weight: 25400kg (56,000lb) loaded
Range: 2071km (1287 miles)	Armament: 12 x 12.7mm (0.5in) guns; 7983kg
Service ceiling: 10,975m (36,000ft)	(17,600) bomb load

▲ **Box formation**

A group of USAAF B-17s head off for a mission over northern Europe. The US Eighth AAF tried a number of box formations to provide powerful interlocking fields of fire so that the bomber units could defend themselves against fighters.

Specifications

Crew: 8–10

Powerplant: 4 x 895kW (1200hp) Wright
  Cyclone radial piston engines

Maximum speed: 475km/h (295mph)

Range: 2071km (1287 miles)

Service ceiling: 10,975m (36,000ft)

Dimensions: span 31.6m (103ft 9in);
  length 22.8m (74ft 9in);
  height 5.85m (19ft 2in)

Weight: 25400kg (56,000lb) loaded

Armament: 12 x 12.7mm (0.5in) MGs; 7983kg
  (17,600lb) of bombs

▲ **Boeing B-17F Flying Fortress**

359th Bomb Squadron / 303rd Bomb Group / US Eighth Army Air Force,
Molesworth, Cambridgeshire, summer 1943

The B-17F was an improved B-17E, with changes including a moulded plexiglas nose, and production totalled 3405 aircraft. This machine has medium-green blotches over the standard olive-drab upper surfaces.

Specifications

Crew: 9–10

Powerplant: 4 x 895kW (1200hp) Wright radial
  engines

Maximum speed: 462km/h (287mph)

Range: 3219km (2000 miles)

Service ceiling: 10,850m (35,800ft)

Dimensions: span 31.62m (103ft 9in);
  length 22.66m (74ft 4in);

height 5.82m (19ft 1in)

Weight: 29710kg (65,000lb) loaded

Armament: 2 x 12.7mm (0.5in) Browning
  trainable MGs in chin, dorsal, ventral and tail
  turrets; 1 x 12.7mm (0.5in) MG in two waist,
  cheek and single dorsal positions; up to
  7983kg (17,600lb) of bombs

▲ **Boeing B-17G Flying Fortress**

535th Bomb Squadron / 381st Bomb Group / US Eighth AAF, Ridgewell,
1943–44

The 381st Bomb Group's units (532nd, 533rd, 534th and 535th Bomb Squadrons)
started to reach the UK in May 1943, and remained at Ridgewell until the group's
deactivation in August 1945. The group flew 296 missions.

Objective: Ploiesti

AUGUST 1943

**The Romanian oil fields and associated refineries around Ploiesti were one of Germany's
primary sources of fuel, and therefore a choice target for destruction. Early efforts achieved
nothing, so a major effort was planned and launched at the start of August 1943.**

PLOIESTI'S OIL FIELDS and eight associated refineries
produced about 10.16 million tonnes (10 million
tons) of fuel annually, and were designated a vital
strategic target for Allied bombing as early as January
1942 after the first attack had been launched on
23 June 1941 by Soviet bombers. The first US attack
was mounted on 11 June 1942 by the 12
Consolidated B-24D Liberator four-engined heavy
bombers of the HALPRO detachment in Egypt.

The major USAAF effort was Tidal Wave under
the control of Major-General Carl A. 'Toohey'
Spaatz's North-West African Air Force. Five groups of
B-24 bombers were allocated to the mission, namely
the North-West African Air Force's own 98th and
376th Bomb Groups; the Eighth AAF's 44th and
93rd Bomb Groups from the UK; and the 389th
Bomb Group, initially allocated to the Eighth AAF
but diverted while still in the United States. The plan

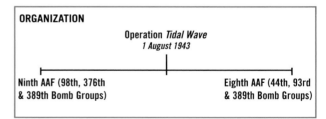

called for the mission to be despatched from
Benghazi for a low-level attack, in the hope of taking
the Germans and Romanians by tactical surprise.

Departure

Some 178 B-24s lifted off on 1 August, and over the
Mediterranean separated into five streams for the
approach flight, which was already being monitored
by the alert Germans. The 376th Bomb Group and
the following 93rd Bomb Group made navigational

EIGHTH AAF ELEMENTS IN 'TIDAL WAVE'		
Unit	Squadrons	Aircraft
44th Bomb Group	66th, 67th, 68th, 506th BSs	B-24
93rd Bomb Group	328th, 329th, 330th, 409th BSs	B-24
389th Bomb Group	564th, 565th, 566th, 567th BSs	B-24

▲ **Consolidated B-24 Liberator**

This remains a classic photograph of a formation of B-24 bombers on a mission, in this instance B-24J aircraft against a Romanian oil refinery at Ploiesti some time in 1944.

Limited damage

Some 40 per cent of the Ploiesti refinery capacity was destroyed, but as the Germans needed only 60 per cent of refinery capacity to process the available oil, the results of the raid were minimal – within a few days, the Germans had restored production to its previous levels.

Ploiesti exercised a fascination for the Americans, and over the following year another 20 raids were launched against the refineries and the complex's transport system before the refineries shut down on 24 August 1944. In the course of 7500 bomber sorties, the Americans dropped about 13,716 tonnes (13,500 tons) of bombs on Ploiesti and lost a total of 350 heavy bombers.

errors and headed for Bucharest before realizing the fact and turning back, only six aircraft of the 376th Bomb Group then bombing Ploiesti while the other aircraft attacked targets of opportunity.

The 44th and 98th Bomb Groups made accurate approaches, but were faced by fully alerted defences. The 389th Bomb Group also bombed with good accuracy. Over the target area and on their exit the bombers were engaged by fighters, and losses were 41 over the target and another 13 on approach or departure.

Specifications

Crew: 10

Powerplant: 4 x 895kW (1200hp) Pratt &
Whitney radial piston engines

Maximum speed: 488km/h (303mph)

Range: 1730km (1080 miles)

Service ceiling: 8540m (28,000ft)

Dimensions: span 33.52m (110ft);

length 20.22m (66ft 4in);

height 5.46m (17ft 11in)

Weight: 27216kg (60,000lb) loaded

Armament: 1 (or 3) x 12.7mm (0.5in) nose

MGs; 6 x 12.7mm (0.5in) MGs: two in dorsal

turret, two in retractable ball turret, two in

waist positions; 3629kg (8000lb) of bombs

▲ **Consolidated B-24D Liberator**

93rd Bomb Group / US Eighth Army Air Force, Hardwick, Norfolk, 1943

'The Travelling Circus' reached Hardwick in December 1942 after spending three months at Alconbury, and remained at this base for the rest of the war. The 93rd Bomb Group possessed the distinction of flying more missions – totalling 396, including 49 from North Africa – than any other Eighth AAF bomb group.

Schweinfurt and Regensburg
AUGUST 1943

These two undertakings were planned in concert so that the German defences would be saturated and major damage would be inflicted on vital war industries. It was a bold plan, but also a plan that went badly wrong and led to very substantial Eighth AAF losses.

THIS DOUBLE mission was conceived as an ambitious plan to cripple the German aircraft industry, and was based on two large forces attacking separate targets in order to dilute the *Luftwaffe's* fighter response. After being postponed several times as a result of adverse weather, the *Juggler* mission was flown on 17 August, the anniversary of the Eighth AAF's first bombing mission. This was the Eighth AAF's 84th mission, and launched 376 bombers of 16 bombardment groups against German heavy industry well beyond the range of escorting fighters. By this time, the B-17 force had been expanded four-fold and was now organized into the 1st and 4th Combat Bomb Wings (CBWs), which were soon to be redesignated as bomb divisions.

The manufacture of the Messerschmitt Bf 109 fighter was centred in Regensburg, and and almost all production of ball bearings was located in Schweinfurt. In its original form, *Juggler* also

ORGANIZATION			
	Schweinfurt mission *17 August 1943*		
201st BW (91st & 381st BGs, & 101st Composite Group)	**202nd BW** (351st & 384th BGs, & 306th Composite Group)	**203rd BW** (92nd, 305th & 306th BGs)	**204th BW** (303rd & 379th BGs, & 1-3rd Composite Group)

envisaged an attack on the Bf 109 factory at Wiener Neustadt in Austria by B-24 bombers, but this mission was in fact flown separately on 13 August. On 17 August, the 4th CBW would attack the fighter factories in Regensburg and then fly on to bases in North Africa, thereby catching the German defences off balance. Following close behind the 4th CBW, the 1st CBW would turn north-east and bomb the ball-bearing factories of Schweinfurt, and by doing so catch the German fighter force on the ground rearming and refuelling after its endeavours against the 4th CBW. P-47 fighters would be able to escort the bombers only as far as Eupen in Belgium. The take-off of the 1st CBW was delayed by fog, so the 4th CBW was therefore well ahead of it.

Fighter response

The Regensburg force was led by the 4th CBW's commander, Colonel Curtis E. LeMay, and comprised seven B-17 groups totalling 146 aircraft. About 15 minutes after it crossed the coast, the Regensburg force encountered the first German fighter response, which continued with growing intensity nearly all the way to the target area. After 90 minutes of combat, the German fighter force broke off the engagement since its aircraft were low on fuel and ammunition, but it had already shot down or fatally damaged at least 15 bombers.

The flak over Regensburg was light and the weather clear, and of the remaining 131 bombers, 126 dropped 303.53 tonnes (298.75 tons) of bombs on the fighter factories with great accuracy. The surviving aircraft then headed south to cross the Alps, losing another eight aircraft.

In all, 24 bombers were lost and more than 60 of the 122 survivors that arrived in Tunisia had suffered battle damage. The 1st CBW, commanded and led by

▲ **Boeing B-17 Flying Fortress**

Almost tailless, this B-17 of the VIII Bomber Command nonetheless made it home safely after a raid on St Omer, France, in 1943.

▲ **Boeing B-17G Flying Fortress**

602nd Bomb Squadron / 398th Bomb Group / US Eighth Army Air Force, Nuthampstead, 1943

The 398th Bomb Group comprised the 600th, 601st, 602nd and 603rd Bomb Squadrons, and deployed from the USA to the UK during April 1944. The group remained at Nuthampstead throughout the war, and redeployed to the USA in May and June 1945 after flying 195 missions.

Specifications

Crew: 9/10	height 5.82m (19ft 1in)
Powerplant: 4 x 895kW (1200hp) Wright radial engines	Weight: 29710kg (65,000lb) loaded
Maximum speed: 462km/h (287mph)	Armament: 2 x 12.7mm (0.5in) Browning trainable MGs in chin, dorsal, ventral and tail turrets; 1 x 12.7mm (0.5in) MGs in two waist, cheek and single dorsal positions; up to 7983kg (17,600lb) bombs
Range: 3219km (2000 miles)	
Service ceiling: 10,850m (35,800ft)	
Dimensions: span 31.62m (103ft 9in); length 22.66m (74ft 4in);	

Brigadier-General Robert B. Williams, comprised nine B-17 groups organized into three provisional combat wings, and followed the same route as the Regensburg force. The first German fighters attacked after the bombers crossed the coast, and over Germany twin-engined fighters joined the battle as more than 300 fighters opposed the raid.

Schweinfurt attacked

The attacking force diverged from the morning's route at Mannheim, alerting the German defenders that the target was Schweinfurt. Losses among the 57 B-17 bombers of the leading wing were so severe that many among its airmen considered the possibility that the wing might be annihilated before reaching the target.

However, 24km (15 miles) from Schweinfurt the opposing fighters, after shooting down 22 bombers, disengaged and landed to rearm and refuel in order to attack the force on its way back. Some 8km (5 miles) from Schweinfurt, the flak lofted a barrage into the path of the bomber force.

At 1459, some 40 B-17 bombers remained as the leading wing dropped its bombs on the target area, followed over a 24-minute period by the remainder of

REGENSBURG FORCE, EIGHTH AAF			
Wing	Group	Base	Sent/lost
403rd BW	96th Bomb Group	Snetterton Hall	21/0
403rd BW	388th BG	Knettishall	21/1
403rd BW	390th BG	Framlingham	20/6
401st BW	94th BG	Bury St Edmunds	21/1
401st BW	385th BG	Great Ashfield	21/3
402nd BW	9th BG	Horham	21/4
402nd BW	100th BG	Thorpe Abbotts	21/9

the force. Each wing found increasingly heavy smoke from preceding bomb explosions a hindrance to accuracy. Three bombers had been shot down by flak over Schweinfurt.

Fifteen minutes after leaving the target, each element of the force circled to rebuild its formation, then continued west. At 15:30, the German fighters renewed their attacks. From 16:30, P-47 and Spitfires covered the withdrawal, claiming 20 fighters shot down, but eight more bombers were lost before the force reached the North Sea, where three more crash-landed. The Schweinfurt force lost a total of 36 bombers.

US Eighth Army Air Force
1944–45

From the spring of 1944, the US Eighth AAF was withdrawn from its strategic role and retasked, together with RAF Bomber Command, to the tactical role in support of the forthcoming invasion of Europe. Only after this could the Eighth AAF complete its strategic task over Germany.

O N 4 JANUARY 1944, the Boeing B-17 and Consolidated B-24 four-engined heavy bombers flew their last missions as part of the US VIII Bomber Command. On this date, the US Eighth AAF and the US Fifteenth AAF, the latter operating from bases in Italy, were combined under central command, namely the new US Strategic Air Forces (USSTAF) with its headquarters at Bushey Hall. In effect, this was a redesignation of the Eighth AAF. The VIII Bomber Command in turn was re-designated as the Eighth AAF on 22 February of the same year and then went out of existence.

General Carl Spaatz returned to England to

ORGANIZATION

VIII Bomber Command
1944

| 1st Bomb Division (1st, 40th, 41st & 94th Combat Bombardment Wings [Heavy]) | 2nd Bomb Division (2nd, 14th & 20th Combat Bombardment Wings [Heavy]) | 3rd Bomb Division (4th, 13th & 45th Combat Bombardment Wings [Heavy]) |

command the USSTAF. At the same time, Major-General 'Jimmy' Doolittle passed command of the Fifteenth AAF to Major-General Nathan F. Twining and assumed command of the new Eighth AAF at High Wycombe. Doolittle's thinking was direct and simple: 'Win the air war and isolate the battlefield.' Spaatz and Doolittle planned to employ the USSTAF in a programme of carefully coordinated attacks under the designation Operation *Argument*. This daylight effort would be supported by Bomber Command's nocturnal programme, and its target was the whittling down of the German aircraft industry as quickly as possible.

By mid-1944, the Eighth AAF had climbed to a strength of more than 200,000 personnel as the human side of an establishment comprising, at its peak, 40 groups of heavy bombers, 15 groups of fighters and four groups of specialized support aircraft. This allowed the Eighth AAF to launch, on a

Specifications

Crew: 10

Powerplant: 4 x 895kW (1200hp) Pratt &
  Whitney Twin wasp radial piston engines

Maximum speed: 488km/h (303mph)

Range: 1730km (1080 miles)

Service ceiling: 8540m (28,000ft)

Dimensions: span 33.53m (110ft);

length 20.22m (66ft 4in); height 5.49m (18ft)

Weight: 32,296kg (71,200lb) loaded

Armament: 1 (usually 3) x 12.7mm (0.5in) nose
MG, plus 2 x 12.7mm (0.5in) MGs each in
dorsal, tail and retractable ball turrets;
2 x MGs in waist positions; up to 3629kg
(8000lb) of bombs

▲ Consolidated B-24D Liberator

491st Bomb Group / US Eighth Army Air Force / North Pickenham, Norfolk, 1944

Each Liberator group possessed one garishly coloured aeroplane designed to facilitate the formation of the group over the UK before the aircraft set off across the English Channel or North Sea to their target. Created out of 'war weary' machines, the unarmed assembly aircraft then returned home.

Specifications

Crew: 8–10

Powerplant: 4 x 895kW (1200hp) Wright
  Cyclone radial piston engines

Maximum speed: 475km/h (295mph)

Range: 2071km (1287 miles)

Service ceiling: 10,975m (36,000ft)

Dimensions: span 31.6m (103ft 9in);
length 22.8m (74ft 9in);
height 5.85m (19ft 2in)

Weight: 25400kg (56,000lb) loaded

Armament: 12 x 12.7mm (0.5in) MGs; 7983kg
(17,600) of bombs

▲ Boeing B-17F Flying Fortress

388th Bomb Group / US Eighth Army Air Force, 1944

This B-17F landed in Rinkaby in neutral Sweden on 29 February 1944, and was later adapted in that country as a 14-passenger transport aeroplane with the markings seen here. This revised aeroplane operated in the civil transport role from 6 October 1944.

1ST AIR DIVISION (MAY 1945)		
Unit	HQ	Groups
1st Bomb Wing	Bassingbourn	91st, 381st, 398th BGs
40th Bomb Wing	Thurleigh	92nd, 305th, 306th BGs
41st Bomb Wing	Molesworth	303rd, 379th, 384th BGs
94th Bomb Wing	Polebrook	351st, 401st, 457th BGs
67th Fighter Wing	Walcot Hall	20th, 352nd, 356th, 359th, 364th FGs

regular basis, more than 2000 four-engined bombers and more than 1000 escorting fighters on a single day's mission to several targets. Within the context of the USSTAF's overall command, the Eighth AAF was primarily responsible for the 'Big Week' air offensive over Germany, the escort fighters tackling the *Luftwaffe*'s fighter arm directly as the German fighters sought to destroy the bombers, which had German aircraft manufacturing facilities as their targets. The heavy bombers of the Eighth AAF also flew missions deep into the heart of Germany, and undertook daylight attacks on Berlin.

Tactical raids

Before the Allied invasion of France in June 1944, the heavy bomb groups of the Eighth AAF conducted tactical raids in preparation for, and in tactical support of, Allied ground forces in and behind the invasion area. They also helped in the airborne assault on Arnhem in the Netherlands during September 1944, and attacked German ground forces during the 'Battle of the Bulge' at the end of the year.

These missions were completed only at a high cost, however, for 50 per cent of the USAAF's casualties in World War II were suffered by the Eighth AAF: 26,000 dead and more than 21,000 wounded. The cost paid by the Eighth AAF, and also its significance in the Allied effort over Europe, is attested by the fact that the personnel of this air force received 17 Medals of Honor, 220 Distinguished Service Crosses and 442,000 Air Medals. The Eighth AAF included 261 fighter aces, 31 of them with more than 15 'kills' each.

Final raids

The Eighth AAF's last raid was flown on 25 April 1945, when B-17s attacked the Skoda armaments factory at Pilsen in Czechoslovakia, and B-24s attacked four railway facilities in the area round Hitler's retreat at Berchtesgaden, and the Fifteenth AAF attacked the mountain passes to prevent German troops from escaping from Italy.

After the end of the war in Europe, some combat units began to move to the Pacific theatre. The HQ of the Eighth AAF reached Okinawa on 16 July 1945, but the Eighth AAF saw no Pacific service.

Specifications

Crew: 2

Powerplant: 2 x 1253kW (1680hp) Merlin 72 engines

Maximum speed: 668km/h (415mph)

Range: 2400km (1300 miles)

Service ceiling: 11,000m (37,000ft)

Dimensions: span 16.52m (54ft 2in); length 12.43m (44ft 6in); height 5.3m (17ft 5in)

Weight: 6490kg (14,300lb) empty

Armament: none

▲ de Havilland Mosquito PR.Mk XVI

653rd Bomb Squadron (Light) / US Eighth Army Air Force, Watton, Norfolk, 1944

The aeroplane was used for weather reconnaissance and visual assessment of bombing attacks. It was completed in PRU blue with black/white 'invasion stripes' on its under surfaces, and its USAAF association was revealed by the national markings, the red tail unit and the 653rd Bomb Squadron's marking on the fin.

Reducing the German fighters
FEBRUARY 1944

To succeed in its strategic bombing campaign, the Eighth AAF needed to be able to reach its targets and bomb accurately. It was therefore a priority that escort fighters were able to accompany the bombers to and from the target, and destroy the German fighter arm.

OPERATION *ARGUMENT* was a six-day major air offensive undertaken between 20 and 25 February 1944 by General Carl Spaatz's US Strategic Air Forces in Europe (Major-General James 'Jimmy' Doolittle's US Eighth AAF in the UK and Major-General Nathan H. Twining's US Fifteenth AAF in Italy), Major-General Hoyt S. Vandenberg's US Ninth AAF in the UK and Air Chief Marshal Sir Arthur Harris' RAF Bomber Command.

It was directed against German fighter strength and production – in this 'Big Week' effort, the Allies used their bombers to attack Germany's major aircraft production centres as the escorting fighters

▶ **Boeing B-17 Flying Fortress**
The two waist gunners of the B-17 operated in exposed positions, and therefore had warm suits and oxygen masks to cope with the conditions at high altitude.

Specifications

Crew: 9–10	height 5.82m (19ft 1in)
Powerplant: 4 x 895kW (1200hp) Wright radial engines	Weight: 29710kg (65,000lb) loaded
	Armament: 2 x 12.7mm (0.5in) Browning
Maximum speed: 462km/h (287mph)	trainable MGs in chin, dorsal, ventral and tail
Range: 3219km (2000 miles)	turrets; 1 x 12.7mm (0.5in) MG in two waist,
Service ceiling: 10,850m (35,800ft)	cheek and single dorsal positions; up to
Dimensions: span 31.62m (103ft 9in);	7983kg (17,600lb) of bombs
length 22.66m (74ft 4in);	

▲ **Boeing B-17G Flying Fortress**
452nd Bomb Group / US Eighth Army Air Force, Deopham Green, 1944
An unusual distinction of the 452nd Bomb Group was that it had more commanding officers, nine in all, than any other bomb group. The group started to reach the UK in December 1943, and remained at Deopham Green until August 1945. The group's 728th, 729th, 730th and 731st Bomb Squadrons flew a total of 250 missions.

a series of missions against German air-related targets on the ground and in the air. The planners designed the operation as the means to lure the *Luftwaffe* into a decisive battle by launching massive attacks on the German aircraft industry. By defeating the *Luftwaffe*, the Allies knew they would have air superiority for the planned *Overlord* amphibious assault on the mainland of Europe.

△ Friendly fire?
These bombs have been dropped from a Boeing B-17 toward a sister aeroplane flying at lower altitude.

used the opportunity to tackle the German fighters that took off to challenge the Allied bomber crews.

The Allied offensive destroyed substantial numbers of German fighters, though the real importance of the battle lay not so much in inflicting severe losses on the *Luftwaffe*, but in forcing the Germans to use irreplaceable fuel supplies and to suffer the loss of yet more experienced pilots at a time when their flying schools were wholly unable to make good such losses with adequately trained replacements.

On 20 February, the US Strategic Air Forces, the US Ninth AAF and RAF Bomber Command started

△ Boeing B-17G Flying Fortress
602nd Bomb Squadron / 379th Bomb Group / US Eighth Army Air Force, Nuthampstead, 1944
The B-17G introduced staggered waist gun positions to provide the gunner with more room, and this aeroplane had radar in place of the ventral 'ball' turret.

Specifications
Crew: 9–10
Powerplant: 4 x 895kW (1200hp) Wright radial engines
Maximum speed: 462km/h (287mph)
Range: 3219km (2000 miles)
Service ceiling: 10,850m (35,800ft)
Dimensions: span 31.62m (103ft 9in); length 22.66m (74ft 4in);
height 5.82m (19ft 1in)
Weight: 29710kg (65,000lb) loaded
Armament: 2 x 12.7mm (0.5in) Browning trainable MGs in chin, dorsal, ventral and tail turrets; 1 x 12.7mm (0.5in) MG in two waist, cheek and single dorsal positions; up to 7983kg (17,600lb) of bombs

△ Boeing B-17G Flying Fortress
91st Bomb Group / US Eighth Army Air Force, Bassingbourn, 1944
The B-17G was essentially an improved B-17F with a remotely controlled chin turret, armed with two 12.7mm (0.5in) Browning machine guns, to cope better with German fighters making head-on attacks.

Specifications

Crew: 10

Powerplant: 4 x 895kW (1200hp) Pratt &
   Whitney Twin wasp radial piston engines

Maximum speed: 467km/h (290mph)

Range: 5955km (3700 miles)

Service ceiling: 8535m (28000ft)

Dimensions: span 33.53m (110ft);

length 20.47m (67ft 2in);

height 5.49m (18ft)

Weight: 25,401kg (56,000lb) loaded

Armament: 2 x 12.7mm (0.5in) Browning
   trainable MGs each in nose, dorsal, ventral
   'ball' and tail turrets, and one each in beam
   positions; up to 5806kg (12,800lb) of bombs

▲ **Consolidated B-24H Liberator**

406th Bomb Squadron / 'Carpetbaggers' Special Operations Group / US Eighth Army Air Force, Cheddington, 1944

This squadron specialized in the nocturnal delivery of leaflet 'bombs', which were laminated paper cylinders, each holding 80,000 leaflets and designed to burst in the air at an altitude between 305m (1000ft) and 610m (2000ft).

'Big Week'
19–25 FEBRUARY 1944

The 'Big Week' campaign was designed to whittle down Germany's fighter strength and cripple Germany's fighter production capability. The campaign was costly for the Americans, but achieved considerable successes, including a strong psychological blow to the Germans.

I N THE 'BIG WEEK' of Operation *Argument*, the USAAF flew heavily escorted missions against airframe manufacturing and assembly plants and other targets in many German cities, including Leipzig, Braunschweig, Gotha, Regensburg, Schweinfurt, Augsburg, Stuttgart and Steyr.

In six days, the bombers of the Eighth and Ninth AAFs flew more than 3250 sorties, the US Fifteenth

▲ **Weary but safe**

The crew of a Boeing B-17G flying Fortress leave their aeroplane to the ground crew after returning from their latest mission.

USAAF RAIDS DURING 'BIG WEEK'			
Date	Target	Sent	Lost
19/20 February	Leipzig & others	921	79 (8.6%)
20/21 February	Stuttgart & others	826	10 (1.2%
21/22 February	various	69	1 (1.4%)
22/23 February	various	134	0
23/24 February	various	22	0
24/25 February	Schweinfurt	1070	36 (3.4%)

AAF more than 500, and Bomber Command some 2350 sorties. The Allied bombers dropped almost 20,320 tonnes (20,000 tons) of bombs and seriously disrupted German fighter production, preventing or delaying the manufacture of hundreds of aircraft at a time when these were badly needed on the Eastern Front and in Italy.

The whole effort cost the US forces 226 heavy bombers and 28 fighters, while Bomber Command lost 157 aircraft. The Allies found the six-day effort costly, the Eighth AAF's losses in February amounting to almost 20 per cent, but this was more than offset by the Germans' loss of two months of fighter production.

Specifications

Crew: 9–10

Powerplant: 4 x 895kW (1200hp) Wright radial engines

Maximum speed: 462km/h (287mph)

Range: 3219km (2000 miles)

Service ceiling: 10,850m (35,800ft)

Dimensions: span 31.62m (103ft 9in); length 22.66m (74ft 4in);

height 5.82m (19ft 1in)

Weight: 29710kg (65,000lb) loaded

Armament: 2 x 12.7mm (0.5in) Browning trainable MGs in chin, dorsal, ventral and tail turrets; 1 x 12.7mm (0.5in) MG in two waist, cheek and single dorsal positions; up to 7983kg (17,600lb) of bombs

▲ Boeing B-17G Flying Fortress

324th Bomb Squadron / 91st Bomb Group / US Eighth Army Air Force, Bassingbourn, 1944

'The Ragged Irregulars' started to reach the UK from September 1942, settling first at Kimbolton before moving to Bassingbourn in October 1942 for the rest of the war. The group's four squadrons were the 322nd, 323rd, 324th and 401st Bomb Squadrons, and the group flew 340 missions under seven commanders.

Specifications

Crew: 10

Powerplant: 4 x 895kW (1200hp) Pratt & Whitney Twin wasp radial piston engines

Maximum speed: 467km/h (290mph)

Range: 5955km (3700 miles)

Service ceiling: 8535m (28000ft)

Dimensions: span 33.53m (110ft);

length 20.47m (67ft 2in); height 5.49m (18ft)

Weight: 25,401kg (56,000lb) loaded

Armament: 2 x 12.7mm (0.5in) Browning trainable MGs in nose, dorsal, ventral 'ball' and tail turrets, and one each in beam positions; up to 5806kg (12,800lb) of bombs

▲ Consolidated B-24J Liberator

446th Bomb Group / US Eighth Army Air Force, Bungay, early 1944

The 'Bungay Buckaroos' group comprised the 704th, 705th, 706th and 707th Bomb Squadrons, and began to reach the UK in November 1943. The group remained at Bungay for the rest of the war, and was redeployed to the USA in June and July 1945 after flying 273 missions.

Another consequence of *Argument* was the Germans' decision to increase still further their dispersion of several industries, particularly aircraft and ball-bearing manufacture, despite the monetary cost and the further dislocation of production. Although this ultimately enabled the Germans to continue and indeed step up fighter production, it also rendered the industry extremely vulnerable to another factor, namely systematic attacks on the transportation network on which dispersed production was reliant.

Morale booster

The week-long offensive also seriously eroded the morale and capability of the *Luftwaffe*. US air crews claimed more than 600 German fighters destroyed and thus achieved almost immediate air superiority, and the *Luftwaffe* never recovered from the loss of so high a proportion of its steadily diminishing pool of skilled fighter pilots. The Germans were therefore forced, in effect, to concede air superiority over occupied Europe and Germany itself to the Allies. The 'Big Week' also bolstered the confidence of US strategic bombing crews.

Until that time, Allied bombers had tended to avoid contact with the *Luftwaffe* whenever possible, but from this time onward the US planners deliberately sought to force the *Luftwaffe* into combat with growing numbers of P-51 escort fighters, which possessed the range to escort the bombers to and from distant targets. This policy allowed the USAAF to consider attacks on Berlin, the German capital. Raiding the German capital, Allied leaders reasoned, would damage important industries and bring the *Luftwaffe* to battle.

Berlin attacks

Thus, on 4 March the USSTAF launched the first of several attacks against Berlin, the fierce air battles which resulted causing heavy losses on each side. But while the Allies could make good their losses without appreciable delay, the Germans could not achieve this and therefore grew steadily weaker. By the spring of 1944, the Allied strategic forces had attacked U-boat construction yards, aircraft factories, transportation and other industrial facilities with limited success. They had fought the *Luftwaffe* in the skies over Europe and, despite suffering severe losses, had never turned back.

When the combined bomber offensive officially ended on 1 April 1944, and the focus of the strategic air effort was switched to support *Overlord*, Allied airmen were well on the way to achieving air superiority over all of Europe.

▲ **Consolidated B-24H Liberator**

566th Bomb Squadron / 389th Bomb Group / US Eighth Army Air Force, Hethel, spring 1944

'The Sky Scorpions' group comprised the 564th, 565th, 566th and 567th Bomb Squadrons, which started to arrived in the UK in June 1943. The group flew 321 missions, 14 of them from North Africa, and was inactivated in September 1945.

Specifications

Crew: 10

Powerplant: 4 x 895kW (1200hp) Pratt & Whitney Twin wasp radial piston engines

Maximum speed: 467km/h (290mph)

Range: 5955km (3700 miles)

Service ceiling: 8535m (28000ft)

Dimensions: span 33.53m (110ft);

length 20.47m (67ft 2in);

height 5.49m (18ft)

Weight: 25,401kg (56,000lb) loaded

Armament: 2 x 12.7mm (0.5in) Browning trainable MGs in nose, dorsal, ventral 'ball' and tail turrets, and one each in beam positions; up to 5806kg (12,800lb) of bombs

Taking the war to Berlin
FEBRUARY–APRIL 1945

A city without the concentrations of war-making industries that the USAAF saw at their primary targets, Berlin did not receive much in the way of American bombing attention until 1945. Then, against the wishes of its commander, the Eighth AAF was ordered to make several raids.

AFTER ITS FAILURE in the battle of Berlin, which involved 16 raids between 18 November 1943 and January 1944 and yielded no major results other than the loss of many bombers and their crews, RAF Bomber Command sensibly decided to avoid Berlin for most of 1944, when its resources were in any case largely diverted to targets in western Germany, France and Belgium in support of the Allied invasion of France in June 1944.

Nevertheless, it was deemed useful to maintain at least a presence over Berlin, thus ensuring that its defences against air attack would not be moved to protect other possible targets, so regular nuisance raids were continued by both the RAF and the USAAF.

Berlin targetted
It was only in early 1945 that Berlin again became a major target for Allied bombing attack. As the Soviet

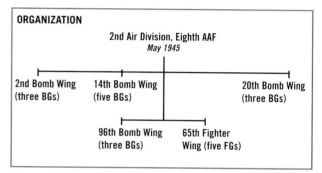

ORGANIZATION

2nd Air Division, Eighth AAF
May 1945

| 2nd Bomb Wing (three BGs) | 14th Bomb Wing (five BGs) | 96th Bomb Wing (three BGs) | 65th Fighter Wing (five FGs) | 20th Bomb Wing (three BGs) |

forces closed on Berlin from the east, the RAF carried out a series of attacks on cities in eastern Germany, swollen with refugees from farther east, to disrupt communications and put more strain on Germany's dwindling manpower and fuel resources. Then a force of almost 1000 B-17 bombers of the Eighth AAF, escorted by large numbers of P-51 single-engined fighters, attacked the German railway system in Berlin during 3 February in an effort to prevent movement of the Sixth *Panzerarmee*, which intelligence sources believed to be travelling through the German capital by rail to fight the Soviet forces on the Eastern Front.

Collateral damage
The raid killed between 2500 and 3000 people, and left another 120,000 persons homeless. This was one of the few occasions on which the USAAF undertook an area attack on a city centre. Lieutenant-General James Doolittle, commanding the Eighth AAF, had objected to the plan but had been overruled by General Carl Spaatz, commanding the US Strategic Air Forces, and General Dwight D. Eisenhower, the supreme commander of the Allied forces in Europe.

The reasoning of Doolittle's two superiors was that the raid might achieve useful military results, but would also help to convince the Soviet Union that the Western Allies were seeking to support them actively. During this raid, Kreuzberg (the newspaper district),

▲ **Top gun**
Forward-firing defensive armament was crucial to the success of the Fortresses' missions. This was finally addressed in the B-17G, which included four machine guns in two turrets as well as two manually operated cheek guns.

Mitte (the central area, as suggested by its name), and other areas such as Friedrichshain were all severely damaged. Among the several government and Nazi party buildings that were also hit were the Reich chancellery, the party chancellery and the headquarters of the Gestapo secret police organization. The Unter den Linden, Wilhelmstrasse and Friedrichstrasse areas were all effectively destroyed.

There was another major US raid on 26 February, and this left another 80,000 persons homeless. The US raids continued until April, when the Soviet forces had reached the outskirts of Berlin, and during the final days of the war the Soviet air forces also bombed Berlin.

Big raid

The largest of the Eighth AAF's raids on Berlin took place on 18 March, when 1327 bombers of three air divisions were committed, together with powerful escort forces. On this occasion the Germans felt that the tactical and weather conditions were favourable for the use of a significant number of Messerschmitt Me 262 jet-powered fighters, each armed with four 30mm (1.18in) cannon. The 1st and 3rd Air Divisions were each attacked by a group of between 10 and 20 Me 262s, which shot down eight bombers within the US losses of 24 bombers on the day. Two Me 262s fell.

Estimates of the dead in Berlin as a result of air raids range from 20,000 to 50,000, the former being more probable. The comparatively low death count for Berlin resulted in part from the city's distance from airfields in the UK, which made the launching of major raids difficult before the liberation of France in late 1944, and in part to the high strength and quality of the city's air defences and shelters.

2ND AIR DIVISION, EIGHTH AAF (MAY 1945)		
Wing	Headquarters	Groups
2nd BW	Hethel	389th, 445th, 453rd BGs
14th BW	Shipdham	44th, 392nd, 491st, 492nd, 489th BGs
20th BW	Hardwick	93rd, 446th, 448th BGs
96th BW	Horsham St Faith	458th, 466th, 467th BGs
65h FW	Saffron Walden	4th, 56th, 355th, 361st, 479th FGs

Specifications

Crew: 9/10

Powerplant: 4 x 895kW (1200hp) Wright radial engines

Maximum speed: 462km/h (287mph)

Range: 3219km (2000 miles)

Service ceiling: 10,850m (35,800ft)

Dimensions: span 31.62m (103ft 9in); length 22.66m (74ft 4in);

height 5.82m (19ft 1in)

Weight: 29710kg (65,000lb) loaded

Armament: 2 x 12.7mm (0.5in) Browning trainable MGs in chin, dorsal, ventral and tail turrets; 1 x 12.7mm (0.5in) MG in two waist, cheek and single dorsal positions; up to 7983kg (17,600lb) of bombs

▲ **Boeing B-17G Flying Fortress**
322nd Bomb Squadron / 91st Group / US Eighth Army Air Force,
Bassingbourn, late 1944–early 1945
The decline of the German fighter arm meant that from April 1944 USAAF bombers increasingly flew in a natural metal finish, reducing cost, maintenance, weight and drag, and boosting performance slightly.

Specifications

Crew: 9/10

Powerplant: 4 x 895kW (1200hp) Wright radial
engines

Maximum speed: 462km/h (287mph)

Range: 3219km (2000 miles)

Service ceiling: 10,850m (35,800ft)

Dimensions: span 31.62m (103ft 9in);
length 22.66m (74ft 4in);

height 5.82m (19ft 1in)

Weight: 29710kg (65,000lb) loaded

Armament: 2 x 12.7mm (0.5in) Browning
trainable machine guns in chin, dorsal,
ventral and tail turrets, 1 x 12.7mm (0.5in)
machine guns in two waist, cheek and single
dorsal positions, up to 7983kg (17,600lb)
bombs

▲ **Boeing B-17G Flying Fortress**

364th Bomb Squadron / 305th Bomb Group / 40th Combat Wing /
US Eighth Army Air Force, 1944–45

Based in Grafton Underwood, the 305th Bomb Group was first activated in
November 1942, and flew its final mission on 25 April 1945. The group dropped
10,144kg (22,363lb) of ordnance over occupied Europe, flying more than 9000
sorties. The 364th Bomb Squadron used the markings 'WF'.

Suppressing the V-2
1944–45

**Once the threat of the German 'V-weapons' was appreciated, the Allies made strenuous efforts
to destroy the production facilities and launch sites. As part of this effort, the US Eighth AAF
visited Peenemünde on three occasions during the course of 1944.**

AFTER THE BRITISH attack on Peenemünde in
Operation *Hydra* on the night of 17/18 August
1943, the Germans deliberately fabricated 'evidence'
of bomb damage in the area, in an effort to persuade
the Allies that this target had in fact been destroyed
beyond the point of any continued operational
viability. They created a number of larger craters in
the sand, deliberately blew up a number of lightly
damaged and minor buildings, and went so far as to
paint simulations of charred beams on the roofs of
undamaged buildings.

Even so, the US Eighth AAF was committed to
three attacks on Peenemünde during 1944, largely in
an effort to ensure that there was no production of
hydrogen peroxide for fuel, one of the essential
ingredients used in the rocket engine of the V-2
ballistic missile, at this site.

The first of these three attacks, which was flown on
18 July 1944, employed 377 B-17 Flying Fortress
four-engined heavy bombers to attack the
experimental establishment at Peenemünde, the
scientific headquarters at Zinnowitz, and the
marshalling yards at Stralsund. The effort of the
bombers was significantly aided by a previous
weather reconnaissance, which had established that
the conditions were just right for the bombers. Such
pre-raid reconnaissance was a new feature in USAAF
planning, and paid handsome dividends. The US
forces lost three B-17s and had another 64 of the
aircraft damaged.

The escort for the raid was provided by 297 P-38
Lightning twin-engined and P-51 Mustang single-
engined fighters, and these claimed the destruction of
21 German fighters for the loss of three P-51s and

another damaged so badly that it had to be scrapped after returning to the UK. General Spaatz commented: 'The finest example of precision bombing I have ever seen.'

Second raid

The second raid, flown on 4 August, also struck at targets in the Peenemünde area. This undertaking involved 221 B-17s against Peenemünde itself, 110 against the airfield at Anklam and 70 against aircraft manufacturing facilities also at Anklam. Three B-17s were lost, one damaged irreparably, and 94 more damaged. The escort force this time comprised 250 P-51 fighters, of which just 223 actually took part on the operation. The Mustangs claimed the destruction of four German fighters and another four damaged on the ground, for the loss of nine of their own number and one more damaged irreparably.

The third raid, on 25 August, committed 376 B-17s against targets in the Peenemünde area: 146 of the bombers attacked the experimental establishment at Peenemünde once again, 108 bombed the airfield at Neubrandenburg and 71 more bombed the airfield at Anklam; 21 other bombers attacked the airfield at Parow, and five

▲ **Boeing B-17G Flying Fortress**
533rd Bomb Squadron / 381st Bomb Group / US Eighth Army Air Force,
Ridgewell, Essex, 1944
The 381st Bomb Group comprised the 532nd, 533rd, 534th and 535th Bomb Squadrons, and reached the UK in June 1943. The group flew 296 missions from Ridgewell before returning to the USA in May and June 1945.

struck at targets of opportunity. Of these B-17s, five were lost and another 75 damaged. On this occasion, the bombers were escorted by 171 P-47 Thunderbolt and P-51 single-engined fighters, and these claimed 36 German aircraft destroyed and another 28 damaged on the ground for the loss of just two of their own number.

Specifications

Crew: 9–10
Powerplant: 4 x 895kW (1200hp) Wright radial engines
Maximum speed: 462km/h (287mph)
Range: 3219km (2000 miles)
Service ceiling: 10,850m (35,800ft)
Dimensions: span 31.62m (103ft 9in);
length 22.66m (74ft 4in);

height 5.82m (19ft 1in)
Weight: 29710kg (65,000lb) loaded
Armament: 2 x 12.7mm (0.5in) Browning trainable MGs in chin, dorsal, ventral and tail turrets; 1 x 12.7mm (0.5in) MGs in two waist, cheek and single dorsal positions; up to 7983kg (17,600lb) bombs

▲ **Boeing B-17G Flying Fortress**
711th Bomb Squadron / 447th Bomb Group / US Eighth Army Air Force,
Rattlesden, 1945
This is a late-production example of the B-17G with a revised tail position. The 447th Bomb Group comprised the 708th, 709th, 710th and 711th Bomb Squadrons, which reached Rattlesden, the group's only English base, in November 1943. The group returned to the USA in August 1945 after flying 257 missions.

The firebombing of Dresden
FEBRUARY 1945

In one of the most controversial campaigns of the strategic air war, the Western Allies bombed Dresden in February 1945. The physical destruction caused by the night and day raids was huge, but the casualties, though still very large, were not as great as has been claimed.

THE ALLIED BOMBING of Dresden, led by Bomber Command of the Royal Air Force and followed by the Eighth AAF of the USAAF, on 13/15 February 1945, remains one of the most controversial Allied campaigns of World War II. Though largely unmilitarized and only little damaged in earlier raids, Dresden was believed early in 1945 to possess the transport network along which the Germans could have passed reinforcements to the Eastern Front. The Western Allies therefore came to the conclusion that the city had to be destroyed despite the fact that it was filled with a possible 200,000 refugees fleeing the Soviet advance from the east.

The railway yards, near the city centre, had already been attacked twice by the Eighth AAF in daylight raids: on 7 October 1944 with 71 tonnes (70 tons) of HE bombs, and once again on 16 January 1945 with 325 tonnes (320 tons) of bombs, including 41.6 tonnes (41 tons) of incendiaries. The new campaign was to have been started by the Eighth AAF during the day of 13 February, but bad weather

prevented USAAF operations during this day. Thus RAF Bomber Command carried out the first raid during the night of 13/14 February.

Then, from just after midday on 14 February, 311 B-17s dropped 783 tonnes (771 tons) of bombs on Dresden, with the railway yards as their aiming point. During this US raid, there was a brief but intense dogfight between US and German fighters around Dresden. The Eighth AAF resumed its attack on 15 February. During the British attack and the two US attacks, some 3962 tonnes (3900 tons) of bombs were dropped.

ORGANIZATION

	US Eighth AAF		
	May 1945		
1st Air Division (four bomb & one fighter wing)	2nd Air Division (four bomb & one fighter wing)	3rd Air Division (four bomb & one fighter wing)	direct reporting units

▲ **Silver flyers**
Camouflage began to disappear from the Eighth AAF's Flying Fortresses from early 1944. These B-17Gs are from the 381st Bomb Group, based at Ridgewell in the UK.

The attacks were designed to create a firestorm: first, a considerable weight of high-explosive (HE) bombs was used to blow the roofs off buildings and so expose the timbers within them; second, incendiary bombs were dropped to ignite the exposed timbers; and third, more HE bombs were dropped to deter the firefighting services. In Dresden, the bombings created a self-sustaining firestorm, with temperatures peaking at more than 1500°C (2700°F). After an area had caught fire, the air in the area immediately above it became very heated and rose rapidly, cold air then being drawn in at very high speed at ground level, sucking other flammable materials into the firestorm and sustaining it.

Devastation

After the main firebombing campaign of 13/15 February, there were two other USAAF attacks on the city's railway marshalling yards: on 2 March 406 B-17s dropped 955 tonnes (940 tons) of HE and 143 tonnes (141 tons) of incendiary bombs, and on 17 April 580 B-17s dropped 1578 tonnes (1554 tons) of HE and 167 tonnes (165 tons) of incendiary bombs. A German police report shortly after the attacks stated that the old town and the inner eastern suburbs had been engulfed in a single fire that had destroyed almost 12,000 buildings, including

3RD AIR DIVISION, EIGHTH AAF (MAY 1945)		
Wing	Headquarters	Bomb groups
4th BW	Bury St Edmunds	94th, 447th, 448th, 487th BGs
13th BW	Horham	95th, 100th, 390th BGs
45th BW	Snetterton Heath	96th, 388th, 452nd BGs
93rd BW	Mendlesham	34th, 385th, 490th, 493rd BGs
66th FW	Sawston Hall	55th, 78th, 339th, 353rd, 357th FGs

residential barracks. The report also said that the raid had destroyed 24 banks, 26 insurance buildings, 31 stores and retail houses, 640 shops, 64 warehouses, two market halls, 31 large hotels, 26 public houses, 63 administrative buildings, three theatres, 18 cinemas, 11 churches, six chapels, five building of cultural and historical significance, 19 hospitals and other medical facilities, 39 schools, five consulates, one zoological garden, one water works, one railway facility, 19 postal facilities, four tram facilities and 19 river craft of various sizes.

Almost 200 factories were damaged, 136 of them badly. The number of dead is difficult to fix, and estimates have varied between 25,000 and 60,000 or more, but modern scholarship suggests a figure toward the lower end of the range between 25,000 and 35,000.

Specifications

Crew: 9/10

Powerplant: 4 x 895kW (1200hp) Wright radial engines

Maximum speed: 462km/h (287mph)

Range: 3219km (2000 miles)

Service ceiling: 10,850m (35,800ft)

Dimensions: span 31.62m (103ft 9in); length 22.66m (74ft 4in);

height 5.82m (19ft 1in)

Weight: 29710kg (65,000lb) loaded

Armament: 2 x 12.7mm (0.5in) Browning trainable MGs in chin, dorsal, ventral and tail turrets; 1 x 12.7mm (0.5in) MGs in two waist, cheek and single dorsal positions; up to 7983kg (17,600lb) bombs

▲ Boeing B-17G Flying Fortress

386th Bomb Squadron / 487th Bomb Group / US Eighth Army Air Force, Lavenham, 1945

The 487th Bomb Group comprised the 836th, 837th, 338th and 839th Bomb Squadrons, which started to reach Lavenham from the USA in July 1944. The group remained at the same base until July and August 1945, where it redeployed to the USA after completing 185 missions.

US Ninth Army Air Force
1943–45

The Ninth AAF of North African service was replaced in October 1943 by a new Ninth AAF based in the UK for support of the US ground forces during and after the *Overlord* invasion of Normandy. The force grow enormously in the winter of 1943–44.

ON 16 OCTOBER 1943, the headquarters of the original US Ninth AAF was inactivated in Egypt and a new headquarters activated in the UK at Burtonwood under the command of Lieutenant-General Lewis H. Brereton, who was succeeded on 7 August 1944 by Major-General Hoyt S. Vandenberg. Initially controlling assets that had previously been part of the Eighth AAF's establishment, but soon swollen enormously by the arrival in the UK of other tactical air units, the new Ninth AAF was created to provide tactical air support for the Allies' planned *Overlord* invasion of German-occupied north-west Europe, and in the periods before, during and after the invasion. As such, the Ninth AAF became a decisive factor in the tactical air power equation in western Europe. With its formation in England, the Ninth AAF was entrusted with the provision of the full range of tactical air support requirements for the US Army in north-western Europe, leaving the Eighth AAF to concentrate its efforts on the strategic bombing mission.

New tactical air force

The core of the new Ninth AAF was created during November 1943 by the transfer from the Eighth AAF of tactical bomber, fighter and troop carrier groups. This transfer created the following: Brigadier-General Samuel E. Anderson's IX Bomber Command with four bomb groups of Martin B-28 Marauder twin-engined medium bombers; Brigadier-General Elwood R. Quesada's IX Fighter Command with one reconnaissance group flying variants of the Lockheed P-38 Lightning twin-engined fighter and three fighter and fighter-bomber groups flying the North American P-51 Mustang single-engined fighters; and Brigadier-General Paul L. Williams' IX Troop Carrier command with three groups of Douglas C-47 twin-engined transport aircraft.

In February 1944, one of the IX Fighter Command's Mustang groups was replaced by another

ORGANIZATION

Ninth AAF
late 1943

| IX Bomber Command (four medium bomber groups) | IX Fighter Command (four fighter groups) | IX Troop Carrier Command (three transport groups) |

flying the Republic P-47 Thunderbolt single-engined heavy fighter and fighter-bomber, and the IX Fighter Command was itself later divided into Major-General Quesada's IX Tactical Air Command with an eventual nine groups to support the US First Army, and Brigadier-General Otto P. Weyland's XIX Tactical Air Command, which had an eventual seven groups to support the US Third Army. This division of responsibilities was eventually formalized on 1 August 1944.

IX BOMBER COMMAND (LATE 1943)

Group	Headquarters	Squadrons	Type
322nd BG	Andrews Field	449th, 450th, 451st, 452nd BSs	B-26
323rd BG	Earls Colne	353rd, 454th, 455th, 456th BSs	B-26
386th BG	Great Dunmow	552nd, 553rd, 554th, 555th BSs	B-26
387th BG	Chipping Ongar	556th, 557th, 558th, 559th BSs	B-26

US ATTACK BOMBER ARMAMENT

Type	Guns	Disposable
Douglas A-20G	9 x 12.7mm (0.5in)	1814kg (4000lb)
Douglas A-26B	18 12.7mm (0.5in)	2722kg (6000lb)
Douglas DB-7B	7 x 7.7mm (0.303in)	907kg (2000lb)
Martin B-26G	11 x 12.7mm (0.5in)	1814kg (4000lb)
North American B-25J	13 x 12.7mm (0.5in)	1814kg (4000lb)

The Ninth AAF grew rapidly during the winter of 1943/44 and the spring of 1944. Thus by the end of May, when its last combat group became operational, the Ninth AAF had grown to no fewer than 45 operational groups with some 5000 aircraft.

Together with its all-important ground support units, without which the air units could not have kept flying, the Ninth AAF thus had a personnel strength of more than 200,000, a total greater than that of the Eighth AAF strategic air force at the same time.

Specifications

Crew: 2–3

Powerplant: 2 x 1193kW (1600hp) Wright radial piston engines

Maximum speed: 546km/h (339mph)

Range: 1754km (1090 miles)

Service ceiling: 12,338m (27,200ft)

Dimensions: span 18.69m (61ft 4in); length 14.63m (48ft);

height 5.36m (17ft 7in)

Weight: 12,338kg (27,200lb) loaded

Armament: 6 x 12.7mm (0.5in) fixed forward-firing MGs in nose; 2 x 12.7mm (0.5in) MGs in power-operated dorsal turret; 1 x manually operated 12.7mm (0.5in) MG in ventral position; up to 1364kg (3000lb) of bombs

▲ **Douglas A-20G Havoc**

646th Bomb Squadron / 410th Bomb Group / US Ninth Army Air Force, Gosfield, 1944

The 410th Bomb Group (Light) comprised the 644th, 645th, 646th and 647th Bomb Squadrons, and with the 409th and 416th Bomb Groups (Light) comprised the IX Bomber Command's 97th Combat Bomb Wing (Medium).

Specifications

Crew: 2–3

Powerplant: 2 x 1193kW (1600hp) Wright radial piston engines

Maximum speed: 546km/h (339mph)

Range: 1754km (1090 miles)

Service ceiling: 12,338m (27,200ft)

Dimensions: span 18.69m (61ft 4in); length 14.63m (48ft);

height 5.36m (17ft 7in)

Weight: 12,338kg (27,200lb) loaded

Armament: 6 x 12.7mm (0.5in) fixed forward-firing MGs in nose; 2 x 12.7mm (0.5in) MGs in power-operated dorsal turret; 1 x manually operated 12.7mm (0.5in) MG in ventral position; up to 1364kg (3000lb) of bombs

▲ **Douglas A-20G Havoc**

646th Bomb Squadron / 410th Bomb Group / US Ninth Army Air Force, Gosfield, 1944

The A-20G was a two/three-seat attack bomber, and in addition to its three defensive machine guns (two in the dorsal turret and one in the ventral position) carried six 12.7mm (0.5in) fixed forward-firing machine guns in the nose, as well as 1361kg (3000lb) of bombs in the lower-fuselage weapons bay.

Specifications

Crew: 2–3

Powerplant: 2 x 1193kW (1600hp) Wright radial piston engines

Maximum speed: 546km/h (339mph)

Range: 1754km (1090 miles)

Service ceiling: 12,338m (27,200ft)

Dimensions: span 18.69m (61ft 4in);

length 14.63m (48ft); height 5.36m (17ft 7in)

Weight: 12,338kg (27,200lb) loaded

Armament: 6 x 12.7mm (0.5in) fixed forward-firing MGs in nose; 2 x 12.7mm (0.5in) MGs in power-operated dorsal turret; 1 x manually operated 12.7mm (0.5in) MG in ventral position; up to 1364kg (3000lb) of bombs

▲ **Douglas A-20G Havoc**

Unknown bomber group / US Ninth Army Air Force, UK, early 1944

With 2850 aircraft built, the A-20G was the most numerous of the A-20 variants, and was a development of the A-20D with a gun-carrying 'solid' nose for improved low-level attack capability.

Softening northern Europe
SPRING 1944

Before *Overlord* could be launched and hope to achieve success, the Allied air forces had to weaken the German defences and also cripple France's transport system, making the arrival of German reinforcements slow and laborious. Here the Ninth AAF came into its own.

THE FIRST OPERATIONAL task undertaken by the Ninth AAF lay within the context of the 'Pointblank' directive issued in January 1943 by the Allied leaders to fix the tasks to be undertaken by their air forces.

Degrading the *Luftwaffe*

Working in tandem with the Eighth AAF, the Ninth AAF was to attack German troop concentrations and military installations, as well as the transport system of northwest Europe, with the IX Bomber Command's aircraft, and to destroy the strength of the *Luftwaffe* on the ground and in the air.

The *Luftwaffe*'s degradation was to be undertaken with the aid of the excellent North American P-51 Musatangs of IX Fighter Command, which would decimate the German fighters that rose to tackle the US bombers.

Ground support role

The Ninth AAF also had to prepare for its major role, which would be the direct tactical support of the US ground forces in the coming invasion. As part of this preparation, the 357th Fighter Group and its P-51 Mustang fighters were transferred to the Eighth AAF in exchange for the 358th Fighter Group and its heavier Republic P-47 Thunderbolt fighter-bombers. The Thunderbolt was an excellent ground attack aircraft and ideal for the role.

The Ninth AAF's missions now grew steadily in pace and intensity, and came to involve attacks on railway marshalling yards; the rail lines themselves, together with the bridges and tunnels they traversed; canal and river barges; airfields; industrial facilities; military installations along and behind the entire north and north-west coasts of France; and other targets in France, Belgium and the Netherlands.

▲ **Douglas A-20G Havoc**

This A-20G served with a unit of the Ninth AAF, which recorded more than 100,000 combat hours in the run-up to D-Day on 6 June 1944.

Specifications

Crew: 7

Powerplant: 2 x 1432kW (1920hp) Pratt &
  Whitney radial piston engines

Maximum speed: 45km/h (282mph)

Range: 1851km (1150 miles)

Service ceiling: 6400m (21,000ft)

Dimensions: span 21.64m (71ft);

length 17.75m (58ft 3in);

height 6.55m (21ft 6in)

Weight: 16,783kg (37,000b) loaded

Armament: 7 x 12.7mm (0.5in) MGs: one in the
  nose, two in dorsal turret, two in tail turret
  and two waist guns; 1818kg (4000lb) of
  bombs

▲ **Martin B-26C Marauder**

557th Bomb Squadron / 387th Bomb Group / US Ninth Army Air Force,
Chipping Ongar, Essex, 1944

One of the four groups constituting the Ninth AAF's 98th Combat Bomb Wing
(Medium), the 387th Bomb Group (Medium) was itself composed of the 556th,
557th, 558th and 559th Bomb Squadrons, all based at Chipping Ongar.

Specifications

Crew: 7

Powerplant: 2 x 1491kW (2000hp) Pratt &
  Whitney radial piston engines

Maximum speed: 455km/h (283mph)

Range: 1770km (1100 miles)

Service ceiling: 6035m (19,800ft)

Dimensions: span 21.64m (71ft);

length 17.09m (56ft 1in);

height 6.20m (20ft 4in)

Weight: 17,327kg (38,200lb) loaded

Armament: 11 x 12.7mm (0.5in) MGs in fixed
  forward-firing, trainable nose and waist
  mounts, power-operated dorsal and tail
  turrets; up to 1813kg (4000lb) of bombs

▲ **Martin B-26C Marauder**

557th Bomb Squadron / 387th Bomb Group / US Ninth Army Air Force,
Chipping Ongar, 1944

Part of the 98th Combat Bomb Wing (Medium), the four squadrons of the 397th
Bomb Group flew the B-26C version of the Marauder medium bomber, itself
identical to the B-26B except for being built in Omaha rather than Baltimore.

Operation *Overlord*
JUNE 1944

The Allied invasion of Normandy was launched on 6 June 1944. Over the ships and men of the invasion forces there roamed the bombers, fighters and fighter-bombers of the Allied tactical air forces. Within them, the Eighth AAF had a major part to play in support of the US landings.

THE ALLIED TACTICAL air forces mustered 2434 fighters and fighter-bombers, together with some 700 light and medium bombers, for the Normandy campaign in the hands of the US Ninth AAF and British 2nd Tactical Air Force. This force first struck against the Germans during the preparatory campaign undertaken before D-Day. Some 60 days before the scheduled start of the invasion, the Allied air forces began their interdiction attacks against rail centres in a campaign that increased steadily in intensity right up to the eve of the invasion and was further enhanced in capability by the collaboration of the Allies' heavy bomber forces.

The campaign against the bridges of northern France began 46 days before D-Day. It was intended to ensure that the forthcoming land battlefield was isolated from the rest of German-occupied Europe by

cutting the bridges over the Seine river below Paris and of the Loire river below Orleans, as well as those over a number of other major and minor rivers and canals. In this task, fighter-bombers proved more effective than medium or heavy bombers, largely because their manoeuvrability allowed them to make pinpoint attacks in a fashion impossible for their larger counterparts with bombing runs in straight and level flight. The fighter-bombers also had the speed, firepower and agility to evade or dominate the *Luftwaffe*'s limited resources in France and the Low Countries. Though flak and fighters brought down some of the fighter-bombers, the loss rate was considerably less than it would have been with conventional attack by level bombers.

By 21 days before D-Day, the Allied air forces were attacking German airfields within a radius of 210km

Specifications

Crew: 7	length 17.09m (56ft 1in);
Powerplant: 2 x 1491kW (2000hp) Pratt &	height 6.20m (20ft 4in)
Whitney radial piston engines	Weight: 17,327kg (38,200lb) loaded
Maximum speed: 455km/h (283mph)	Armament: 11 x 12.7mm (0.5in) MGs in fixed
Range: 1770km (1100 miles)	forward-firing, trainable nose and waist
Service ceiling: 603500m (19,800ft)	mounts, power-operated dorsal and tail
Dimensions: span 21.64m (71ft);	turrets; up to 1813kg (4000lb) of bombs

▲ **Martin B-26G Marauder**

585th Bomb Squadron / 394th Bomb Group / US Ninth Army Air Force, Cambrai, France, 1944

Another element of the Ninth AAF's 98th Combat Bomb Wing (Medium), based at Boreham before D-Day, the 394th Bomb Group (Medium) moved its 584th, 585th, 586th and 587th Bomb Squadrons to France as soon as suitable airfields were available.

(130 miles) of the area of Normandy selected for the initial lodgement, and this effort was also sustained up to the eve of *Overlord*.

On D-Day itself, 6 June 1944, the IX Troop Carrier Command flew more than 2000 sorties to deliver the paratroopers and infantry-filled gliders of the US 82nd and 101st Airborne Divisions to Normandy. Other elements of the Ninth AAF, namely the IX Bomber Command and IX Tactical Air Command, carried out massive air attacks with B-25 Mitchell and B-26 Marauder medium bombers, and with P-47 Thunderbolt and P-51 Mustang fighter-bombers.

Air cover during the amphibious assault of the Allied forces on the beaches of France during the morning of 6 June was flown mostly by P-38 Lightnings, which encountered almost nothing in the way of German 'trade'. During the assault, a total of 171 British and US fighter squadrons undertook a variety of tasks in support of the invasion: 15 flew shipping cover, 54 provided cover over the assault beaches, 33 were committed to bomber escort and offensive fighter sweeps, 33 hit targets inland of the assault beaches and 36 provided direct air support to invading forces. Of greater importance by far, given that the German air opposition was almost non-existent, was the direct support provided to the forces landed in Normandy.

▲ **Bombing run**

A Martin B-26B of the 556th Bomb Squadron, 387th Bomb Group, releases a stick of bombs over a target in German-occupied Europe.

The French campaign

JUNE–SEPTEMBER 1944

The Ninth AAF helped the US First Army to consolidate its lodgement in Normandy, expand this by taking the Cotentin peninsula and then break out at St Lô and Avranches, and then supported the US Twelfth Army Group as it raced across France toward western Germany.

A S THE US TROOPS came ashore on 'Omaha' and 'Utah' Beaches, they discovered that the air and naval bombardments of the German coastal defences had failed to destroy a considerable portion of those defences. This was especially evident on 'Omaha' Beach, where the US forces suffered heavy casualties and were badly delayed.

ORGANIZATION

9th Bomb Division
September 1944

97th Bomb Wing (three medium bomber groups with 12 sqns)	98th Bomb Wing (four medium bomber groups with 16 sqns)	99th Bomb Wing (four medium bomber groups with 16 sqns)

Invasion support

Despite a series of attacks by heavy and medium bombers in the early hours of 6 June, the invading troops were checked on the beach itself. The air commanders had predicted that the air and naval bombardments would not wholly destroy the German defensive positions, but the army commanders had believed otherwise and were now sadly disabused. It was only the success of fighter-

bombers in later battlefield operations that then restored the confidence of army commanders in the efficacy of air support.

Throughout the advance from the Normandy lodgement, it was the fighter-bomber that emerged as being more useful in the ground-attack role than the heavy or even the medium bomber. With the lodgement secure, the Ninth AAF's tactical air units

▲ **Martin B-26 Marauders**
The 'PN' codes identify these B-26B medium bombers as aircraft of the 449th Bomb Squadron, 322nd Bomb Group. This latter was the first B-26 group to be assigned to the European theatre.

then provided the air support for the US forces' break-out from the beach-head.

Contact cars

The most significant development in terms of tactical air support during the Normandy campaign was the establishment of a system of close liaison between air and armoured forces. In the Italian campaign, the British had initiated the use of 'contact cars' to operate as mobile air/surface control posts, and continued this successful practice in Normandy. Thus tactical air units always knew the exact position of the relevant British and German forces. The contact cars worked with reconnaissance aircraft, reducing the time required to summon air support. Brigadier-General Quesada developed a comparable system for the US forces in Normandy.

Shortly before the break out from St Lô to Avranches, Quesada felt that General Omar N. Bradley was unwilling to concentrate his armoured strength in the face of the Germans' strong defences. He therefore offered Bradley potent air support for an armoured concentration, from dawn to dusk, if he was provided with an armoured vehicle in which the relevant radio equipment and an air force pilot could be located for real-time communication with the fighter-bombers, which would be loitering overhead. Bradley agreed, and an initial two M4 Sherman medium tanks were modified. The concept worked

excellently, and immediately became a standard feature of the operations of the US First Army, and then of the US Twelfth Army Group.

By early in August 1944, most of the Ninth AAF's fighter and bomber groups had been moved to bases in France and assigned to support of the new US Twelfth Army Group. These groups were then assigned to tactical air commands which were allocated to specific armies: Brigadier-General Richard E. Nugent's XXIX Tactical Air Command supported the US Ninth Army in the north, Major-General Quesada's IX Tactical Air Command supported the US First Army in the centre, and Major-General Weyland's XIX TAC supported the US Third Army in the south.

Air cover over the US-controlled areas on the continent was provided by the new IX Air Defense Command, and bomber support by Major-General Anderson's 9th Bomb Division with three wings of 45 squadrons. As the land campaign moved west, the groups of the Ninth AAF kept pace with it in a succession of moves within France, then the Low Countries and finally western Germany. This ensured that the tactical air groups were always within range and, perhaps more importantly, could respond with minimum reaction time to emergencies.

▲ **Martin B-26B Marauder**

598th Bomb Squadron / 397th Bomb Group (Medium) / US Ninth Army Air Force, Dreux, France, September 944

Based at Rivenhall before D-Day but moving to France when this became feasible, the 397th Bomb Group was one of the 98th Combat Bomb Wing (Medium)'s four groups, and consisted of the 596th, 597th, 598th and 599th Bomb Squadrons.

Specifications

Crew: 7	length 17.75m (58ft 3in);
Powerplant: 2 x 1432kW (1920hp) Pratt &	height 6.55m (21ft 6in)
Whitney radial piston engines	Weight: 16,783kg (37,000b) loaded
Maximum speed: 453km/h (282mph)	Armament: 7 x 12.7mm (0.5in) MGs: one in the
Range: 1851km (1150 miles)	nose, two in dorsal turret, two in tail turret
Service ceiling: 6400m (21,000ft)	and two waist guns; 1818kg (4000lb) of
Dimensions: span 21.64m (71ft);	bombs

Germany defeated

JANUARY–MAY 1945

The beginning of 1945 found the Germans at the end of their tether after their offensive in the 'Battle of the Bulge' had been defeated. The warplanes of the Ninth AAF kept pounding at German tactical targets, and the US ground forces drove the Germans steadily back to the east.

DURING OPERATION *Dragoon*, the Franco-American invasion of southern France in August 1944, two fighter groups of the Ninth AAF were transferred to Major-General Ralph Royce's US/Free French 1st Tactical Air Force (Provisional), which had been created specifically to provide air support for the invasion force's advance to the north along the line of the Rhone river.

Battle of the Bulge

In the following month, as part of the intertwined but failed Operations Market and Garden to secure a crossing of the lower Rhine in the area of Arnhem in the Netherlands, the Ninth AAF transferred the whole of its IX Troop Carrier Command (14 groups with C-47 transports) to the Allied First Airborne Army in September 1944.

In December 1944 and January 1945, the fighters and bombers of the Ninth AAF played a decisive part in defeating the German offensive in the 'Battle of the Bulge': the Germans had timed the start of the offensive for adverse weather that would keep the Allied air forces on the ground, but fell behind schedule and were then caught and crushed with the aid of Allied air power as soon as the weather cleared sufficiently for the bombers and fighter-bombers to carry out ground attacks.

In overall terms, its support for the US Twelfth Army Group as this drove across France and through Luxembourg and Belgium toward the Netherlands and western Germany, had been the heyday of the Ninth AAF's existence in terms of its capabilities and the support provided. There was much very hard fighting on the ground, but the Ninth AAF was on

Specifications

Crew: 7	length 17.09m (56ft 1in);
Powerplant: 2 x 1491kW (2000hp) Pratt &	height 6.20m (20ft 4in)
Whitney radial piston engines	Weight: 17,327kg (38,200lb) loaded
Maximum speed: 455km/h (283mph)	Armament: 11 x 12.7mm (0.5in) MGs in fixed
Range: 1770km (1100 miles)	forward-firing, trainable nose and waist
Service ceiling: 6035m (19,800ft)	mounts, power-operated dorsal and tail
Dimensions: span 21.64m (71ft);	turrets; up to 1813kg (4000lb) of bombs

▲ **Martin B-26G Marauder**

456th Bomb Squadron / 323rd Bomb Group (Medium) / US Ninth Army Air Force, Laon, France, late 1944

Another element of the four-group 98th Combat Bomb Wing (Medium), and based at Horham before D-Day, the 323rd Bomb Group (Medium) comprised the 453rd, 454th, 455th and 456th Bomb Squadrons all flying in the medium bomber role.

hand to provide accurate and timely air support wherever the terrain permitted this and the weather made flying possible.

Glider operations

During the spring of 1945, the troop carrier groups of the Ninth AAF were instrumental in the delivery of paratrooper and glider units during the Allies' Operation *Varsity* assault crossing of the Rhine river on 24 March 1945: this was the single largest airborne operation in history, and its worst aspect was the 28 per cent losses suffered by the Curtiss C-49 Commando transports making their debut in Europe.

The Ninth AAF continued to provide its now-traditional level of tactical support to the ground forces of the US Army right to the end of the European war in May 1945, but was then cut back by rapid demobilization. Most personnel were returned to the USA and their units inactivated. Others were assigned to the new US Air Forces in Europe (USAFE) command on ex-*Luftwaffe* bases for occupation duties. Some transport units were relocated to France. Finally, the Ninth AAF was inactivated at the headquarters of the USAFE on 2 December 1945.

▲ **Bombing run**

This Martin B-26B-50-MA served with the 558th Bomb Squadron, flying 29 missions with the 'Mighty Eighth', before transferring to the Ninth Air Force in August 1944.

Specifications

Crew: 3

Powerplant: 2 x 1491kW (2000hp) Pratt & Whitney radial piston engines

Maximum speed: 600km/h (373mph)

Range: 2253km (1400 miles)

Service ceiling: 6735m (22,100ft)

Dimensions: span 21.34m (70ft);

length 15.62m (51ft 3in);

height 5.56m (18ft 3in)

Weight: 15,876kg (35,000lb) loaded

Armament: 6 x 12.7mm (0.5in) MGs: two each in nose, dorsal and ventral positions; up to 1814kg (4000lb) of bombs

▲ **Douglas A-26B Invader**

552nd Bomb Squadron / 386th Bomb Group / US Ninth Army Air Force, Beaumont sur Oise, France, April 1945

Part of the 99th Combat Bomb Wing (Medium), the 386th Bomb Group (552nd, 553rd, 554th and 555th Bomb Squadrons) had been based at Great Dunmow before D-Day, but switched from the B-26 to the A-26 after arriving in Europe.

US Air Forces in North Africa and the Mediterranean
1942–45

The North African and Italian campaigns of World War II were seen by the Americans largely as a 'sideshow', since they did not commit the main weight of the US forces directly against the primary enemy, Germany. Even so, three numbered air forces operated in this theatre.

THE ALLIED CAMPAIGNS in North Africa and Italy were supported by three numbered air forces: the Ninth, Twelfth and Fifteenth AAFs. The first was essentially a tactical air force, the second was a more evenly balanced formation, and the third was dedicated almost exclusively to the strategic role. This reflected the fact that as World War II continued, the offensive air forces of the USAAF were progressively classified as strategic or tactical.

The former's mission was to attack the enemy's war effort (in essence, weapon manufacture, supplies of essential raw materials and fuel, and transportation) deep behind the front. The mission of the latter was to support the ground forces (in or immediately behind the frontline) with objectives normally chosen through a process of cooperation with the field forces. In Europe, the Eighth AAF was the first of the

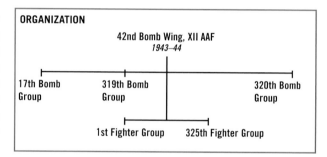

ORGANIZATION

42nd Bomb Wing, XII AAF
1943–44

17th Bomb Group — 319th Bomb Group — 320th Bomb Group

1st Fighter Group — 325th Fighter Group

USAAF's strategic air forces, with a mission to pave the way for an invasion of continental Europe from the UK. The Eighth AAF originally included a number of tactical units, but many of these were transferred to the Twelfth AAF, which was formed in the UK during the autumn of 1942 as a tactical air force to provide air support for the Allied invasion

▲ **North American B-25A Mitchell**

17th Bomb Group (Medium) / USAAF, McChord Field, 1942

The 17th Bomb Group was the first USAAF unit to receive the new B-25 medium bomber (24 built). Production of the following B-25A, with self-sealing fuel tanks, totalled only 40 aircraft.

Specifications

Crew: 5

Powerplant: 2 x 1268kW (1700hp)

Maximum speed: 483km/h (300mph)

Range: 3219km (2000 miles)

Service ceiling: 7163m (23,500ft)

Dimensions: span 20.7m (68ft);

length 16.2m (53ft); height 0m (0ft)

Weight: 14,061kg (31,000lb) loaded

Armament: 1 x 7.6mm (0.3in) nose-mounted MG; 4 x 12.7mm (0.5in) MGs (pair in top and pair in bottom turret); 1361kg (3000lb) of bombs of French north-west Africa in November of the same year.

The USAAF had begun planning for the development of a significant US air power capability in the Middle East as early as January 1942 in response to a request from the British. The first unit to arrive was designated as HALPRO and, under command of Colonel Harry A. Halverson, comprised 23 Consolidated B-24D Liberator four-engined heavy bombers with carefully selected crews.

HALPRO raids

On 12 June 1942, 13 of the the HALPRO B-24s took off from Fayid, Egypt to bomb the oil fields at Ploiesti in Romania. Only 12 aircraft actually completed the the attack at dawn. Four of the 13 landed at the Iraqi base designated for the task, three landed at other Iraqi airfields, two landed in Syria, and four were interned in Turkey. Though damage to the target was negligible, the raid was significant because it was the first USAAF combat mission in the North African and European theatres of operations in World War II.

On 15 June, seven HALPRO aircraft attacked units of the Italian fleet attempting to intercept a convoy from Alexandria to Malta. The Liberators achieved at least one direct hit on the battleship *Littorio*, but the convoy did not reach Malta because of the threat of the Italian warships.

On 17 June, HALPRO became part of the new US Army Forces in the Middle East, commanded by Major-General Russell L. Maxwell. The new command comprised HALPRO and a detachment of Boeing B-17Ds from the 7th Bomb Group at Allahabad in India under the command of Major-General Lewis H. Brereton.

The B-17Ds had been assigned to the China-Burma-India Theatre to attack targets in Japan from airfields in China. But the British loss of Burma allowed the Japanese to cut the Burma Road, and this prevented the logistical support of the bombers, which were therefore diverted to India.

To Egypt

On 2 July 1942, additional B-17Es from the 7th Bomb Group arrived from India at Lydda, Palestine, and on 20 July the B-24s and B-17s were formed into the 1st Provisional Group in Cairo. Soon after this, the USAAF deployed to this theatre the Curtiss P-40F single-engined fighter-bombers of the 57th Fighter Group, the North American B-25C twin-engined medium bombers of the 12th Bombardment Group (Medium), and the B-24D four-engined bombers of the 98th Bombardment Group (Heavy), together with a number of Douglas C-47 Skytrain twin-engined transport aircraft, to bases in Egypt and Palestine. US Air Forces in the Middle East (USAFIME) units took part in the British victory at

Specifications	
Crew: 5	length 16.2m (53ft); height 0m (0ft)
Powerplant: 2 x 1268kW (1700hp)	Weight: 14,061kg (31,000lb) loaded
Maximum speed: 483km/h (300mph)	Armament: 1 x 7.6mm (0.3in) nose-mounted
Range: 3219km (2000 miles)	MG; 4 x 12.7mm (0.5in) MGs (pair in top and
Service ceiling: 7163m (23,500ft)	pair in bottom turret); 1361kg (3000lb) of
Dimensions: span 20.7m (68ft);	bombs

▲ **North American B-25A Mitchell**

34th Bomb Squadron / 17th Bomb Group (Medium), Pendleton, Oregon, 1942
The 17th Bomb Group was operational with the US Twelfth AAF before the end of December 1941, the month in which the United States entered World War II. Within a year, the Twelfth AAF would be in action in North Africa.

the second battle of El Alamein in November 1942, and its operations demonstrated the importance of having in this theatre a heavy bomber capability as well as tactical air assets. On 12 November 1942, the USAFIME was terminated and succeeded by the US Ninth Air Force, under the command of Lieutenant-General Frank M. Andrews, with triple tactical tasks: winning air superiority, denying the Axis forces the ability to resupply or make good their losses, and the provisiong of close air support for the Allied forces in North Africa.

Ninth AAF structure

At this time, the Ninth AAF North Africa comprised the IX Bomber Command, IX Fighter Command and 316th Troop Carrier Group. The IX Bomber Command controlled the 12th Bomb Group (Medium) with B-25C squadrons detached to the RAF, 98th Bomb Group (Heavy) with B-24Ds, 340th Bomb Group (Medium) with B-25Cs, and 376th Bomb Group (Heavy) with B-24Ds (previously the 1st Provisional Group USAAF).

The IX Fighter Command controlled the 57th Fighter Group with squadrons detached to RAF, 79th Fighter Group and 324th Fighter Group: all of these groups had P-40F fighter-bombers. By the end of 1942, some 370 aircraft had reached the Ninth Air Force. While the great majority were the B-24, B-25 and P-40 aircraft already mentioned, there were also more than 50 C-47 twin-engined transports, making it possible to create an effective local air transport service.

▲ Consolidated B-24 Liberator

The B-24D *Teggie Ann* kicks up the dust of a Libyan base while preparing for a mission. These aircraft were finished in a light shade known as desert pink.

First Ploiesti raid
JUNE 1942

The HALPRO raid on the Romanian oil facilities at Ploiesti was the first attack by bombers of the USAAF against a target in continental Europe. The raid was small and ineffective, but showed that Ploiesti was within range of North African bases, and that the USAAF meant business.

COMMANDED BY Colonel Harry A. Halverson, CHALPRO (Halverson Project no. 63) was a provisional unit equipped with 23 examples of the new Consolidated B-24D Liberator four-engined heavy bomber, a type already making a good name for itself as a long-range bomber as a result of the considerable efficiency of its high-aspect-ratio wing. This range capability suggested the initial deployment of the B-24D for operations against Japan. HALPRO therefore left its base in Florida to reach the Tenth AAF in Burma. From here, it was proposed that the aircraft should be based around Chengtu in the province of Szechwan in China, and from a forward base at Chekiang launch a raid or raids on Tokyo, the capital of Japan.

However, after it had reached Khartoum in Sudan, HALPRO was instructed to wait since the April 1942 'Doolittle raid' on Japanese targets, undertaken by B-25 Mitchell bombers launched from a US Navy aircraft carrier, had persuaded the Japanese that the aircraft must be operating from China, and they therefore launched an offensive toward Chekiang.

Specifications

Crew: 10

Powerplant: 4 x 895kW (1200hp) Pratt & Whitney Twin wasp radial piston engines

Maximum speed: 467km/h (290mph)

Range: 5955km (3700 miles)

Service ceiling: 8535m (28000ft)

Dimensions: span 33.53m (110ft);

length 20.47m (67ft 2in); height 5.49m (18ft)

Weight: 25,401kg (56,000lb) loaded

Armament: 2 x 12.7mm (0.5in) Browning trainable MGs in nose, dorsal, ventral 'ball' and tail turrets, and one each in beam positions; up to 5806kg (12,800lb) of bombs

▲ Consolidated B-24D Liberator

98th Bomb Group / IX Bomber Command / USAAF, Benghazi, Libya, 1943

On 20 February 1943, this aircraft became lost and landed inadvertently on the Italian airfield at Pachino in Sicily, where it was captured after an earlier attack on Naples.

Specifications

Crew: 10

Powerplant: 4 x 895kW (1200hp) Pratt & Whitney Twin wasp radial piston engines

Maximum speed: 467km/h (290mph)

Range: 5955km (3700 miles)

Service ceiling: 8535m (28000ft)

Dimensions: span 33.53m (110ft);

length 20.47m (67ft 2in); height 5.49m (18ft)

Weight: 25,401kg (56,000lb) loaded

Armament: 2 x 12.7mm (0.5in) Browning trainable MGs in nose, dorsal, ventral 'ball' and tail turrets, and one each in beam positions; up to 5806kg (12,800lb) of bombs

▲ Consolidated B-24D Liberator

376th Bomb Group / 47th Bomb Wing / US Fifteenth AAF, Libya, 1943

This aeroplane, wearing a desert-pink finish under its mix of US and British national markings, was on the strength of the 'Liberandos', or 376th Bomb Group, during their attack of 1 August 1943 on the Romanian oil fields at Ploiesti.

HALPRO was then ordered to proceed to Fayid near the Great Bitter Lake in Egypt, and prepare for a raid on Ploiesti before flying south-east to a base in British Iraq, a distance of some 4185km (2600 miles). There were no accurate maps, the raid would be flown at night, and the crews were wholly inexperienced in combat. They were also flying aircraft of a variant that had not been blooded.

Limited success

Thirteen aircraft took off late in the night of 11/ 12 June, and 12 of these reached the vicinity of the target, where they bombed without success but also without loss over the target before departing to a number of safe locations. Eight bombs fell into the Black Sea, two on Constanza, six on Ploiesti, six on Teisani and several on Ciofliceni. In total, three people were killed.

There was no publicity of the type that had followed the 'Doolittle raid', but the USAAF had entered combat over Europe in a raid that confirmed its ability to strike at distant targets.

US Ninth Army Air Force: Mediterranean operations 1942–45

The Ninth AAF cut its operational teeth in North Africa in support of the British Eighth Army, and moved steadily west with the advance to meet forces, including the new Twelfth AAF, moving from the west. The Allied junction in Tunisia spelled the end for the Axis forces in North Africa.

THE FIGHTERS OF THE Ninth Army Air Force supported the westward drive of the British Eighth Army across Egypt and Libya, with bomber escort as well as ground-attack and dive-bombing missions against Axis airfields, lines of communication and troop concentrations. The Ninth AAF also attacked shipping and harbour installations in North Africa, Sicily, Italy, Crete and Greece as part of the Allied effort to cut the supply lines used by the Axis powers to nourish their forces in North Africa.

In February 1943, after the Axis forces had been compressed into Tunisia, the Germans took the offensive and pushed through the Kasserine Pass before being stopped. Units of both the US Ninth and Twelfth AAFs were involved in this part of the campaign, in which the Allies checked the Kasserine Pass and other Axis thrusts before driving the surviving German and Italian forces back into a coastal lodgement around Bizerta and Tunis. Here the last Axis forces surrendered in May.

The victory not only ended the North African campaign, but gave the Allies the use of Tunisia as the springboard from which to launch an amphibious

ORGANIZATION

US 9th AAF
Spring 1943

| IX Bomber Command (two heavy & two medium bomb groups) | IX Fighter Command (three fighter groups) | 316th Troop Carrier Group |

IX BOMBER COMMAND UNITS		
Unit	Type	Aircraft type
12th Bomb Group	Medium	B-25C
98th Bomb Group	Heavy	B-24D
340th Bomb Group	Medium	B-25C
376h Bomb Group	Heavy	B-24D
57th Fighter Group	Fighter-bomber	P-40F
79th Fighter Group	Fighter-bomber	P-40F
324th Fighter Group	Fighter-bomber	P-40F

descent on Sicily as the prelude to an assault on Italy proper. Following the Allied victory in Tunisia, Ninth AAF groups attacked airfields and rail facilities in Sicily and Italy.

Transport elements of the Ninth AAF were involved in Operation *Husky*, the Allied amphibious invasion of Sicily, delivering paratroopers and flying reinforcements to the ground forces. The heavy bomber elements also participated in the *Tidal Wave* low-level attack on the oil refineries at Ploiesti on 1 August 1943. In August and September 1943, Ninth AAF units in North Africa were transferred to the Twelfth AAF as preparations were made for the reconstitution of the Ninth AAF in the UK for service in and after the *Overlord* invasion of Normandy. The Ninth AAF was inactivated in Egypt on 16 October 1943.

In mid-1942, a series of Allied planning meetings was held to develop an overall strategy for the prosecution of the war in North Africa against Germany and Italy, whose forces held the central coastal part of North Africa, with the Vichy French colonial forces holding the portion farther to the west and round onto the Atlantic coast of French Morocco south-west of the Strait of Gibraltar.

The first step in this process was to be Operation *Torch,* the landing of the Allied First Army in French north-west Africa during November 1942, to take French North Africa and then advance east to meet the British Eight Army advancing from the east.

Specifications

Crew: 5	length 16.2m (53ft); height 0m (0ft)
Powerplant: 2 x 1268kW (1700hp)	Weight: 18,960kg (41,800lb) loaded
Maximum speed: 457km/h (284mph)	Armament: 2 x 12.7mm (0.5in) nose-mounted
Range: 3219km (2000 miles)	MGs; 4 x 12.7mm (0.5in) MGs (pair in top
Service ceiling: 7163m (23,500ft)	and pair in bottom turret); 2359kg (5200lb)
Dimensions: span 20.7m (68ft);	of bombs

▲ **North American B-25C Mitchell**

487th Bomb Squadron / 340th Bomb Group / USAAF, Catania, Sicily, September 1943

Wearing a mix of USAAF and RAF markings, the latter exemplified by the fin flashes, this aeroplane has desert-sand upper surfaces and sky-blue under surfaces.

Specifications

Crew: 5	length 16.2m (53ft); height 0m (0ft)
Powerplant: 2 x 1268kW (1700hp)	Weight: 18,960kg (41,800lb) loaded
Maximum speed: 457km/h (284mph)	Armament: 2 x 12.7mm (0.5in) nose-mounted
Range: 3219km (2000 miles)	MGs; 4 x 12.7mm (0.5in) MGs (pair in top
Service ceiling: 7163m (23,500ft)	and pair in bottom turret); 2359kg (5200lb)
Dimensions: span 20.7m (68ft);	of bombs

▲ **North American B-25C Mitchell**

81st Bomb Squadron / 12th Bomb Group / USAAF, Gerbini, Sicily, August 1943

By this time, the Allies had taken Sicily and were quickly developing its facilities, and especially its air bases and airfields, to accommodate the tactical warplanes that would be required for the September 1943 invasion of the Italian mainland at Salerno, and the operations which would follow that.

US Twelfth Army Air Force
1942–45

Because Operation *Torch* required a new air organization to provide enough manpower and equipment, plans for the creation and outfitting of a new Twelfth AAF were developed alongside the preparations for the invasion proper and subsequent campaign.

THE TWELFTH AAF was activated on 20 August 1942 at Bolling air base in Maryland, and on 23 September 1942 Brigadier-General James 'Jimmy' Doolittle formally assumed command of the Twelfth AAF with Colonel Hoyt S. Vandenberg as his chief of staff. Barely four months after it had been conceived, the Twelfth AAF was able to make its first contributions to World War II, for when the North African invasion was launched on 8 November 1942, the Twelfth AAF was ready to undertake the role intended for it by providing tactical air support for the Allied First Army as it moved to link with the British Eighth Army and encompass the overwhelming defeat of the Axis forces in North Africa by May 1943.

XII Bomber Command reactivated

The XII Bomber Command was activated at MacDill air base in Florida on 13 March, was assigned to the Twelfth AAF in August and transferred, without personnel and equipment, to High Wycombe in England, where it was re-established. It moved to Tafaraoui in Algeria on 22 November 1942 in the immediate aftermath of the Torch landings in

ORGANIZATION

US Twelfth AAF
Summer 1944

| XII Bomber Command (four bomb wings) | XII Tactical Air Command (one heavy bomber, two medium bomber & one fighter wings) | XXII Fighter Command (three fighter wings) |

5TH BOMB WING, TWELFTH AAF (1943–44)		
Unit	Type	Aircraft type
2nd Bomb Group	Heavy bomber	B-17
47th Bomb Group	Attack bomber	A-20 & A-26
97th Bomb Group	Heavy bomber	B-17
98th Bomb Group	Heavy bomber	B-24
99th Bomb Group	Heavy bomber	B-17
301st Bomb Group	Heavy bomber	B-17
376th Bomb Group	Heavy bomber	B-24
463rd Bomb Group	Heavy bomber	B-17
483rd Bomb Group	Heavy bomber	B-17
1st Fighter Group	Fighter	P-38
14th Fighter Group	Fighter	P-38
82nd Fighter Group	Fighter	P-38
325th Fighter Group	Fighter	P-38
68th Recce Group	Reconnaissance	varied

▲ **North American B-25 Mitchells**
A section of B-25 Mitchells gets airborne from Sousse in Tunisia, some time late in 1943, for a mission to Italy.

North Africa. The Twelfth AAF later saw large-scale action over Sicily, Italy and southern France in support of the US Fifth and Seventh Armies and their allies. The Twelfth AAF acquired an excellent reputation, and by VE-Day in May 1945 had flown some 430,680 sorties, claimed the destruction of 2857 German and Italian aircraft, and lost 2667 of its own aircraft.

With hostilities over, the Twelfth AAF was inactivated at Florence, in northern Italy, on 31 August 1945. The Twelfth AAF had incorporated three subordinate formations, namely the XII Bomber Command, XII Tactical Air Command (originally XII Air Support Command) and XXII Tactical Air Command.

The XII Bomber Command was operational in the Mediterranean theatre until 1 November 1943, when most of its manpower was withdrawn, but it then received additional personnel in January 1944 and was operational once more to 1 March 1944 before

being inactivated in Corsica on 10 June 1944. The XII Tactical Air Command was initially planned as the XII Ground Air Support Command on 10 September 1942, activated on 17 September, assigned to the Twelfth AAF as the XII Air Support Command, and redesignated as the XII Tactical Air Command in April 1944.

The command moved to French Morocco on 9 November 1942 as part of the Torch campaign, and

Specifications

Crew: 5	length 16.2m (53ft); height 0m (0ft)
Powerplant: 2 x 1268kW (1700hp)	Weight: 18,960kg (41,800lb) loaded
Maximum speed: 457km/h (284mph)	Armament: 2 x 12.7mm (0.5in) nose-mounted
Range: 3219km (2000 miles)	MGs; 4 x 12.7mm (0.5in) MGs (pair in top
Service ceiling: 7163m (23,500ft)	and pair in bottom turret); 2359kg (5200lb)
Dimensions: span 20.7m (68ft);	of bombs

▲ **North American B-25C Mitchell**

488th Bomb Squadron / 340th Bomb Group / US Twelfth AAF, Sfax, Tunisia, April 1943

With a disruptive olive-drab pattern over the original desert sand finish, this B-25C has the yellow ring round the national markings (used in North Africa up to June 1943) and British fin flashes. The dorsal turret was adopted on the B-25B.

▲ **Douglas A-20B Havoc**

84th Bomb Squadron / 47th Bomb Group / US Twelfth AAF, Mediouna, Morocco, December 1942

The A-20B light attack bomber was the USAAF's counterpart of the DB-7A delivered by Douglas to the French Air Force. The aeroplane could carry 1179kg (2600lb) of bombs internally, and had two fixed forward-firing machine guns.

Specifications

Crew: 2–3	Weight: 9414kg (20,710lb) loaded
Powerplant: 2 x 1192kW (1600hp) Wright radials	Armament: 2 x 12.7mm (0.5in) forward-firing
Maximum speed: 563km/h (350mph)	MGs in forward fuselage; 1 x 12.7mm (0.5in)
Range: 3701km (2300 miles)	MG in flexible dorsal position; 1 x 7.62mm
Service ceiling: 8687m (28,500ft)	(0.3in) MG in ventral tunnel; 2 x rearward-
Dimensions: span 18.69m (61ft 4in);	firing 7.62mm (0.3in) MGs in engine nacelles;
length 14.63m (48ft); height 5.51m (18ft 1in)	1179kg (2600lb) bombs

served operationally in the Mediterranean and European theatres until May 1945. It then remained in Europe as part of the US Air Forces in Europe until inactivated at Bad Kissingen in Germany on 10 November 1947.

The XXII Tactical Air Command was activated on 5 March 1942, and redesignated as the XII Fighter Command in May 1942 before becoming the XXII Tactical Air Command in November 1944. The command was assigned to the Twelfth AAF during August 1942 and moved to Wattisham in England during September before reaching Tafaraoui in Algeria on 8 November 1942. The command was operational in the Mediterranean until the end of the war, and was inactivated at Pomigliano in Italy on 4 October 1945.

57TH BOMB WING, TWELFTH AAF (1944)		
Unit	Type	Aircraft type
12th Bomb Group	Medium bomber	B-25
310th Bomb Group	Medium bomber	B-25
319th Bomb Group	Medium bomber	B-25
321st Bomb Group	Medium bomber	B-25
340th Bomb Group	Medium bomber	B-25
47th Bomb Group	Attack bomber	A-20 & A-26
57th Fighter Group	Fighter-bomber	P-40
79th Fighter Group	Fighter-bomber	P-40

Specifications

Crew: 7

Powerplant: 2 x 1400kW (1900hp) Pratt & Whitney R-2800-43 radial engines

Maximum speed: 4600km/h (287mph)

Range: 4590km (2850 miles)

Service ceiling: 6400m (21,000ft)

Dimensions: span 21.65m (71ft); length 17.8m (58ft 3in); height 6.55m (21ft 6in)

Weight: 17,000kg (37,000lb) loaded

Armament: 12 x 12.7mm (0.5in) Colt-Browning MGs; 1800kg (4000lb) bomb load

▲ **Martin B-26B Marauder**

444th Bomb Squadron / 320th Bomb Group / US Twelfth Army Air Force, Decimomannu, Sardinia, 1945

Operating primarily over northern Italy, the aircraft of the 444th Bomb Squadron all gained shark's mouth markings on the forward fuselage during the last months of the war.

▲ **Douglas A-20 Havoc light attack bombers**

These A-20Bs were flown by the 84th Bomb Squadron, 47th Bomb Group, from the base at Mediouna, Morocco, during December 1942. Large patches of brown were applied over the original olive-drab finish to create a makeshift but nonetheless effective North African camouflage.

US Fifteenth Army Air Force
1943–45

The Fifteenth AAF was established on 1 November 1943 in Tunis. It was conceived specifically as a strategic rather than tactical air force.

THE FIFTEENTH AAF began combat operations on 2 November, the day after its establishment, under the command of Major-General Doolittle, whose previous command, the Twelfth AAF, was now led by Major-General Carl Spaatz and, from 21 December of the same year, Major-General John K. Cannon.

The Fifteenth AAF was not an altogether new formation, for it drew its initial forces from the IX Bomber Command when the Ninth AAF was relocating to the UK to become a tactical air force for north-west European operations, and through a diversion of other bomb groups that had originally been destined for service with the Eighth AAF in England.

The Fifteenth AAF moved to Bari in south-eastern Italy on 1 December 1943, and operated from a growing number of bases in this flat region in raids over German-held northern Italy, Germany, Austria, Hungary and the Balkans.

European remit

The Fifteenth AAF grew quickly and strongly in power and, with the Eighth AAF and RAF Bomber Command, became one of the primary weapons in the Allied strategic air offensive against German targets in occupied Europe and Germany. The Fifteenth AAF eventually grew to six Boeing B-17 and 15 Consolidated B-24 groups, and it lost some 2110 of its aircraft, while its seven fighter groups claimed 1836 German aircraft destroyed. The Fifteenth AAF was inactivated in Italy on 15 September 1945.

▲ Consolidated B-24J Liberator

449th Bomb Group / US Fifteenth Army Air Force, Mediterranean Theatre, late 1944

With its wing characterized by a high aspect ratio, the B-24 was aerodynamically efficient, and its primary advantage over the B-17 was therefore greater range.

Specifications

Crew: 10

Powerplant: 4 x 895kW (1200hp) Pratt & Whitney Twin wasp radial piston engines

Maximum speed: 467km/h (290mph)

Range: 3380km (2100 miles)

Service ceiling: 8535m (28,000ft)

Dimensions: span 33.53m (110ft); length 20.47m (67ft 2in); height 5.49m (18ft)

Weight: 32,296kg (71,200lb) loaded

Armament: 2 x 12.7mm (0.5in) Browning trainable MGs in nose, dorsal, ventral 'ball' and tail turrets, and one MG in each beam position; up to 5806kg (12,800lb) of bombs

US maritime operations
1941–45

Before World War II, the maritime defence of the United States had been largely a prerogative of the US Army Air Corps, which commissioned aircraft such as the Boeing B-17 for this purpose. In World War II, the primary responsibility switched steadily to US naval aviation.

JUST FOUR DAYS after Germany's invasion of Poland started World War II, President Franklin D. Roosevelt declared the neutrality of the USA, and also that nation's intention of ensuring this neutrality, by force if necessary.

Roosevelt was, in fact, strongly pro-British, and the US military of the period was poorly prepared for real military operations. The US Navy was ordered to establish a Neutrality Patrol to 555km (345 miles) off the US east coast, running south along the boundary of the Caribbean. The entry of any foreign warship entering the zone was to be reported immediately, and a force, more imposing on paper than in reality, was available to enforce the patrol: four battleships, five cruisers, some 40 destroyers and two aircraft carriers.

In fact, most of the required patrol work fell on the shoulders of five flying boat squadrons supported by four tenders. In all, 36 Consolidated PBY and 18 older Consolidated P2Y flying boats were based at Newport, Rhode Island; Norfolk, Virginia; and in Cuba and Puerto Rico. Detachments were also sent to Charleston, South Carolina, and Key West, Florida. In 1940, two patrol squadrons were commissioned at Norfolk.

Convoy protection

A support organization was established in March 1941 as the Support Force Atlantic Fleet destroyers and a patrol wing of five squadrons. Directed to prepare for operations in northern waters, the patrol crews practised convoy escort and anti-submarine warfare. The intent was to prevent German commerce raiders and U-boats from severing the maritime route linking the USA and UK. Elements of Patrol Squadron 52 (VP-52) arrived at Argentia in Newfoundland during mid May 1941. Only six days after their arrival, the news that the German

▲ Consolidated LB-30B

Unknown squadron / USAAF, Bolling Field, 1941

This was an aeroplane ordered by the British as a night bomber but taken over by the USAAF before delivery to the UK and adapted as a transport. The RAF roundels were overpainted but just evident on the fuselage sides, and large US flags were painted on each side of the nose and above the fuselage to indicate neutrality.

Specifications

Crew: 10	Service ceiling: 8535m (28000ft)
Powerplant: 4 x 895kW (1200hp) Pratt &	Dimensions: span 33.53m (110ft);
Whitney Twin wasp radial piston engines	length 20.47m (67ft 2in); height 5.49m (18ft)
Maximum speed: 467km/h (290mph)	Weight: 25,401kg (56,000lb) loaded
Range: 5955km (3700 miles)	Armament: N/A

battleship *Bismarck* had sunk the British battle-cruiser *Hood* in the Denmark Strait led to the lift-off of 11 of VP-52's PBYs to search for the German warship, but the aircraft became lost and scattered, and it was several days before they all returned to Argentia.

Hunting the *Bismarck*

Some 17 PBY pilots had been sent to the UK in April to instruct Coastal Command of the RAF in Catalina operations. US Navy pilots then started to fly search missions with Coastal Command squadrons, one of these men being Ensign Leonard B. Smith, who was assigned to No. 209 Squadron at Lough Erne in Northern Ireland. Flying his second operational sortie, Smith spotted the German battleship. The Catalina's crew watched the *Bismarck* for the next four hours, awaiting relief. Each of the next two Catalinas to arrive on station also had a US Navy pilot on board, and finally a British battleship and cruiser force caught and destroyed the *Bismarck*. British and US cooperation continued during the summer as six new Martin PBM Mariners of VP-74 and six PBY-5s of VP-73 moved to Skerjafjord in Iceland during August.

US FIRST-LINE AIR STRENGTHS			
Date	USAAF	USN & USMC	Total
January 1942	1622	1915	3573
January 1943	3174	8268	11,442
January 1944	4911	13,065	17,976
January 1945	5827	14576	20,403
July 1945	7260	14648	21,908

Though supported by a US Navy tender, the aircraft also used RAF moorings, and the area of the Atlantic that could be covered was radically increased. In October, four Catalinas also deployed to Greenland for three weeks.

Three aircraft carriers were also involved in the Neutrality Patrol, operating from Norfolk, Virginia, for most of the period. The *Ranger*, *Wasp* and *Yorktown* undertook periodic sorties into the Atlantic and Caribbean, but these were more training exercises than operational cruises. The *Wasp* was at sea on 7 December 1941 with the *Yorktown's* VF-5 fighter squadron on board. The *Yorktown* was rushed to the Pacific, and VF-5 did not catch up with its parent air group for more than six months.

▲ **Consolidated PBY-5**

VP-12 (Patrol Squadron 12) / US Navy, 1942

Long-ranged and reliable, the flying boats of the PBY series were at the heart of the US Navy's maritime reconnaissance capability in World War II. And with the ability to carry two torpedoes, or four depth charges or four 454kg (1000lb) bombs, the PBY was also a very useful 'bomber'.

Specifications

Crew: 7–9

Powerplant: 2 x 895kW (1200hp)

Maximum speed: 288km/h (179mph)

Range: 4096km (2545 miles)

Service ceiling: 4480m (14,700ft)

Dimensions: span 31.7m (104ft);

length 19.47m (63ft 11in);

height 6.15m (20ft 2in)

Weight: 16,066kg (35,420lb) loaded

Armament: 3 x 7.62mm (0.3in) trainable MGs: two in the bow turret, one firing aft of the hull step; 1 x 12.7mm (0.5in) MG in each of the two beam positions; up to 1814kg (4000lb) of bombs or depth charges

Specifications

Crew: 7

Powerplant: 2 x 1300kW (170hp) Wright R-
2600-12 14-cylinder radial engines

Maximum speed: 330km/h (205mph)

Range: 4800km (3000 miles)

Service ceiling: 6040m (19,800ft)

Dimensions: span 36m (118ft);

length 23.50m (77ft 2in); height 5.33m
(17ft 6in)

Weight: 25,425kg (56,000lb) loaded

Armament: 4 x 12.7mm (0.5in) MGs (one each
in nose and dorsal turrets, blisters
amidships), plus 1800kg (4000lb) of bombs
or depth charges or 2 x Mark 13 torpedoes

▲ **Martin PBM-1 Mariner**

VP-74 / US Navy, USA, 1942

The PBM-1 was the first production model of the Mariner family, and only 20 of
this variant were built. The PBM-1 was equipped with retractable wing landing
floats that were hinged inboard. The following PBM-3 had longer nacelles, each
possessing a bay for four 227kg (500lb) bombs or depth charges, and fixed rather
than retractable underwing stabilizing floats.

Anti-submarine warfare
1942

**The squadrons and airmen of the US Navy soon found that the intensity of real combat
operations off the USA's eastern seaboard and over the North Atlantic was considerably more
taxing than the Neutrality Patrol, but after a slow start started to come to grips with the task.**

N OW THE USA was no longer neutral, and US
Naval Aviation was faced with altogether more
pressing demands on two fronts. The war in the
Atlantic was primarily an anti-submarine effort. For
the first 18 months of the US entry into World War
II, anti-submarine warfare squadrons were exclusively
land-based.

U-boat threat

Though based extensively on each side of the
Atlantic, the aircraft had only modest ranges, and this
left large holes in the trade routes in which the U-
boats could operate with little fear of air attack. Once
Germany had declared war on the USA on
11 December 1941, Admiral Karl Dönitz ordered his
packs of U-boats to start operating in US waters from
January 1942. Here the U-boats found perhaps their
best hunting of the whole war. Ill-prepared for

▲ **Consolidated PBY-6A**

Production of this amphibious flying boat totalled 235 machines. Some 48 were
delivered to the USSR, and 75 to the USAAF, by which the type was known as the
OA-10B.

hostilities, the Atlantic coast continued to glow with city lights and navigational beacons operating normally, and many ships sailed independently and without escort.

The U-boats sank 26 ships off the US and Canadian coasts in January 1942. In February, the U-boats slipped into the Gulf of Mexico, attacking oil tankers and other merchant ships, and achieving 42 sinkings.

A shooting war

The situation improved but little in the rest of 1942, for Allied shipping losses were greater than new construction. However, measures were being implemented to improve the situation, albeit only slowly. Some parts of the Neutrality Patrol were already in position as the shooting war started. Patrol Wing Seven covered the northern routes from Newfoundland and Iceland, Patrol Wing Five operated from Norfolk, Virginia, and Patrol Wing Three flew from the Panama Canal Zone.

With some foresight, Natal in Brazil had been prepared as an anti-submarine warfare (ASW) base during December 1941, and by late in 1942 three patrol squadrons were based there. Eventually they

▲ **Catalina blister gunner**
Possessing good fields of fire and observation, the blister gunner/observer provided a measure of defence against beam attacks and watched the sea.

were joined by Martin PBMs and Lockheed Venturas of Fleet Air Wing 16 during 1943.

Meanwhile, the German U-boats continued to enjoy success in its campaign in US east coast waters.

Specifications

Crew: 7–9

Powerplant: 2 x 895kW (1200hp) engines

Maximum speed: 288km/h (179mph)

Range: 4096km (2545 miles)

Service ceiling: 4480m (14,700ft)

Dimensions: span 31.7m (104ft);

length 19.47m (63ft 11in);

height 6.15m (20ft 2in)

Weight: 16,066kg (35,420lb) loaded

Armament: 3 x 7.62mm (0.3in) trainable MGs: two in the bow turret, one firing aft of the hull step; 1 x 12.7mm (0.5in) MG in each of the two beam positions; up to 1814kg (4000lb) of bombs or depth charges

▲ **Consolidated PBY-5 Catalina**
VP-44 (Patrol Squadron 44) / US Navy, 1942
The large blistered transparencies on the waist of the PBY's hull to the rear of the wing pylon provided excellent vantage points for a pair of observers, each armed with a single 7.62 or 12.7mm (0.3 or 0.5in) Browning trainable machine gun.

May was the worst month to date, with 72 ships sent to the bottom. While few U-boats were lost, the patrol squadrons did score occasional successes. During the summer, for example, a PBY of VP-73 scored a direct hit with a depth charge on the wooden deck planking of a surfaced U-boat. The charge was pushed overboard, sank to its preset detonation depth and exploded, sinking the boat.

▲ **Douglas B-18B Bolo**

Unknown squadron / USAAF, USA, 1942

Lacking adequate coastal and maritime reconnaissance aircraft when it entered the war, the USAAF converted 122 B-18A bombers as B-18B anti-submarine aircraft with search radar (antenna in the nose radome) and the Magnetic Anomaly Detector Mk IV with its sensor to the rear of the tail unit.

Specifications

Crew: 6

Powerplant: 2 x 750kW (1000hp) Wright R-1820-53 radial engines

Maximum speed: 346km/h (215mph)

Range: 1850km (1150 miles)

Service ceiling: 7280m (23,900ft)

Dimensions: span 27.3m (89ft 6in); length 17.6m (57ft 10in); height 4.6m (15ft 2in)

Weight: 10,030kg (22,123lb) loaded

Armament: 3 x 7.62mm (03in) MGs, plus a bom load of up to 2200kg (4500lb)

North Atlantic operations
1943–44

Despite all their efforts to out-think and outfight the Allied air squadrons, the U-boat arm was steadily matched in 1942 and outmatched in 1943. By 1944, the US Navy's patrol bomber and anti-submarine squadrons were in the ascendant, and there was nothing the Germans could do.

SLOWLY AND METHODICALLY, the ASW squadrons assimilated their experience and evolved an effective tactical method. The advent of new equipment, such as improved search radar, more effective weapons and more efficient aircraft, was critical. The submarine war was perhaps the most technological of all, and small improvements in detection or warning equipment gave each side a useful if temporary advantage.

Perhaps best-suited for the long-range ASW role was the Consolidated Liberator four-engined bomber. Designed for the US Army Air Corps as the B-24, the Liberator became the US Navy's PB4Y-1, later evolved into the PB4Y-2 Privateer with a single than twin vertical tail surfaces. With exceptional range and the ability to carry heavy offensive and defensive armament, the PB4Y was a very capable submarine hunter and killer. But so were aircraft as different as the PBM Mariner flying boat and the slow, and generally under-rated, 'blimp' airship.

Another way in which the U-boat was countered was the 1942 creation of 15 inshore patrol squadrons

▲ **A-29 submarine hunter**
The first submarines sunk by US aircraft were claimed by US Navy patrol VP-82, equipped with A-29s originally intended for British use under the Lend-Lease scheme.

for service along the USA's eastern seaboard and in the Caribbean. Another 15 such squadrons were also established for service along the USA's western seaboard, at Coco Solo in the Panama Canal Zone, and Pearl Harbor.

On 17 October 1942, these inshore patrol squadrons came under the control of the patrol wings. Originally equipped with the Vought OS2U floatplane, the squadrons were bolstered by the arrival of Douglas SBD Devastators for the ASW role. By the middle of 1944, the U-boat threat had largely disappeared, and the inshore patrol squadrons were steadily inactivated, all having disappeared by the end of World War II.

Central Atlantic operations

In the Atlantic theatre, the establishment of new bases helped to close the 'Atlantic Gap' in which air

▲ **Lockheed A-29**
Unknown group / USAAF, USA, 1943
While early examples of Hudson repossessed by the USAAF for service with the designation A-29 retained the Boulton Paul turret specified by the British, later aircraft such as that seen here had an open gunner's position with a 12.7mm (0.5in) machine gun. The British camouflage and serial were retained.

Specifications

Crew: 6

Powerplant: 2 x 820 kW (1100 hp) Wright Cyclone 9-cylinder radial engines

Maximum speed: 397km/h (246mph)

Range: 3150km (1960 miles)

Service ceiling: 7470m (24,000ft)

Dimensions: span 19.96m (65ft 6in); length 13.51m (44ft 4in); height 3.62m (11ft 10in)

Weight: 7930kg (17,500lb) loaded

Armament: 4 x 9.7mm (0.303in) Browning MGs, 2 in nose, 2 in dorsal turret; 340kg (750lb) of bombs or depth charges patrol had previously been impossible. Airfields in the West Indies, along the Brazilian coast and finally on Ascension Island did much to enhance the overall level of protective air cover that could be provided to convoys. New aircraft and improved technology could not in themselves ensure the defeat of the U-boat, however. Before the end of 1942, US Navy patrol squadrons were operating on both sides of the Atlantic. Fleet Air Wing 15's two original squadrons were operational from Casablanca and Port Lyautey in French Morocco within hours of the Vichy French surrender of 11 November.

Squadrons of Lockheed Ventura twin-engined and Liberator four-aircraft patrol aircraft increasingly supplemented the PBY in the first half of 1943, covering the North Atlantic convoys routes from Iceland to Morocco as far as their ranges permitted. But the Germans were themselves slightly on the ascendant once more. As the Allied coastal air patrols increased, *Luftwaffe* maritime aircraft became increasingly aggressive during May 1943. While Focke-Wulf Fw 200 and other long-range aircraft had previously been content to shadow convoys and radio reports of their positions, courses and speeds, they now attacked ships more frequently in the Bay of Biscay, diverting Allied squadrons from ASW work to

▲ Lockheed Hudson

This view of a Hudson Mk IV shows developments to boost capability: the eight under-wing rocket projectiles were potent submarine killers, and ASV.Mk II radar (antennae under the wing and on the nose) was a capable search equipment.

convoy air defence. In the summer, the U-boats were ordered to fight it out with aircraft: fitted with ever heavier batteries of light flak weapons, they remained on the surface and resisted as they made high-speed passage to and from their operational areas.

▲ Consolidated PBY-5A

Unknown squadron / US Navy, mid war years

The general versatility of the PBY series was enhanced in the PBY-5A variant by the adoption of retractable tricycle landing gear to turn the type from a pure flying boat into an amphibian also able to use conventional runways.

Specifications

Crew: 7–9

Powerplant: 2 x 895kW (1200hp) engines

Maximum speed: 288km/h (179mph)

Range: 4096km (2545 miles)

Service ceiling: 4480m (14,700ft)

Dimensions: span 31.7m (104ft);

    length 19.47m (63ft 11in);

height 6.15m (20ft 2in)

Weight: 16,066kg (35,420lb) loaded

Armament: 3 x 7.62mm (0.3in) trainable MGs: two in the bow turret, one firing aft of the hull step; 1 x 12.7mm (0.5in) MG in each of the two beam positions; up to 1814kg (4000lb) of bombs or depth charges

Losses on both sides were heavy: for instance, the Gibraltar-based FAW-15 made 16 attacks on U-boats during the first half of June 1943, claiming five kills, but lost one PBY and three Liberators to the U-boats' flak guns.

Biscay patrols

Flights over the Bay of Biscay and the approaches to the Mediterranean now regularly encountered aggressive patrols of Junkers Ju 88s. Meanwhile, FAW-7 had been located to Dunkeswell in Devon as the US Navy's most important ASW unit in the UK, and here, late in July, the original VP-103 and VP-105 with Liberators were supplemented by the VP-63 squadron flying a variant of the PBY with MAD (magnetic anomaly detection) gear for the detection of submerged submarines. The wing's start was problematic, with a number of losses and only limited success. But things started to improve from August, in which only two merchant ships sunk in areas patrolled by US Navy aircraft. Even so, the wing's aircraft generally operated alone, and were never a match for the faster and better armed aircraft which the *Luftwaffe* operated over the area. On sighting a German (and sometimes aggressively neutral Spanish) warplanes, therefore, the pilots of PBY and PB4Y aircraft generally turned west in an effort to use their machines' greater range to outstay the opposition. The solution was found in the movement to Agadir in Morocco of a pair of well-armed and considerably faster and agile Venturas to take over the PBYs' patrol route.

Operating under the direction of RAF Coastal Command, Fleet Air Wing 7 played a major role in the D-Day landings in Normandy in June 1944 with dawn-to-dusk patrols, helping to ensure that not one of the thousands of Allied vessels was lost to U-boat attack in the three weeks after D-Day.

End of Atlantic operations
1944–45

By mid 1943 the Germans had lost the technological race on which success in the Battle of the Atlantic hinged. From this point to the German capitulation in May 1945, substantial numbers of U-boats were sunk, usually with all hands, as the Allies maintained their sea and air superiority.

FROM LATE 1943 the rate at which men and equipment reached the UK from North America paved the way for the June 1944 invasion of France. This fact was evident to the Germans, who tried every expedient that they could think of to reassert their offensive in the Atlantic. They therefore made several attempts at reviving the fortunes of their numerically important Type VII class U-boat force, including much heavier anti-aircraft batteries, radar detection equipment, and the addition of the *Schnorchel* (snorkel) device to allow them to run underwater off their diesel engines and so reduce the chances of detection by radar.

None of these expedients was genuinely effective, however, and by the autumn of 1943 Allied air power was so strong that the U-boats were being attacked in the Bay of Biscay as they left or tried to return to port. The development of German torpedoes was also stepped up, paving the way for weapons which ran a

U-BOAT LOSSES, ATTRIBUTED TO US NAVY				
Year	1942	1943	1944	1945
Sunk/captured	9	43	16	2

US NAVY AVIATION, ATLANTIC OPERATIONS				
Aircraft types	Action sorties	Tons bombs dropped	Enemy aircraft destroyed	Aircraft lost
Carrierborne	1,103	174	40/40	32/8
Land-based	58	3	2/0	12/1
Overall totals	1,161	177	42/30	44/9

pre-programmed course criss-crossing the convoy path. Perhaps the most dangerous were the electrically powered G7e/T4 Falke acoustic-homing torpedo and G7es/T5 Zaunkönig (known to the

▲ **Consolidated PBY-6A Catalina**

US Navy, 1944–45

This was an amphibious flying boat (built by Convair in New Orleans) of the type designed by Consolidated on the basis of the PBY-5A with the revised nose and tail unit created for the PBN-1 Nomad, a development of the PBY-5 by the Naval Aircraft Factory. The PBY-6A was generally deemed the best Catalina variant.

Specifications

Crew: 7–9	Weight: 16,066kg (35,420lb) loaded
Powerplant: 2 x 895kW (1200hp) engines	Armament: 3 x 7.62mm (0.3in) trainable MGs:
Maximum speed: 288km/h (179mph)	two in the bow turret, one firing aft of the hull
Range: 4096km (2545 miles)	step; one 12.7mm (0.5in) MG in each of the
Service ceiling: 4480m (14,700ft)	two beam positions; up to 1814kg (4000lb) of
Dimensions: span 31.7m (104ft);	bombs or depth charges
length 19.47m (63ft 11in); height 6.15m	
(20ft 2in)	

Specifications

Crew: 10	length 20.47m (67ft 2in); height 5.49m (18ft)
Powerplant: 4 x 895kW (1200hp) Pratt &	Weight: 25,401kg (56,000lb) loaded
Whitney Twin wasp radial piston engines	Armament: 2 x 12.7mm (0.5in) Browning
Maximum speed: 467km/h (290mph)	trainable MGs in nose, dorsal, ventral 'ball'
Range: 5955km (3700 miles)	and tail turrets, and one each in beam
Service ceiling: 8535m (28000ft)	positions; up to 5806kg (12,800lb) of bombs
Dimensions: span 33.53m (110ft);	

▲ **Consolidated PB4Y-1**

VPB-110 / US Navy, Devon, UK, winter 1944

Operated in the long-range patrol bomber role out over the southwestern Approaches to the UK and farther afield into the Atlantic, this aeroplane has non-specular sea-blue upper surfaces, intermediate blue vertical surfaces and insignia-white under surfaces.

Allies as the GNAT, or German Navy Acoustic Torpedo), which homed on the propeller noise of a target. Late-war developments were the *Elektroboot* series, comprising the Type XXI and short-range Type XXIII classes. The design was finalised in January 1943 but production started only in 1944–45. The Type XXI ran at 17 knots submerged, but full-scale production began only in 1944 and only one combat

patrol was carried out by a Type XXI boat before the war ended.

Even if the new boats and new weapons had been available in larger numbers, the strength of the Allied air forces, on both sides of the Atlantic, on islands such as Iceland and the Azores, and on large numbers of escort carriers dedicated to the anti-submarine role, would have made their task impossible.

Specifications

Crew: 7	length 24.50m (80ft); height 5.33m
Powerplant: 2 x 1300kW (170hp) Wright R-	(17ft 6in)
2600-12 14-cylinder radial engines	Weight: 25,425kg (56,000lb) loaded
Maximum speed: 330km/h (205mph)	Armament: 4 x 12.7mm (0.5in) MGs (one each
Range: 4800km (3000 miles)	in nose and dorsal turrets, blisters
Service ceiling: 6040m (19,800ft)	amidships), plus 3629kg (8000lb) of bombs
Dimensions: span 36m (118ft);	or depth charges or 2 x Mark 13 torpedoes

▲ Martin PBM-5 Mariner
US Navy, 1945

With two rather than four engines, and a bomb load of 3629kg (8000lb) rather than 5443kg (12,000lb), the Mariner was smaller and lighter than the heavyweight Coronado, and was designed for operations over shorter ranges. Again, the radar was located above the hull just to the rear of the flight deck.

Carrier operations
1942–44

While it was the war in the Pacific theatre that captured most of the attention for aircraft carrier operations, US Navy carriers were also involved in the North African and European theatres in a tactical role in support of the land forces.

THE FIRST US CARRIER involved in the European war was the USS *Wasp*, which left the US east coast late in March 1942 and reached the British base at Scapa Flow on 4 April. After taking on 47 Supermarine Spitfire land-based fighters for delivery as reinforcements for the British bastion on the Mediterranean island of Malta, the USS *Wasp* undertook the first delivery on 20 April. The carrier returned to its base in Scapa Flow, Scotland, some six days later. Facing overwhelming German and Italian air strength, Malta's air units suffered a heavy rate of losses, and a second reinforcement was launched on 2 May, 47 more Spitfire fighters being delivered on 9 May. The *Wasp* returned to the United States almost immediately after this and prepared to redeploy into the Pacific. The USS *Ranger* also ferried fighters, but in this instance Curtiss P-40 Warhawk fighter-

bombers of the US Army Air Forces: the carrier delivered 68 such aircraft to the Gold Coast in West Africa during April, and a second batch of aircraft in June.

Operation *Torch*

Soon after this, the USS *Ranger* embarked its air group and began to train for the most ambitious naval operation yet conducted in the African and European theatres: three groups of simultaneous amphibious landings by Anglo-US forces in Morocco and Algeria early in November 1942 as Operation *Torch*. Supporting the US portion of the undertaking were four carriers operating in three task groups, with 62 Douglas SBD-3 and Grumman TBF-1 bombers and 109 Grumman F4F fighters. Floatplanes operating from battleship and cruisers were also committed for the scouting, observation and search-and-rescue roles.

The US landings were centred on and round Casablanca. The USS *Ranger* and the escort carrier USS *Suwanee* operated to the west of Casablanca while two other smaller carriers, the USS *Sangamon* and USS *Santee*, operated to the west of the northern and southern landing areas respectively. The experience of most naval fliers was distinctly limited, but the task force had been assembled and dispatched so rapidly that there had been almost no opportunity to train in any realistic manner, and some pilots had not flown in two weeks.

More important that the experience of the aircrews, however, was the way in which the Vichy French armed forces would react: all agreed that they would fight the British, but opinion was divided as to their reaction to the Americans. The Vichy air force and naval air arm approached some 200 aircraft, including many US-built Martin and Douglas bombers and Curtiss fighters, and many of the Vichy French pilots were veterans of the Battle of France.

Landings begin

The landings began at dawn on 8 November, and to reduce the chances of triggering any reaction, the US aircrew were forbidden to shoot unless first fired upon. Matters got off to a poor start as a flight of seven fighters from the USS *Santee* became lost and ran low on fuel. One ditched in the sea and five crash-landed ashore: six of the pilots eventually reached safety, but one disappeared and was later reported killed. The pilots of the USS *Ranger*'s VF-4 and VF-9 soon discovered that that they could not dogfight the agile French fighters, and also encountered automatic weapons fire from the ground.

The focus of the undertaking in this part of French Morocco was Casablanca harbour, in which lay the French battleship *Jean Bart*, whose 381mm (15in) guns supplemented the efforts of the shore batteries. Eighteen of the USS *Ranger*'s dive-bombers attacked the port's naval facilities, submarine moor¬ings and the *Jean Bart*. The battleship was hit and damaged, and one submarine was sunk. When a French light cruiser, escorted by destroyers, emerged from Casablanca in a sortie against the US naval force, SBD and F4F warplanes attacked with bombs and machine gun fire at low level, and the cruiser and two destroyers had to be beached to prevent their sinking.

The subsidiary objectives, Fedala and Safi in the north and south respectively, were captured on the first day of Operation *Torch*. During this period SBD and TBF bombers flew anti-submarine patrols and

▲ **Douglas SBD-3 Dauntless**

VS-41 / USS Ranger, *Northwest Africa, November 1942*

The slightly ragged yellow circling of the US National insignia was applied by hand on all US Navy aircraft involved in Operation *Torch*, the Allied landings in French north-west Africa.

Specifications

Crew: 2

Powerplant: 895kW (1200hp) Wright R-1820-
60 radial engine

Maximum speed: 410km/h (255mph)

Range: 1243km (773 miles)

Service ceiling: 7780m (25,5300ft)

Dimensions: span 12.65m (41ft 6in);
length 10.08m (33ft 1in); height 4.14m
(13ft 7in)

Weight: 4843kg (10,676lb) loaded

Armament: 2 x 12.7mm (0.5in) forward-firing
machine guns

attacked Vichy French airfields and defensive positions. Casablanca's batteries continued to fire on the American forces during 9 November, and nine SBDs from the USS *Ranger* attacked them with 454kg (1,000lb) bombs, scoring two direct hits which finally put the *Jean Bart* out of action. The French surrender came early on the morning of 11 November. As far as the US Navy was concerned, Operation *Torch* had been invaluable in providing its aircrews with a relatively mild introduction to combat. Ground support tactics had been proved in real operations, and anti-submarine techniques tested, not least as the TBFs of the USS *Suwanee* sank at least one Vichy French boat at sea.

In the air, the unblooded F4F pilots achieved a kill/loss rate of about 5/1 after learning very rapidly that mutual support and the maintenance of high speed were vital. But the losses of carrierborne warplanes to ground fire and operational causes were heavy. As its aircraft losses had reached almost 25 pecent over a three-day period, the task force could have sustained operations for only a very short time longer.

Norwegian operation

The next operation undertaken by a US Navy carrier in European waters took place almost a year later, and this again involved the air group of the USS *Ranger*. Collaborating with the British Home Fleet, the USS *Ranger* was involved in an attack on German shipping in and around the harbour of Bodø on the Norwegian coast. The US carrier reached position about dawn on 3 October 1943, closely escorted by a powerful Royal Navy force, and here launched two waves of warplanes: 20 SBDs followed by 10 TBFs, each escorted by six to eight F4Fs.

After a low-level approach to reduce the chances of detection by radar, each wave climbed to attack altitude within visible distance of the coast, and the bombers then attacked coastal targets and shipping anchored in the harbour. There was no aerial opposition over the target area. Between them, the SBDs of VB-4 and the TBFs of VT-4 destroyed six ships and damaged another three. The attackers lost three of their number, and one fighter was badly damaged. This very successful undertaking marked the end of the USS *Ranger*'s combat career, for the carrier was then used as a training carrier off the west coast of the United States for the rest of the war.

▲ **Douglas SBDs in the Atlantic**
Douglas SBD Dauntless divebombers sit aboard USS *Yorktown* while on Atlantic patrol in 1943. USS *Ranger* can be seen in the background.

Final raids

The next, and indeed final, undertaking by US carriers in the European theatre took place in the Mediterranean, where two escort carriers provided air support for Operation *Dragoon*, the invasion of southern France. Here both the carriers and their aircraft were different from those that had been used in Operation *Torch*. By August 1944 the escort carriers USS *Tulagi* and USS *Kasaan Bay* each had a squadron of Grumman F6F-5 Hellcat fighters far superior to the F4F machines they replaced. Each of the carriers had 24 of these large fighter-bombers. On 15 August, the first day of the landings, the two American squadrons flew 100 sorties, directing naval gunfire against German troop concentrations and supply routes. In the succeeding days the wide variety of missions undertaken including low-altitude bombing, machine-gun strafing, attacks on ground targets with rockets, and armed reconnaissance. The two squadrons were operational over the south of France for 13 days, and in this time lost 11 F6Fs, including five on 20 August, but in exchange had destroyed more than 800 road vehicles and 84 locomotives.

So ended US carrier aviation's operations against the western Axis powers, but the escort carriers' war against the U-boats continued.

Chapter 4

Soviet Union

A leading exponent of the concept
of long-range bombing during the 1930s, a period in which
it developed some of the world's first genuinely heavy
bombers, the Soviet Union then stepped back from the
notion of the strategic bomber and decided to
concentrate its efforts on tactical bombing with light and
medium bombers. Validated in the Spanish Civil War
(1936–39) by machines such as the Tupolev SB-2,
the new Soviet concept was based on fast bombers
operating at no greater than medium altitude over and
immediately behind the battlefield, providing the ground
forces with immediate and short-term support.
The concept proved useful but limited, and late in World
War II the Soviet Union began once again to consider
long-range strategic heavy bombing.

◀ Ilyushin Il-2
Well protected, possessing adequate performance and agility, but notably well armed with cannon,
machine guns, light bombs and rocket projectiles, the Il-2 was a war-winning battlefield weapon.

Soviet Frontal Aviation
1941–43

In the first months of the war, the FA (Frontal Aviation) lost the majority of its aircraft on the ground and in the air. Even so, the surviving Soviet light and medium bomber elements fought with courage, if not with great skill, but achieved little and had to be almost wholly rebuilt.

THE LIGHT AND MEDIUM bomber elements of the FA (Frontal Aviation), representing the vast majority of the bombing capability available to the Soviet Union, were tasked from the very start of hostilities with attacks on German tactical targets right on the battlefield, and only slightly later and also to a lesser degree with rear-area targets such as airfields, troop, artillery and vehicle (especially armoured) concentrations, and chokepoints typified by bridges and railway junctions.

Flying as a mix of many obsolescent and few modern aircraft, the Soviet bomber regiments initially operated largely by day and without fighter escort, although fighters started to become available, initially to no great effect, after about the first month of the campaign. The bombers' losses were very great, and their successes minimal. They did, however, have

ORGANIZATION

Air Force Command
1941

Composite air divisions (one reconnaissance, one bomber, one fighter & one ground-attack regiments)	Bomber divisions (three bomber regiments)	Fighter divisions (three fighter regiments)

ORGANIZATION

Bomber Division
June 1941

Bomber regiment with four sqns (36 aircraft)	Bomber regiment with four sqns (36 aircraft)	Bomber regiment with four sqns (36 aircraft)	Bomber regiment with four sqns (36 aircraft)

Specifications

Crew: 4	height 3.25m (10ft 8in)
Powerplant: 2 x 619kW (830hp) M-100 V-12 piston engines	Weight: 5732kg (12,636lb) loaded
	Armament: 2 x 7.62mm (0.3in) MGs in nose
Maximum speed: 410km/h (255mph)	turret; 1 x 7.62mm (0.3in) ShKAS MG in
Range: 1200km (746 miles)	dorsal turret and 1 x 7.62mm (0.3in) ShKAS
Service ceiling: 8500m (27,885ft)	MG in ventral position; maximum bomb load
Dimensions: span 20.33m (66ft 9in);	1000kg (2205lb)
length 12.27m (40ft 3in);	

▲ **Tupolev SB-2M**

Unknown bomber regiment / Soviet Air Force, 1941–42

Developed for high-speed bombing, and eventually built to the extent of 6967 aircraft, the SB-2 series is here exemplified by an aeroplane in winter camouflage. The ANT-40 prototype first flew in October 1934, and the type made its combat debut on the Republican side in the Spanish Civil War (1936–39). Always powered by liquid-cooled engines, though initially with frontal rather than chin radiators, the SB-2 was obsolescent by 1941 but remained in first-line service to 1944.

the effect of clearing from the Soviet inventory the high proportion of inferior types. Thus they facilitated the entry of more modern bombers as and when these were delivered from the factories uprooted from western Russia in the face of the German advance and relocated to the safety of areas lying to the east of the Ural mountains.

The rate and weight of the Soviet bombing attacks increased steadily from the end of August 1941, although they tended still to be made against short-range tactical targets: to this extent the bombers attacked essentially the same types of targets as the

Specifications

Crew: 4

Powerplant: 2 x 619kW (830hp) M-100 V-12
  piston engine

Maximum speed: 410km/h (255mph)

Range: 1200km (746 miles)

Service ceiling: 8500m (27,885ft)

Dimensions: span 20.33m (66ft 9in);
  length 12.27m (40ft 3in);

height 3.25m (10ft 8in)

Weight: 5732kg (12,636lb) loaded

Armament: 2 x 7.62mm (0.3in) machine guns
  in nose turret, 1 x 7.62mm (0.3in) ShKAS in
  dorsal turret and 1 x 7.62mm (0.3in) ShKAS
  in ventral position; maximum bomb load
  1000kg (2205lb)

 Tupolev SB-2M

Unknown bomber regiment / Soviet Air Force, 1941–42

This is a somewhat atypical example of the SB-2M fast bomber with no dorsal turret (its location being fitted with a sliding transparency) and the original type of ventral protection by means of a 7.62mm (0.3in) ShKAS machine gun in a ventral hatch position.

Specifications

Crew: 4

Powerplant: 2 x 619kW (830hp) M-100 V-12
  piston engines

Maximum speed: 410km/h (255mph)

Range: 1200km (746 miles)

Service ceiling: 8500m (27,885ft)

Dimensions: span 20.33m (66ft 9in);
  length 12.27m (40ft 3in);

height 3.25m (10ft 8in)

Weight: 5732kg (12,636lb) loaded

Armament: 2 x 7.62mm (0.3in) MGs in nose
  turret; 1 x 7.62mm (0.3in) ShKAS MG in
  dorsal turret and 1 x 7.62mm (0.3in) ShKAS
  MG in ventral position; maximum bomb load
  1000kg (2205lb)

▲ **Tupolev SB-2bis-3**

Unknown bomber regiment / Soviet Air Force, 1942–43

This is an example of the final production version of the SB-2 fast bomber with an MV-3 dorsal turret and remotely controlled ventral barbette, each carrying one 7.62mm (0.3in) ShKAS machine gun. The aeroplane is depicted in standard summer camouflage.

ground-attack aircraft, and in tactical terms the efforts of the ground-attack and bomber regiments can be regarded as little more than an extension of the fire plan ordained for the Soviet long-range artillery.

While short-range attack remained a major part of the bombers' efforts, the importance of targets deeper in the Germans' rear gradually registered with the Soviets and the number of attack on such targets increased. Typical of such efforts were the raids delivered on German-held airfields in the region of Kiev on 21–26 July 1941. In these raids the number of attacking bombers was between three and 10, and some of the crews managed to make good tactical use of cloud to conceal their approaches. The bombing was then carried out at various altitudes, without fighter escort and without any attempt at evasive manoeuvres, and in most of the attacks all of the Soviet bombers were destroyed by the German fighters and/or anti-aircraft fire without inflicting anything but very minor damage, which in no way impeded the tempo of German air operations.

Increased production

So remained the basic nature of Soviet bombing operations until well into 1942. Numbers of more modern aircraft were being delivered, and the flying schools were beginning to churn out an ever-increasing flood of pilots and other aircrew, but the newer bombers were often delivered before they were in fact fully ready for service, and the aircrews were both short of flying experience and lacking in operational training before they were committed to operations. The *Luftwaffe*, on the other hand, was flying fully developed fighters in the hands of highly experienced pilots, and the toll they exacted from the Soviet bombers continued to be very high.

The toll was also exacerbated by the Soviet demand that the vast majority of bombing efforts were directed against targets in or immediately behind the battlefield, where the density of the German fighters and flak guns was greatest.

Nevertheless, the Soviet tactical bombing arm did slowly begin to become more effective as the last teething problems of the new-generation bombers were eliminated, and as aircrews gained experience, where they survived, and could thus pass on the fruits of their survival to fresh aircrews. The Soviet tactical bombing effort thus began to improve late in 1942 and early in 1943. It was increasingly well coordinated within the overall operational plan to provide the infantry, armour and artillery with the support they needed to check the Germans advances and start to develop their own strategic offensives, which the Germans lacked the strength to beat back.

▲ **Petlyakov Pe-8**

Unknown bomber regiment / Soviet Air Force, 1943

The only genuinely long-range heavy bomber operated by the Soviet Union in World War II, the Pe-8 was built to the extent of only 79 aircraft for service from 1940. The type was well armed both defensively and offensively, but suffered constantly from powerplant problems.

Specifications

Crew: 11	height 6.20m (20ft 4in)
Powerplant: 1100kW (1350hp)	Weight: 27,000kg (59,400lb) loaded
Maximum speed: 443km/h (276mph)	Armament: 2 x 20mm (0.79in) ShVAK cannons
Range: 3600km (2245 miles)	(dorsal and tail turret); 2 x 12.7mm (0.5in)
Service ceiling: 9300m (30,504ft)	UBT MGs (engine nacelles); 1 x 7.62mm
Dimensions: span 39.10m (128ft 3in);	(0.3in) ShKAS MG (nose turret); up to 4000kg
length 23.59m (77ft 5in);	(8800lb) of bombs

Facing *Barbarossa*
JUNE–DECEMBER 1941

The German *Barbarossa* invasion of the Soviet Union caught the Soviets completely by surprise, with their forces deployed too far forward in a cordon behind the frontier. The Germans swept forward, killing and capturing vast numbers of Soviet personnel on their way to Moscow.

THE *BARBAROSSA* INVASION started on 22 June 1941, and the Germans swept all before them as their infantry and armoured forces, supported by tactical warplanes, punched through the Soviet line and began a series of pincer envelopments that killed or captured vast number of men and took huge amounts of weapons and equipment.

The pace of the advance slowed later, but the Germans were poised outside Moscow in November, only to be denied the prize by the onset of winter and the determination of the Soviet government and forces, and then falling back.

During this period, the FA's bomber regiments made many attacks, but to no real effect. Each attack was made by a squadron of typically six to eight but never more than 10 aircraft flying at between 600m

ORGANIZATION

	Composite Air Division		
	June 1941		
Reconnaissance regiment (four sqns with 36 aircraft)	Fighter regiment (four sqns with 48 aircraft)	Ground-attack regiment (four sqns with 48 aircraft)	Bomber regiment (four sqns with 36 aircraft)

▶ ***Shturmovik* fighter-bomber**

In combination with its successor (the Ilyushin Il-10), the Ilyushin Il-2 is the single most produced military aircraft design in all of aviation history. A total of 36,163 were built by the Soviets during World War II.

Specifications	
Crew: 2	length 10.46m (34ft 4in);
Powerplant: 1 x 1134kW (1520hp)	height 3.80m (12ft 6in)
Maximum speed: 486km/h (302mph)	Weight: 3273kg (7216lb) loaded
Range: 1100km (683 miles)	Armament: 4 x 7.62mm (0.3in) fixed wing MGs
Service ceiling: 8800m (28,870ft)	and 1 x 7.62mm (0.3in) MG in dorsal turret;
Dimensions: span 14.30m (46ft 11in);	400kg (880lb) of bombs

▲ **Sukhoi Su-2**

Unknown regiment / Soviet Air Force, 1941–42

Designed as a light reconnaissance bomber role with ground-attack capability, the Su-2 was built to the extent of 500 or slightly more aircraft in 1940–42. Early operational experience against German fighters revealed that the Su-2 lacked the performance, agility, armament and protection for battlefield survival.

(1970ft) and 825m (2700ft) in tight formation, despite the attentions of flak. The attacking squadron sometimes attempted to manoeuvre in formation, and tended to become more widely spaced only after the arrival of German fighters.

The whole attack was delivered in level flight 'by the book', with a rigid adherence to a preconceived plan that made no allowance for the realities of the tactical situation. In combination with the slow speed of the formation, this resulted in very heavy losses, many such formations losing all of their number. Moreover, the inaccuracy of the bombing, even from the low altitude from which it was delivered, meant that the results of most attacks were very poor.

▲ Ilyushin Il-2

Unknown attack regiment / Soviet Air Force, winter 1941–42

The original version of the Il-2, first flown in TsKB-55P prototype form during December 1940, was rushed into service during 1941 as a single-seater with the gun armament of two 20mm (0.79in) ShVAK cannon with 420 rounds and two 7.62mm (0.3in) ShKAS machine guns with 1500 rounds.

Specifications

Crew: 2

Powerplant: 1 x 1320kW (1770hp) Mikulin
    AM-38F liquid-cooled inline engine

Maximum speed: 404km/h (251mph)

Range: 800km (497 miles)

Service ceiling: 6000m 19,685ft)

Dimensions: span 14.6m (47ft 11in);
    length 11.60m (39ft); height 3.4m (11ft 2in)

Weight: 6360kg (14,023lb) loaded

Armament: 2 x 20mm (1.79in) ShVAK cannon
    and 2 x 7.62mm (0.3in) MGs

Night harassment
1941–45

The Soviets were adept at exploiting the equipment they did possess in useful quantities, even if this equipment was technically obsolete. One such type of aeroplane was the old training and liaison biplane, which was used to disturb the Germans' opportunity to rest at night.

THE SOVIETS were quick to appreciate that they could achieve good results at minimal cost by simple harassment of the Germans at night using obsolete biplanes such as the Polikarpov Po-2 (or U-2).

Silent attack

Equipped with a single defensive machine gun and carrying a small load of bombs, often of the anti-

NIGHT HARASSMENT AIRCRAFT			
Type	Engine	Bomb load	Speed
Polikarpov U-2VS	1 x radial	200kg (441lb)	147km/h (91mph)
Polikarpov R-5	1 x V	400kg (882lb)	228km/h (142mph)
Yakovlev UT-2	1 x radial	light bombs	192km/h (20mph)

personnel bomblet type, an irregular stream of these aircraft at intervals of between five and 15 minutes would cruise over the German lines at a height of between 225m (740ft) and 1500m (4920ft) to drop their bombs and fire at anything evident on the ground. The U-2 aircraft often made a gliding approach to arrive without warning, and then

gunned their engines as they dropped their bombs before turning back.

The Germans' direct casualties were small, but the effort had a cumulative effect in keeping the Germans psychologically off balance and disturbing their opportunity to rest. As such, an obsolete aircraft performed a militarily useful service.

Specifications

Crew: 3
Powerplant: 2 x 820kW (1100hp)
Maximum speed: 540km/h (336mph)
Range: 1500km (932 miles)
Service ceiling: 8800m (28,870ft)
Dimensions: span 17.16m (56ft 4in);
length 12.66m (41ft 7in);
height 4m (13ft 2in)
Weight: 8496kg (12,943lb) loaded
Armament: 2 x 7.62mm (0.3in) ShKAS MGs in nose and 1 x 7.62mm (0.3in) ShKAS MG in ventral or dorsal station; maximum bomb load 1200kg (2646lb)

▲ Petlyakov Pe-2FT
Unknown dive-bomber regiment / Soviet Air Force, 1943

Fast, agile and well protected, the Pe-2 was one of the finest warplanes to serve with any of the combatants in World War II. The original crew was three, but the bomb-aimer's glazed position in the nose was later removed as redundant, leaving the pilot and gunner as the two members of the crew.

▲ Polikarpov U-2VS
Unknown Polish-manned regiment / Soviet Air Force, 1942

Built to the extent of 33,000 or more aircraft, the Po-2 was a 'maid-of-all-work' aeroplane in a host of variants. The U-2VS was the night harassment variant.

Specifications

Crew: 2
Powerplant: 1 x 75kW (100hp)
Maximum speed: 156km/h (97mph)
Range: 400km (249 miles)
Service ceiling: 4000m (13,125ft)
Dimensions: span 11.4m (37ft 5in);
length 8.17m (26ft 10in);
height 3.10m (10ft 2in)
Weight: 890kg (1962lb) loaded
Armament: 1 x 7.62mm (0.3in) rear-facing MG and up to 250kg (551lb) of bombs under the lower wing.

Checking the German offensive
1942–43

In 1942, the Germans switched their focus south, where they hoped to reach the Caspian Sea and secure the oilfields of the Caucasus. Time and distance slowed the advance, and then Hitler decided that the objective was to be Stalingrad, where the Germans suffered a huge defeat.

THE LURE OF THE Caucasian oilfields drew the Germans' primary offensive of 1942 off to the south-east and into a vastness of open country and great heat. Suffering from acute strategic indecision as the Soviet forces melted away and no tangible benefit accrued from his armies' efforts, Hitler then decided that the industrial city of Stalingrad on the Volga river should be taken.

A trap is sprung

As the exhausted Germans approached and entered Stalingrad, the Soviets prepared a major counterstroke, which trapped the German Sixth Army and part of the Fourth Panzer Army in the city, where some of the war's bloodiest fighting took place. *Reichsmarschall* Hermann Göring assured Hitler that his *Luftwaffe* could keep the garrison supplied, but Soviet pressure and deteriorating weather meant that this was not achieved.

The remnants of the starving garrison surrendered in February 1943, and with them disappeared

Germany's last real chance of victory on the Eastern Front. Throughout 1942, the quality of the Soviet bombing effort improved, but only slowly and hesitantly.

Each bomber unit generally flew in a V formation of between 12 and 30 aircraft, followed at a varying distance by the next unit probably at a different altitude, while the rare attacks by complete bomber divisions were normally made with the regiments abreast of each other. The attack was generally started at dawn or at midday, and the last attack of the day,

ORGANIZATION

| | Ground-Attack Division | | |
	1942		
Ground-attack regiment of four sqns (48 aircraft)	Ground-attack regiment of four sqns (48 aircraft)	Ground-attack regiment of four sqns (48 aircraft)	Ground-attack regiment of four sqns (48 aircraft)

Specifications

Crew: 2

Powerplant: 1 x 1320kW (1770hp) Mikulin
 Am-38F liquid-cooled inline piston engine

Maximum speed: 404km/h (251mph)

Range: 600km (375 miles)

Service ceiling: 5945m (19,500ft)

Dimensions: span 14.6m (47ft 11in);

length 11.6m (38ft 0.5in);

height 3.4m (11ft 1in)

Weight: 6360kg (14,021lb) loaded

Armament: 2 x 37mm (1.46in) cannon, 2 x
7.62mm (0.3in) MGs; 1 x 12.7mm (0.5in) MG
in rear cockpit; 200 x 2.5kg (5.5lb) PTAB anti-
tank bombs, or 8 x RS-82 or RS-132 rockets

▲ **Ilyushin Il-2m3**

Unknown attack regiment / Soviet Air Force, Stalingrad Front, 1943

The aircraft of the Il-2 series were known universally by the soubriquet *Shturmovik*, meaning 'assaulter' or 'attacker'. The weight of the protective armour incorporated in each aeroplane was typically 990kg (2183lb), and much of this also served a structural purpose.

▲ **Ilyushin Il-2 attack aircraft, 1942**
Reliable, easy to maintain and simple to manufacture in large numbers (it was produced in only a small number of variants), the Il-2 was rugged, as demanded by the indifferent quality of the airfields from which it had to operate, and became the heart of the Soviet ground-attack capability at low level over the armoured battlefield.

often the most intense, was always delivered before the fall of night.

The attack altitude was varied in accordance with circumstances, including the tactical situation and the weather, and were recorded by the Germans between rare lower and upper limits of 300m (985ft) and 8000m (26,245ft). Targets in or close behind the frontline were normally attacked from between 1000m (3810ft) and 2500m (8200ft), while those farther to the rear were tackled by bombing from between 3000m (9845ft) and 4000m (16,405ft).

All of the aircraft bombed simultaneously under command of the lead bomb-aimer, and the bombs were of the light and medium types. Several attacks were made until the whole bomb load had been dropped, and then the bombers turned for home.

▲ **Ilyushin Il-2m3**

Unknown attack regiment / Soviet Air Force, 1943–44

The original Il-2 single-seater had offered good offensive capability but, despite its sturdy structure and much armour, proved vulnerable to fighter attack from the rear. The Il-2m3 introduced a gunner with one 12.7mm (0.5in) machine gun, and formations of Il-2m3 aircraft could put up a powerful weight of defensive fire.

Specifications

Crew: 2

Powerplant: 1 x 1320kW (1770hp) Mikulin Am-38F liquid-cooled inline piston engine

Maximum speed: 404km/h (251mph)

Range: 600km (375 miles)

Service ceiling: 5945m (19,500ft)

Dimensions: span 14.6m (47ft 11in); length 11.6m (38ft 0.5in); height 3.4m (11ft 2in)

Weight: 6360kg (14,021lb) loaded

Armament: 2 x 23mm (0.9in) VYa-23 cannon, 2 x 7.62mm (0.3in) MGs, 1 x 12.7mm (0.5in) rear-mounted MG; and 8 x 82mm (3.2in) RS-82 or 132mm (5.2in) RS-132 rocket projectiles

Soviet Frontal Aviation
1943–45

The qualitative improvement of the FA's bombing capability in the last two years of the war mirrored that of the Soviet Union's fighter and ground-attack capabilities, albeit on a smaller scale and reflecting the importance placed by the Soviets on battlefield air power.

BY THE MIDDLE OF 1943, the improvements in Soviet tactical bombing that had become discernible in the previous 18 months were becoming more pronounced. While tactical bombing still lagged somewhat behind fighter and ground-attack operations in the repertoire of Soviet air power capabilities, the Germans were the first to admit that it nonetheless achieved useful results.

Bomber development

The slower pace of the bomber arm relative to the fighter and ground-attack arms reflected a number of factors: industrial limitations meant that all three air elements could not be developed at the same rate, the development of the bomber arm presented problems not typical of the fighter and ground-attack arms, Soviet military doctrine emphasized the importance

ORGANIZATION

Air Force High Command
mid 1943

Central Administration — Long-Range Air Force — Air Defence Command

Air Force of the Airborne Troops — Civil Air Fleet

of battlefield rather than rear-area air power, and for attacks on Germany's cities and industrial base the Soviets could leave matters to the Western Allies.

Even though the bomber arm lagged behind the fighter and ground-attack arms, it benefited

Specifications

Crew: 2	height 3.4m (11ft 1in)
Powerplant: 1 x 1320kW (1770hp) Mikulin Am-38F liquid-cooled inline piston engine	Weight: 6360kg (14,021lb) loaded
	Armament: 2 x 23mm (0.9in) VYa-23 cannon,
Maximum speed: 404km/h (251mph)	2 x 7.62mm (0.3in) MGs, 1 x 12.7mm (0.5in)
Range: 600km (375 miles)	rear-mounted MG; and 8 x 82mm (3.2in) RS-
Service ceiling: 5945m (19,500ft)	82 or 132mm (5.2in) RS-132 rocket
Dimensions: span 14.6m (47ft 11in);	projectiles
length 11.6m (38ft 0.5in);	

▲ **Ilyushin Il-2m3**

Unknown attack regiment / Soviet Air Force, 1944

A decisive tactical warplane built to the extent of some 36,250 aircraft, the Il-2 was an excellent aeroplane in the ground-attack and anti-armour roles. It reached its definitive form as the Il-2m3 with a gunner added behind the pilot for rearward protection. The gunner's glazing was not infrequently removed to improve the field of fire for the one or occasionally two 12.7mm (0.5in) machine guns. The slogan on the side of the fuselage translates as 'Avenger'.

considerably from the decline of the German fighter and anti-aircraft artillery branches in achieving useful results. It is estimated that by March 1944 the Soviet tactical bomber arm totalled some 4560 aircraft, including about 1810 nocturnal harassment machines and excluding about 860 long-range bombers (February 1944 figure). The latter almost doubled to about 1600 in January 1945.

During September 1944, the tactical bomber arm comprised six bomber corps with 30 bomber divisions incorporating 110 bomber regiments, these figures rising to seven, 35 and 135 respectively by the

Specifications

Crew: 2
Powerplant: 1 x 1320kW (1770hp) Mikulin Am-
    38F liquid-cooled inline piston engine
Maximum speed: 404km/h (251mph)
Range: 600km (375 miles)
Service ceiling: 5945m (19,500ft)
Dimensions: span 14.6m (47ft 11in);

length 11.6m (38ft 0.5in);
height 3.4m (11ft 2in)
Weight: 6360kg (14,021lb) loaded
Armament: 2 x 23mm (0.9in) VYa-23 cannon,
    2 x 7.62mm (0.3in) MGs, 1 x 12.7mm (0.5in)
    rear-mounted MG; and 8 x 82mm (3.2in) RS-
    82 or 132mm (5.2in) RS-132 rocket projectiles

▲ Ilyushin Il-2m3

Unknown attack regiment / Soviet Air Force, winter 1943–44

Seen in winter camouflage, this Il-2m3 retains the gunner's glazing. The wing carried two 23mm (0.9in) VYa-23 cannon and two 7.62mm (0.3in) machine guns and eight 82mm (3.2in) or four 132mm (5.2in) rocket projectiles, while the bomb load was six 100kg (220lb) bombs or a smaller number of lighter bombs, the later including anti-armour bomblets.

▲ Tupolev Tu-2S

Unknown bomber regiment / Soviet Air Force, 1943–45

The Tu-2 series was optimized for mass production by a demand for the minimum number of parts, the use of very accurate drawings and tooling to ensure accuracy of fit, and pre-prepared wiring looms and pipe runs. The result was a major reduction in the number of man hours required to build each aeroplane.

Specifications

Crew: 4
Powerplant: 2 x 1380kW (1850hp) Shvetsov
    ASh-82FN radial piston engines
Maximum speed: 547km/h (340mph)
Range: 2000km (1243 miles)
Service ceiling: 9500m (31,170ft)
Dimensions: span 18.86m (61ft 11in);

length 13.8m (45ft 4in);
height 4.56m (14ft 11in)
Weight: 12,800kg (28,219lb) loaded
Armament: 2 x 20mm (0.79in) ShVAK cannon
    in wing roots; 3 x 12.7mm (0.5in) UBT MGs
    (one in both dorsal positions and ventral
    station); max. bomb load 3000kg (6614lb)

end of the year. At the same time, the long-range bomber arm comprised nine corps with 18 divisions incorporating 48 regiments. At this time, the establishment of the bomber regiment was 33. However, most squadrons in fact had between three and five more aircraft, and also a number of crews in reserve as combat attrition replacements.

Improved capabilities

The growing experience that helped to make the tactical bomber arm more capable was reflected in the fact that, by September 1944, the Soviets reckoned that some 70 per cent of their crews could be deemed experienced. Another way of looking at the same trend is provided by losses, which had been 5100 aircraft in 1943 and 5200 in 1944, the very slight increase in losses being considerably more than offset by the numbers of aircraft in service.

The role in which the Soviets employed their tactical bomber arm reflected not only their overall military philosophy but, of course, the nature of the land war on the Eastern Front. Up to the end of 1942, the Soviets had in general responded to German offensives, and mustered significant bomber strength in the areas in which the Germans were trying to effect a breakthrough.

After the surrender of the German Sixth Army at Stalingrad in February 1943, however, the Soviets generally had the strategic initiative, and therefore grouped their bomber strength to support their own great offensive movements. Up to April 1944, the ADD was concentrated primarily in the north for attacks on Finland, but after that time it was shifted south to the area of Kiev to support the great offensives through Ukraine and Poland and into the northern Balkans.

Ground support

Over the same period, the tactical bomber arm was grouped to support the efforts within the various grand schemes by fronts (army groups), armies and corps. By this stage of the war, there was a high level of coordination between the ground forces and their supporting air strength, and the bombers were able to go about their tasks increasingly unmolested by German fighters because of the latter's declining capability and the conduct of bombing operations with fighter escort or, over the battlefield, in collaboration with fighter patrols.

Night bombers

A notable feature evident from the middle of 1944 was the greater use made of night bombing of all types, and the commitment of the Soviet bombers to attacks deeper in the German rear areas. For the latter, several waves of bombers were employed, each

Specifications	
Crew: 4	height 4.56m (14ft 11in)
Powerplant: 2 x 1380kW (1850hp) Shvetsov	Weight: 12,800kg (28,219lb) loaded
ASh-82FN radial piston engines	Armament: 2 x 20mm (0.79in) ShVAK cannon
Maximum speed: 547km/h (340mph)	in wing roots and 3 x 12.7mm (0.5in) UBT
Range: 2000km (1243 miles)	MGs (one each in both dorsal positions and
Service ceiling: 9500m (31,170ft)	ventral station); maximum bomb load of
Dimensions: span 18.86m (61ft 11in);	3000kg (6614lb)
length 13.8m (45ft 4in);	

▲ **Tupolev Tu-2S**

Unknown bomber regiment / Soviet Air Force, possibly Kalinin front, 1943–45

The subject of protracted development, as indicated by a first flight in January 1941 but entry into service only at a time early in 1944, the four-seat Tu-2 was a superlative medium attack bomber and ground-attack warplane. More than 1000 aircraft were delivered before the end of World War II, and more than 1500 after the war. The Tu-2S was the first full-production model, and the dorsal and ventral positions each carried 12.7m (0.5in) machine guns.

▼ Soviet bomber regiment / Frontal Aviation, 1943–44

The regiment was the smallest tactical unit of the Soviet Air Force, and in organizational terms was subordinated to the air division or, in some cases, was controlled directly by an air army. The bomber regiment comprised three bomber squadrons, each with an establishment of 11 aircraft, giving the bomber regiment a total establishment of 33 aircraft, a figure often exceeded by up to five aircraft later in the war.

1st Squadron

2nd Squadron

3rd Squadron

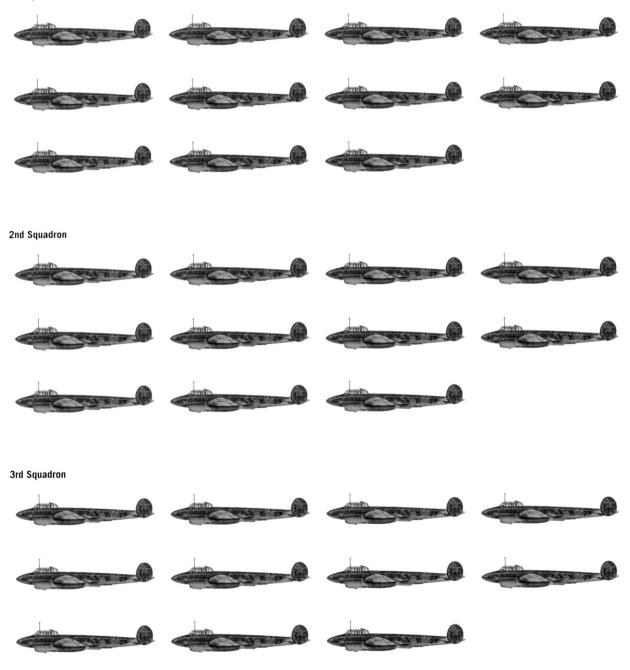

wave comprising one regiment that attacked in a tight concentration at altitudes between 2000m (6560ft) and 4000m (13,125ft), all of the aircraft releasing their bombs in level flight on receipt of the order from the leading aeroplane. Bombing accuracy was better than it had been in 1943 and the first part of 1944, but was still not as great as that achieved by the Western Allies, and losses to flak were heavy.

▲ **Petlyakov Pe-2 Series 359**

Unknown dive-bomber regiment / Soviet Air Force, 1944–45

This is an example of a late variant with individual ejector exhaust stubs.

Specifications

Crew: 3	height 4m (13ft 2in)
Powerplant: 2 x 820kW (1100hp)	Weight: 8496kg (12,943lb) loaded
Maximum speed: 540km/h (336mph)	Armament: 2 x 7.62mm (0.3in) ShKAS MGs in
Range: 1500km (932 miles)	nose and 1 x 7.62mm (0.3in) ShKAS MG in
Service ceiling: 8800m (28,870ft)	ventral or dorsal station; maximum bomb
Dimensions: span 17.16m (56ft 4in);	load 1200kg (2646lb)
length 12.66m (41ft 7in);	

Specifications

Crew: 4	length 13.8m (45ft 4in);
Powerplant: 2 X 1380kW (1850hp) Shvetsov	height 4.56m (14ft 11in)
ASh-82FN radial piston engines	Weight: 12,800kg (28,219lb) loaded
Maximum speed: 547km/h (340mph)	Armament: 2 x 20mm (0.79in) ShVAK cannon
Range: 2000km (1243 miles)	in wing roots,;3 x 12.7mm (0.5in) UBT MGs
Service ceiling: 9500m (31,170ft)	(one in both dorsal positions and ventral
Dimensions: span 18.86m (61ft 11in);	station; max. bomb load of 3000kg (6614lb)

▲ **Tupolev Tu-2S**

Unknown bomber regiment / Soviet Air Force, summer/autumn 1944

With two 20mm ShVAK cannon in the wing roots, and rearward defence provided by three 12.7mm (0.5in) UBT machine guns (single guns in the two dorsal and one ventral positions), the Tu-2S had good gun armament and provision for a standard bomb load of 3000kg (6614lb) carried internally or overload of 4000kg (8814lb), including two 500kg (1102lb) weapons under the wing roots.

Drive to victory
1943–45

Germany's defeat at Stalingrad made the Soviet Union's eventual victory all but certain, though there was still more than two years of bitter fighting still to come. During this period, the Soviet bomber arm matured slowly but steadily as a potent adjunct to the Soviet ground forces.

A FTER ITS VICTORY at Stalingrad, the Soviet Army drove forward to retake the region between the Don and Donets rivers, in the process creating the great Kursk salient, which the Germans tried but failed to retake during July 1943 in their last major attempt to regain the initiative on the Eastern Front. The Soviets then swept across the Dniepr river to re-enter Ukraine in the south, freeing Leningrad from siege in the north, liberating south Ukraine in spring 1944, and Belorussia and north Ukraine in the summer before moving into Poland during late summer 1944.

Without real pause, the Soviets then moved into the northern Balkans and retook the Baltic states in the south and north respectively, and then in January 1945 moved remorselessly into Germany proper, where their capture of Berlin on 2 May 1945 signalled the end of the 'Great Patriotic War'.

Operations in the Crimea

Throughout this series of grand offensives, which placed huge demands on men and machines, and required a vast logistical effort that seldom faltered in any major way for more than a short period, the ground forces were covered by the fighter arm of the V-VS, and supported by the heavier warplanes of the same service's ground-attack and bomber arms.

The nature of the bombing undertaken by the bomber arm of the V-VS in these decisive later stages

ORGANIZATION

Air Army
mid-1943 (typical)

| Air corps (one bomber, one fighter & one ground-attack divisions) | Air corps (two fighter divisions) | Air corps (two bomber divisions) | Direct reporting formations (one fighter, two ground-attack & one composite divisions) |

SOVIET LIGHT AND MEDIUM BOMBER AIRCRAFT

Type	Engines	Bomb load	Speed
Ilyushin Il-2m3	1 x V	600kg (1323lb)	404km/h (251mph)
Nyeman R-10	1x V	300kg (661lb)	370km/h (230mph)
Petlyakov Pe-2FT	2 x V	1200kg (2465lb)	540km/h (336mph)
Sukhoi Su-2	1 x radial	600kg (1323lb)	378km/h (235mph)
Tupolev SB-2	2 x V	1000kg (2205lb)	410km/h (255mph)
Tupolev Tu-2S	2 x radial	3000kg (6614lb)	547km/h (340mph)
Yakovlev Yak-4	2 x V	600kg (1323lb)	540km/h (335mph)

SOVIET GROUND ATTACK AIRCRAFT, 1941–45

Year	Total
1941	1543
1942	8219
1943	11,177
1944	11,110
1945	c. 5500
Total	37,549

of the war can first be discerned in the campaign of the first part of 1944, which aimed for the expulsion of the Germans from Crimea and the recapture of the great fortress city of Sevastopol.

The campaign fell into four parts, and in the first of these (the German withdrawal into Sevastopol and the unsuccessful Soviet attempt to storm the city) bombers were not used at all. Thereafter the air tactics employed by the bombers focused on using long-ranged and more heavily armed counterparts of those used by the ground-attack arm.

In the second phase of the campaign, the Soviets attempted to take Sevastopol in a major assault. Long-range support was provided by bombers operating from airfields in the area of Kiev to deliver day and night attacks on targets located deep in Germany's fortified area round Sevastopol, but the accuracy of the bombing was poor and the Germans losses, in men and materiel, were therefore small.

In the third phase of the campaign, the Soviet bombers undertook a carefully pre-planned offensive against the fortress of Sevastopol and the German airfields in the fortified area round Sevastopol. This third phase, flown primarily by day, was more successful than the second phase.

The fourth and final phase was flown over the western Crimea as the Germans tried to evacuated

Specifications

Crew: 3
Powerplant: 2 x 820kW (1100hp)
Maximum speed: 540km/h (336mph)
Range: 1500km (932 miles)
Service ceiling: 8800m (28,870ft)
Dimensions: span 17.16m (56ft 4in);
  length 12.66m (41ft 7in);
height 4m (13ft 2in)
Weight: 8496kg (12,943lb) loaded
Armament: 2 x 7.62mm (0.3in) ShKAS MGs in
  nose and 1 x 7.62mm (0.3in) ShKAS MG in
  ventral or dorsal station; maximum bomb
  load 1200kg (2646lb)

▲ **Petlyakov Pe-2FT**

Unknown dive-bomber regiment / Soviet First Air Army, spring 1945

The Pe-2FT was the first standard variant of the Pe-2 series, of which 11,427 examples were delivered between early 1941 and the end of World War II. The Pe-2 was the Soviets' most important tactical bomber of World War II, and the slogan on the side of this aeroplane translates as 'Leningrad-Konigsberg'.

Specifications

Crew: 3
Powerplant: 2 x 820kW (1100hp) Klimov
Maximum speed: 540km/h (336mph)
Range: 1500km (932 miles)
Service ceiling: 8800m (28,870ft)
Dimensions: span 17.16m (56ft 4in);
  length 12.66m (41ft 7in);
height 4m (13ft 2in)
Weight: 8496kg (12,943lb) loaded
Armament: 2 x 7.62mm (0.3in) ShKAS MGs in
  nose and 1 x 7.62mm (0.3in) ShKAS MG in
  ventral or dorsal station; maximum bomb
  load 1200kg (2,646lb)

▲ **Petlyakov Pe-2FT**

Unknown dive-bomber regiment / Soviet Air Force, 1944–45

The vane above the forward edge of the MVT turret immediately to the rear of the cockpit was an aerodynamic balance area to offset the drag of the 12.7mm (0.5in) machine gun as the turret was traversed, and so obviate the need for the turret to be power-operated.

their forces by sea to Ukraine. Here the main targets of the Soviet bombers were the ports the Germans were using for the evacuation, and the troop transports plying to and from these ports.

This phase of the bombing effort was successful, the bombs killing large numbers of troops awaiting evacuation, sinking two 3048-tonne (3000-ton) transport ships as well as larger numbers of 1016-tonne (1000-ton) transport vessels. This tactical pattern was repeated, with changes as demanded by the situation, in other areas wherever the Germans tried to make a stand and then withdraw in the face of overwhelming Soviet ground strength. The basic element of the Soviet bombing attacks was a double concentration on the German-held area and its associated lines of communication.

▲ **Ilyushin Il-10**

Unknown attack regiment / Soviet Tactical Air Force, Poland 1945

The Il-10 was the second-generation successor to the classic Il-2 *Shturmovik*, and retained only its predecessor's basic concept. It had an improved engine and enclosed rear-gunner's cockpit, as well as heavier armaments.

Specifications

Crew: 2
Powerplant: 1 x 1492kW (2000hp)
Maximum speed: 530km/h (329mph)
Range: 800km (497 miles)
Service ceiling: 7250m (23,785ft)
Dimensions: span 13.4m (43ft 12in);
  length 11.06m (36ft 4in);
height 4.18m (13ft 9in)
Weight: 6535kg (14,407lb) loaded
Armament: 2 x 7.62mm (0.3in) MGs; 2 x 23mm
  (0.9in) cannon on wings and 1 x 20mm
  (0.8in) cannon or 12.7mm (0.5in) MG in
  dorsal position; up to 500kg (11290lb) bombs
  and 4 x rockets

Specifications

Crew: 2
Powerplant: 1 x 1492kW (2000hp)
Maximum speed: 530km/h (329mph)
Range: 800km (497 miles)
Service ceiling: 7250m (23,785ft)
Dimensions: span 13.4m (43ft 12in);
  length 11.06m (36ft 4in);
height 4.18m (13ft 9in)
Weight: 6535kg (14,407lb) loaded
Armament: 2 x 7.62mm (0.3in) MGs; 2 x 23mm
  (0.9in) cannon on wings and 1 x 20mm
  (0.79in) cannon or 12.7mm (0.5in) MG in
  dorsal position; up to 500kg (11290lb) bombs
  and 4 rockets

▲ **Ilyushin Il-10**

Unknown attack regiment / Soviet Air Force, 1945

Total Soviet production of the Il-10 to 1949 (when the tooling was transferred to Czechoslovakia for the manufacture of 1200 B-33 and BS-33 trainers), and of the Il-10M in 1951–55, was 4966 aircraft.

Soviet Long-Range Aviation
1939–45

During the 1930s, the Soviet Union allowed its air force to become a semi-independent force, and this expanded its belief in the desirability of long-range bombing. The situation did not last long, however, and for most of World War II long-range aviation was a very limited asset.

I N 1935, THE SOVIET authorities allowed the slight disentanglement of the air force from the army and navy, of which it had been a part. By the following year, it had established itself as a semi-independent force in terms of its structure, but was still required to cooperate with the two older services and furnish them with the type of air support they needed.

This emphasis stemmed from a factor at the very heart of Soviet military thinking, namely that it was the forces on the ground that were the arbiters of war, and therefore that air power should be an adjunct of these. Even so, the V-VS (Soviet Air Force) had already started to experiment with a long-range heavy bomber capability designed to secure strategic results. The effort had been spurred by Soviet attempts to create, primarily for political and social reasons, a generation of very large and moderately advanced multi-engined aircraft whose existence would

▲ **Petlyakov Pe-8**
A Pe-8 bomber used to transport diplomats to Britain refuels at an RAF base somewhere in Scotland, 1942.

highlight the scientific and industrial advances being made by the Soviet Union. These technical developments led to the Tupolev TB-1 and TB-3, and the Kalinin K-7 heavy bombers, and it was these

Specifications

Crew: 4	length 14.8m (48ft 6in);
Powerplant: 2 x 821kW (1100hp) 88B radial	height 4.10m (13ft 6in)
piston engines	Weight: 10,000kg (22,046lb) loaded
Maximum speed: 410km/h (255mph)	Armament: 12.7mm (0.5in) MGs in nose,
Range: 2600km (1616 miles)	dorsal turret and ventral positions; maximum
Service ceiling: 10,000m (32,810ft)	bomb load 1000kg (2205lb)
Dimensions: span 21.44m (70ft 4in);	

▲ **Ilyushin Il-4**
Unknown bomber regiment / Soviet Air Force, 1945
Initially known as the DB-3F, the Il-4 was built to the extent of 5256 aircraft in a programme extending from 1941 to 1945. Differentiated from predecessor variants by its more streamlined and glazed nose, the Il-4 provided the backbone of the Soviet Union's longer-range bomber capability throughout World War II.

SOVIET LONG-RANGE BOMBERS			
Type	Engines	Bomb load	Speed
Ilyushin DB-3F (Il-4)	2 x radial	2500kg (5511lb)	507km/h (305mph)
Petlyakov Pe-8	4 x V or radial	4000kg (8818lb)	438km/h (272mph)
Tupolev TB-1	2 x V	3000kg (6614lb)	198km/h (121 mph)
Tupolev ANT-3	4 x V	4000kg (8818lb)	288km/h (179mph)

ungainly machines that constituted the Soviet heavy bomber arm in the late 1930s.

Further operational thinking and technical development had by now started the pendulum swinging back toward the tactical bomber able to intervene directly over the battlefield. The 'modern' aeroplane, of light alloy construction with a cantilever monoplane wing, retractable landing gear and enclosed accommodation, was by now standard, and the new generation of Soviet bombers was developed on the basis of this concept.

Bomber types

The Petlyakov Pe-8 was created as a four-engined heavy bomber, but was then built only in very small numbers, while far more ambitious manufacture was undertaken of twin-engined medium bombers typified by the Ilyushin DB-3 (Il-4), Petlyakov Pe-2 and Yermolayev Yer-2 and Yer-6 as successors to the

pioneering Tupolev SB-2, which saw service in the Spanish Civil War on the Republican government side. The process of rebuilding the V-VS' bomber force with modern aircraft and the tactics to serve the ground forces over the battlefield was still incomplete as German forces invaded the Soviet Union in June 1941. Even though the Soviets had more than four times as many aircraft as the Germans, the aircraft's general obsolescence and the poor training of their crews meant that those which managed to get into the air were shot down in droves. Large numbers were also destroyed on the ground.

The situation of the Soviet Union became ever more critical in the first four months of the war as the Germans drove steadily east, and the Soviets had recourse to all manner of expedients in an effort to stem the German tide. One of these expedients was the committal of bomber units to unescorted attacks in daylight against German forces shielded by potent anti-aircraft artillery under an umbrella of *Luftwaffe* fighters. The Soviet bomber force was largely destroyed in vain efforts to inflict tactical reverses on the Germans. After the immediate crisis had passed, a smaller and leaner long-range bomber arm was created in March 1942 as the ADD (Long-Range Aviation). The ADD's two main types were a few Pe-8 aircraft for limited long-range attacks and altogether larger numbers of Il-4s for more numerous medium-range efforts. In December 1944, the ADD came under the direct control of the V-VS as the Eighteenth Air Force.

▲ **Tupolev Tu-2S**

Unknown bomber regiment / Soviet Air Force, 1944–45

The Tu-2 was an outstanding design, in which great care had been taken to minimize drag. The result was high performance on modest power.

Specifications

Crew: 4

Powerplant: 2 X 1380kW (1850hp) Shvetsov ASh-82FN radial piston engines

Maximum speed: 547km/h (340mph)

Range: 2000km (1243 miles)

Service ceiling: 9500m (31,170ft)

Dimensions: span 18.86m (61ft 11in);

length 13.8m (45ft 4in);

height 4.56m (14ft 11in)

Weight: 12,800kg (28,219lb) loaded

Armament: 2 x 20mm (0.79in) ShVAK cannon in wing roots; 3 x 12.7mm (0.5in) UBT MGs (one in both dorsal positions and ventral station); max. bomb load of 3000kg (6614lb)

Soviet Naval Air Force
1941–45

The task of the Soviet Naval Air Force was, not surprisingly, the protection of ships and naval facilities from the attentions of Axis warplanes, and attacks on Axis shipping, especially in the Arctic Ocean, the Baltic Sea and the Black Sea as well as on major rivers.

L IKE THE V-VS, the Soviet Naval Air Force was structured and equipped for tactical support, and where necessary the two forces could assume a limited part of each other's roles. In the last two years of the war, for example, the Germans found that V-VS bombers were notably active in the anti-ship role. Up to 1943 it was mainly in the Black Sea that the Soviet Naval Air Force operated, but its attentions were spread more widely after that, and in 1944–45 the service was strongly evident in the Baltic Sea and the Arctic Ocean.

Medium-altitude bombing

The primary Soviet targets were convoys, supply vessels and troop transports, and attacks on German warships and naval installations were altogether less frequent. A type of target much favoured by the Soviets was the seaborne evacuation, in which the

ORGANIZATION

Morskaya Aviatsiya
mid 1944

| Northern Fleet Air Force | Baltic Fleet Air Force | Black Sea Air Force | Pacific Fleet Air Force |

sinking of a laden transport not only cost the Germans the troops being evacuated, but the subsequent use of the ship for further evacuations.

The bombers of the Soviet Naval Air Force operated in regiments, squadrons and flights according to the importance of the target, and the standard tactic was medium-altitude level bombing at between 3000m (9845ft) and 4000m (13,125ft). Only occasionally was dive-bombing used, Petlyakov Pe-2 warplanes then being employed in dives at

▲ **Handley Page Hampden TB.Mk I**

Unknown bomber regiment / Northern Fleet Air Force / Soviet Naval Air Force, Vaenga, Murmansk, October 1942

The Soviet Union took over 10 or more of these aircraft when the British pulled out the personnel of the two torpedo-bomber squadrons deployed temporarily to the Soviet Union earlier in 1942 for anti-shipping operations off northern Norway.

Specifications

Crew: 4

Powerplant: 2 X 746kW (1000hp) Bristol Pegasus XVIII radial piston engines

Maximum speed: 409km/h (254mph)

Range: 3034km (1885 miles)

Service ceiling: 5790m (19,000ft)

Dimensions: span 21.08m (69ft 2in); length 16.33m (53ft 7in); height 4.55m (14ft 11in)

Weight: 8508kg (18,756lb) loaded

Armament: 1 x 7.7mm (0.303in) Vickers or Browning fixed forward-firing MGs in port side of upper fuselage; 7.7mm (0.3in) Vickers K trainable forward-firing MGs in nose, dorsal position, ventral positions; 907kg (2000lb) of bombs, or 4 or 6 x 227kg (500lb) bombs or mines, or 1 x 457mm (18in) Mk XII torpedo between 60 and 70 degrees. The size of bomb carried was generally between 150kg (331lb) and 250kg (551lb), and the aircraft of each flight followed the leader to release their bombs at an altitude of about 1000m (3280ft). Wherever possible, the bombers had strong fighter escort to provide protection, and the aircraft also carried parachute-retarded fragmentation bombs for release over German fighter units as a (questionable) means of self-defence. Torpedo-bombing by Ilyushin Il-4s and Douglas A-20s became standard only late in the war.

Specifications

Crew: 3	length 14.63m (48ft); height 5.36m (17in 7in)
Powerplant: 2 x 1193kW (1600hp) Wright	Weight: 10,964kg (24,127lb) loaded
radial piston engines	Armament: 6 x 12.7mm (0.5in) Browning M2
Maximum speed: 510km/h (217mph)	fixed forward-firing MGs; 2 x similar weapons
Range: 1521km (945 miles)	in power-operated dorsal turret, and one
Service ceiling: 7225m 23,700ft)	rearward-firing through ventral tunnel; up to
Dimensions: span 18.69m (61ft 4in);	1814kg (4000lb) of bombs

▲ Douglas A-20C

Unknown bomber regiment / Northern Fleet Air Force / Soviet Naval Air Force, 1944

The Soviet Union received 665 and 48 examples respectively of the A-20B and A-20C variants of the Havoc, known to the British as the Boston, and made extensive first-line use of these aircraft.

Specifications

Crew: 3	length 14.63m (48ft); height 5.36m (17ft 7in)
Powerplant: 2 x 1193kW (1600hp) Wright	Weight: 10,964kg (24,127lb) loaded
radial piston engines	Armament: 6 x 12.7mm (0.5in) Browning M2
Maximum speed: 510km/h (217mph)	fixed forward-firing MGs, and 2 x similar
Range: 1521km (945 miles)	weapons in power-operated dorsal turret, and
Service ceiling: 7225m 23,700ft)	one rearward-firing through ventral tunnel;
Dimensions: span 18.69m (61ft 4in);	up to 1814kg (4000lb) of bombs

▲ Douglas A-20G

Unknown bomber regiment / Soviet Naval Air Force, March 1944

The Soviet Union received 3125 aircraft of the DB-7 series as part of US Lend-Lease deliveries, many of them receiving a number of local modifications such as the Soviet dorsal turret evident here. The Soviet Naval Air Force operated its aircraft in the anti-ship role from the Arctic Ocean to the Black Sea.

Appendices

During World War II, for the first time, bombers could strike directly at the enemy's means of waging war. By destroying industries and vital resources, vast fleets of Allied bombers waged the first truly strategic air campaign in history.

▼ **Combat strengths, all countries**

Germany started the war in Europe in 1939 with a large and powerful airforce, but as the conflict expanded to include the United States and Soviet Union, the Reich was quickly out-produced by the titanic industrial muscle arrayed against it.

FRONTLINE COMBAT AIRCRAFT, COMPARATIVE STRENGTHS (1939–45)					
Date	Germany	USA	USSR	UK	Total Allied
September 1939	2916	–	–	1660	1660
August 1940	3015	–	–	2913	2913
December 1940	2885	–	–	1064	1064
June 1941	3451	–	8105	3106	11,211
December 1941	2561	4000	2495	4287	6782
June 1942	3573	1902	3160	4500	9562
December 1942	3440	4695	3088	5257	13,040
June 1943	5003	8586	8290	6026	22,902
December 1943	4667	11,917	8500	6646	27,063
June 1944	4637	19,342	11,800	8339	39,481
December 1944	5041	19,892	14,500	8395	42,787
April 1945	2175	21,572	17,000	8000	46,752

▼ **Bomber aircraft production, all Allied and Axis forces**

Bombers are essentially offensive weapons, but although Germany was the aggressor in the early stages of the war, it did not produce as many aircraft of this type as the British. Albert Speer's rearmament program in the later stages of the war meant that German production increased, even in the face of intense Allied attacks, but the entire Axis production throughout the war was matched by the production of United States industry in 1944 alone. The British also built more bombers than the Germans, though the Soviets concentrated more on fighters and ground-attack aircraft.

ANNUAL ALLIED BOMBER AIRCRAFT PRODUCTION (1939–45)				
Year	USA	USSR	UK	Total
1939	–	–	1837	?
1940	623	3571	3488	7682
1941	4115	3748	4668	12,531
1942	12,627	3537	6253	22,417
1943	29,355	4074	7728	41,157
1944	35,003	4186	7903	47,092
1945	16,087	c 2,000	2812	20,899
TOTAL	97,810	21,116	34,689	153,615

ANNUAL AXIS BOMBER AIRCRAFT PRODUCTION (1939–45)				
Year	Germany	Italy	Japan	Total
1939	737	?	?	?
1940	2852	640	?	?
1941	3373	754	1461	5588
1942	4502	566	2433	7501
1943	4789	103	4189	9081
1944	1982	–	5100	7082
1945	–	–	1934	1934
TOTAL	18,235	2063	15,117	35,415

TONS BOMBS DROPPED AND SORTIES FLOWN BY ALLIED AIR FORCES IN EUROPE (AUGUST 1942 – MAY 1945)									
	Bomber Command			US Eighth Air Force		US Fifteenth Air Force		Balkan Air Force	
Date	Tons	Day Sorties	Night Sorties	Tons	Sorties	Tons	Sorties	Tons	Sorties
Aug 1942	4162	186	2454	151	114	–	–	–	–
Sept	5595	127	3489	189	183	–	–	–	–
Oct	3809	406	2198	278	284	–	–	–	–
Nov	2423	127	2067	604	519	–	–	–	–
Dec	2714	200	1758	340	353	–	–	–	–
TOTAL 1942	**18,703**	**1046**	**11,966**	**1411**	**1453**	–	–	–	–
Jan 1943	4345	406	2556	594	338	–	–	–	–
Feb	10,959	426	5030	568	526	–	–	–	–
Mar	10,591	284	5174	1483	956	–	–	–	–
Apr	11,467	316	5571	858	449	–	–	–	–
May	12,290	360	5130	2555	1672	–	–	–	–
Jun	15,271	–	5816	2330	2107	–	–	–	–
Jul	16,830	–	6170	3475	2829	–	–	–	–
Aug	20,149	–	7807	3999	2265	–	–	–	–
Sept	14,855	–	5513	7369	3259	–	–	–	–
Oct	13,773	–	4638	4548	2831	–	–	–	–
Nov	14,495	–	5208	5751	4157	5392	1785	–	–
Dec	11,802	–	4123	10,655	5973	7752	2039	–	–
TOTAL 1943	**157,367**	**1792**	**62,736**	**44,185**	**27,362**	**13,144**	**3824**	–	–
Jan 1944	18,428	–	6278	10,532	6367	11,051	4720	–	–
Feb	12,054	45	4263	16,480	9884	6747	3981	–	–
Mar	27,698	18	9031	19,892	11,590	10,176	5996	–	–
Apr	33,496	10	9873	22,447	14,464	21,256	10,182	–	–
May	37,252	16	11,353	32,450	19,825	30,355	14,432	–	–
Jun	57,267	2371	13,592	54,204	28,925	27,466	11,761	–	–
Jul	57,615	6298	11,500	40,784	23,917	32,183	12,642	132	2509
Aug	65,855	10,271	10,013	44,120	22,967	27,859	12,194	277	3437
Sept	52,587	9643	6428	36,332	18,268	20,856	10,056	480	3698
Oct	61,204	6713	10,193	38,961	19,082	16,257	9567	430	3416
Nov	53,022	5055	9589	36,091	17,003	17,297	9259	342	4604
Dec	49,040	3656	11,239	36,826	18,252	18,757	10,050	761	4653
TOTAL 1944	**525,518**	**44,096**	**113,352**	**389,119**	**210,544**	**240,260**	**114,840**	**2422**	22,317
Jan 1945	32,923	1304	9603	34,891	16,702	6784	4002	395	2460
Feb	45,889	3685	13,715	46,088	22,884	24,508	13,444	1085	4690
Mar	67,637	9606	11,585	65,962	31,169	30,265	14,939	1086	3954
Apr	34,954	5001	8822	41,632	20,514	29,258	15,846	1561	4546
May	337	1068	349	–	2276	84	42	101	373
TOTAL 1945	181,740	20,664	44,074	188,573	93,545	90,899	48,273	4228	16,023
GRAND TOTAL	**883,328**	**67,598**	**232,128**	**623,288**	**332,904**	**344,303**	**166,937**	**6650**	**38,340**

RAF medium/heavy bomber strengths by theatre

Medium and heavy bombers are the primary offensive weapon of any air arm. The Royal Air Force was a firm believer in the efficacy of the heavy bomber as a strategic platform, but it was not until the introduction of large numbers of heavy four-engined bombers in 1942 that Bomber Command was able to hit German industry hard. The 'UK (other)' column refers mainly to Coastal Command squadrons.

RAF MEDIUM AND HEAVY BOMBER SQUADRONS (1939–45)						
Date	Bomber Command	UK (other)	NW Europe	Med	Far East	Total
September 1939	37	3	–	2	2	44
July 1940	38	3	–	2	2	45
December 1941	50	12	–	7	3	72
December 1942	60	17	–	14	7	98
December 1943	72	19	–	21	8	120
September 1944	86	23	1	19	9	138
March 1945	96	30	2	16	15	159

RAF light bomber strengths by theatre

Light bombers formed a high proportion of the RAF's bomber inventory at the beginning of World War II, but experiences in France in 1940 showed that such aircraft had no place in a modern strategic bombing campaign. Later in the war light bombers returned to favour, primarily as tactical weapons operating in support of armies on the ground.

RAF LIGHT BOMBER SQUADRONS (1939–45)					
Date	UK	NW Europe	Med	Far East	Total
September 1939	12	6	8	5	31
July 1940	19	–	9	4	32
December 1941	22	–	10	2	34
December 1942	8	–	17	9	34
December 1943	17	–	13	5	35
September 1944	12	3	7	6	28
March 1945	8	9	6	5	28

USAAF bomber combat groups by theatre

The Group was the basic tactical unit of the American air forces. Usually consisting of three or four squadrons with up to 72 aircraft in heavy units and 96 aircraft in lighter units, Bomb or Bombardment Groups were classified as Very Heavy (operating Boeing B-29s or Consolidated B-32s and only used in the Pacific); Heavy (equipped with Boeing B-17s or Consolidated B-24s); Medium (using North American B-25s or Martin B-26s) and light (flying Douglas A-20s or A-26s). Ground attack aircraft such as the Republic P-47 Thunderbolt and P-38 Lightning were classified as fighters.

USAAF BOMBER COMBAT GROUPS BY THEATRE (1941–45)						
Date	Pacific	CBI	UK	NW Europe	Med	Total
December 1941	3	–	–	–	–	3
December 1942	8	2	11	–	9	30
December 1943	14	3	34	–	17	68
September 1944	19	7	44	9	27	106
March 1945	30	6	43	9	27	115

RAF Bomber Command operational strength

The actual number of aircraft available for operations was much lower than the total number on strength, with many bombers being unserviceable, under repair or being used for operational conversion and training.

AVAILABLE CREWS											
Date	Hampden	Blenheim	Mosquito	Wellington	Whitley	Stirling	Halifax	Manchester	Lancaster	US Type	Total
Sept 1939	71	140	–	77	61	–	–	–	–	–	280
Nov 1941	150	79	–	250	62	18	17	31	–	3	506
May 1942	27	29	–	214	15	45	62	15	29	44	417
Jan 1943	–	–	17	128	–	56	104	–	178	99	515
Mar 1944	–	–	58	–	–	63	328	–	594	–	974
Apr 1945	–	–	203	–	–	–	353	–	1087	–	1609

▲ Rest and relaxation

US aircrews watch as a B-17 Flying Fortress from the 1st Combat Wing (Heavy) lands at an East Anglian air base following an attack on a German munitions factory in the Autumn of 1943.

Total bombs dropped by weight (1942–45)

Although the US Eighth Air Force flew more sorties than RAF Bomber Command, the larger payload of the British bombers meant that they actually dropped more bombs.

BOMB TONNAGES DROPPED IN EUROPE		
Year	Bomber Command	US Eighth Air Force
1942	18,703	1411
1943	157,367	44,185
1944	525,518	389,119
1945	181,740	188,573
Totals	883,328	623,288

FAA torpedo-bomber strengths by theatre

The bomber strength of the Fleet Air Arm in 1939 was provided by the Fairy Swordfish torpedo bomber. These were later supplemented by the Albacore, Barracuda and Avenger.

FLEET AIR ARM TORPEDO-BOMBER SQUADRONS (1939–45)			
Date	Total	Far East	Aircraft
September 1939	12	2	140
September 1940	19	–	169
September 1941	29	–	198
September 1942	28	1	209
September 1943	29	1	349
September 1944	37	6	549
April 1945	27	8	500
September 1945	27	14	205

USAAF bomber strengths by type (1939–45)

The USAAF grew to become the largest bomber force in the history of air warfare during the course of World War II, fielding an extremely high proportion of B-17 and B-24 heavy bombers.

USAAF BOMBER AIRCRAFT BY TYPE (1939–45)			
Date	Heavy	Med & Light	Total bombers
December 1939	39	738	777
December 1940	92	639	731
December 1941	288	1544	1832
December 1942	2079	3757	5836
December 1943	8118	6741	14,859
December 1944	13,790	9169	22,959
August 1945	13,930	8463	22,393

Index

Page numbers in *italics* refer to illustrations.